Keith Floyd was born in 1943 and educated at Wellington School, Somerset. Since then he has devoted his life to cooking food, except for a few brief and fatal excursions into the army, antiques and wine trades. Happily released from the rigours of running a restaurant by a chance meeting with a television producer, Keith Floyd has now presented five television cookery series and written several bestselling books. When not hurtling around the world, he spends his time in Devon reading, fishing and watching rugby as well as worrying about spending too much money.

DEDICATION

This book is for cooks and chefs who have encouraged me *and* for all the home economists, food stylists and editors who have toiled on my untidy manuscripts, painfully correcting some glaring errors! Thanks very much. I'm sorry I've been such a nuisance.

A FEAST OF
Floyd

This special edition published in 1998
by HarperCollins*Publishers*
77–85 Fulham Palace Road
Hammersmith, London W6 8JB

Published by Grafton Books 1990

Commissioning Editor: Louise Haines
Art Director: Janet James
Photographer: Laurie Evans
Home Economist: Berit Vinegrad
Stylist: Leslie Richardson
Cookery Adviser: Carol Bowen
Illustrator: Richard Eckford

Printed and bound in Great Britain

CONTENTS

FOREWORD

This is a book of fun and feasts. What is a feast? A feast is an occasion where food, friends and drinks are harmoniously celebrated, no matter how humble or grand the occasion.

To Parson James Woodforde, a gluttonous old eccentric who gleefully recorded a lifetime of eating and drinking in the eighteenth century in *The Diary of a Country Parson*, feasting was about, 'A Calf's Head, Boiled Fowl and Tongue, a Saddle of Mutton rosted [sic] on the side table and a fine Swan rosted with Currant Jelly Sauce' – and that was only for starters!

According to Charles Gattey, the Archbishop of York, George Neville, took feasting extremely seriously. When he was enthroned in 1464, he ordered some 5,000 oxen, wild bulls, sheep, pigs, geese, capons, swans, peacocks, quails and fish of various kinds to be delivered to 62 cooks in the kitchens, together with 300 tuns of ale, 100 of wine, and one pipe of hippocras.

An earlier Archbishop had celebrated his enthronement in 1295 with a fish course consisting of 300 ling, 600 cod, 40 fresh salmon, 7 barrels of salt salmon, 14 of white herrings, 20 of red herrings, 5 of salt sturgeon, 2 of salt eels, 60 fresh eels, 8,000 whelks, 100 pike, 400 tench, 100 carp, 800 bream, 80 fresh, large Severn lampreys, 1,400 small lampreys, 124 salt conger eels, 200 large roach, as well as a selection of porpoises and seals.

The most prodigal and notorious banquet, however, was given by the Roman Tigellinus, joint commander of the Praetorian Guard. To avoid another litany of extravagance, let's just say it was a model of its kind, with the entertainment taking place on a raft constructed on Marcus Agrippa's lake, towed about by other vessels decked out in gold and ivory. Old Tigellinus brought in birds and animals and fish from the four corners of the empire, and all along the quays were brothels stocked with high-ranking ladies.

In my own, slightly more humble way, I have feasted at the tables of such culinary geniuses as the remarkable Albert Roux at Le Gavroche, and the innovative Brian Turner at Turner's in London's Walton Street. I have feasted on caviar and champagne in the bar of The Dorchester, and boiled beef and carrots at The Dukes Hotel in St James's. And I have had far flung feasts in The

Mandarin in Bristol. I have feasted on porridge made from army issue oatcakes, and I have feasted off mackerel hand-lined off the end of a yacht.

What I'm trying to say, dear Gastronaut, is that you don't have to throw a Roman orgy to enjoy a feast, and this haphazard little book, this eclectic list of delightful dishes, contains a highly personal selection of my favourite dishes, the kind of things that anyone, with a little patience and love, a few good friends, a little ambience, and a bottle or several of something cheering, can turn into a feast of the first order.

They are dishes prepared by the likes of George Perry Smith, Claud Arnaud, my Mum or my Uncle Ken. They are not people with an academic, high faluting, didactic approach to cookery. You won't find *them* sitting around discussing the relative merits of black or white truffles, because they understand the *real* meaning of a feast.

They are people who have the pride, skill and imagination necessary to lift cooking from the routine of making sandcastles and mud pies to the art of giving pleasure.

It doesn't matter a jot if your repertoire of dishes is small – though you have about 400 in this book to choose from! In fact, some of the best cooks I know produce only half-a-dozen dishes, but they do them so well that it is always a pleasure to be invited to their table. As Elizabeth David noted in *French Country Cooking*: 'Know your limitations is a copy book maxim which could be applied more often; many a reputation for skilful entertaining has been founded on the ability to cook one dish to perfection.'

And that one dish doesn't have to be grand. Frankly, I would prefer a fresh cauliflower cheese with a smooth, creamy sauce and hunks of good bread and butter, or a wonderful beef stew any day, to a more exotic dish that was ill conceived and fell short of its promise. Although, having said all that, these days my life is so hectic that I am more likely to offer guests a piece of toasted cheese or to take them out to dinner, rather than cook myself.

However, while I have included new recipes for these simple dishes, this doesn't, of course, mean that you shouldn't be prepared to experiment with new ideas. And so you will find in this book not only the elements of the most basic feasts but also of the most sumptuous. Whichever you choose, enjoy it and remember that a feast is what you want it to be.

INTRODUCTION

Food does not taste better just because you are sitting in evening dress under crystal chandeliers munching 'Turbot Brillat-Savarin' to the strains of a Bach concerto. A freshly caught perch grilled on whim by the river bank on a November morning with makeshift spit and a fire of twigs, nuts and pine cones is exquisite, while often the glittering formal dinner produces nothing more than the animalistic and ritual chomping of pigs at a trough.

Simplicity is the key to good cooking, no matter how deft at handling saucepans you may be, or how well equipped your kitchen. You can think out complicated recipes, work from cookery books, experiment with microwaves, test tubes and thermometers and yet the humble stew simmered long under a tight-fitting lid before being laid on the family table will always give most pleasure when the lid is removed and the fine aroma escapes into our nostrils.

Beware, though, of confusing simplicity with mediocrity. How often do people think that a well done steak is a straightforward thing to prepare? So easy they say. Yet to cook a plain steak so that it is slightly charred on the outside, its fat is crunchy and golden, but not oily, and it remains pink and tender inside is no easy task. Yet all you have to do is apply the meat to a hot grill for a moment or two, turn it over, cook a little longer and serve. But all depends on the temperature and the quality of the meat, the thickness of its cut, the heat of the grill, and so on. Not to mention the unpredictable interruptions. Simplicity needs a long apprenticeship. Paradoxically, though, you won't find that good cooks are themselves simple. You need to be very rounded in experience to prepare food simply.

A simple meal is one of the most complicated things to prepare.

The kitchen at Cobhay Farm was large with a softly worn yellow tiled floor, doors with latches and windows that overlooked the cow yard and barns. On one wall a ten pound brown trout was mounted, a fine specimen indeed, but it was not the real thing, simply a perfectly carved reproduction. It was a model of great beauty and evidence of the country-man's perfect compromise: Mr Ratsey (my schooldays chum's Dad) wanted to stuff it, Mrs Ratsey naturally wanted to cook it. And though I forget the year, maybe 1958, I shall never forget eating it for lunch at the huge kitchen table that dominated the room.

The farmhouse was quite big, but when I was a regular visitor there over thirty years ago, I seldom entered any other room. Occasionally, and with tiptoed confidence, I would creep down the passage to the sitting room. This was a cool, dark room with glass cabinets of decorated china and bottles of plum wine. There were display cases of stuffed specimen fish: perch, a tench and roach. In the hall there was a big bell, but visitors seldom entered by the front door – always through the kitchen, past the piles of muddy boots, sticks and water-proofs. You had to step carefully through packs of outdoor cats who slept on the sacks of meal stored in the porch, or dodge the odd elderly balding chicken. And woe betide you if you didn't take off your shoes before you came in.

When I first met the Ratseys – Lynn had invited me back for tea after the Wednesday rugby match – they terrified me. Mrs Ratsey had penetrating eyes that could see through you, even into your pockets, as if to tell you not even to think of using your catapult around here, and from behind his owl-like eyebrows, Mr Ratsey left you feeling you'd just been found guilty of pinching rare birds' eggs, at the very least. But over the next five years or so, from the age of ten, Cobhay Farm became almost a second home to me. Summer times we'd play cricket in the field, mornings we'd fish. Winter evenings Mr Ratsey would make me fishing rods, hand-built, varnished and beautiful. We'd make floats from feathers and spinners from redundant copper cistern balls.

Some evenings I'd walk, late, the three miles home and they always gave me a shilling. 'Indemnity against arrest as a vagrant,' they said. It was a house without fuss, fiction or cer-emony, but love, real love was spread thick like butter on home-made bread.

Sometimes I used to hang around the cow-sheds during milking, hoping to be asked to help, but though I lived in a village that the most advanced spy satellite would have diffi-culty in locating, they thought of me as a townie, so I tended to wander back into the kit-chen and annoy Mrs Ratsey shelling the peas or stringing the beans – in the hope that I'd be invited for tea, or lunch, or supper.

The food there was fabulous. It was the kind of table that always had two or three puddings; half a rhubarb tart left over from yesterday, today's treacle pudding and maybe some stewed fruit, because it was in season and had to be used. Tea-times had those pots, not jars, of jam in which the little greaseproof discs were crunchy with sugar crystals and the fruit was thick. There were fruitcakes and breadcakes and crunchy slabs made with trea-cle. Soups were thick and meaty, and although the table always groaned under the weight of these home-produced delights, there was never enough to eat. I didn't know it, but I was a gourmand even in those days. Hungry from rabbiting, bird-nesting or fishing; but never tired from homework.

There was a larder of chutneys and pickles and bottles of raspberry vinegar (this sometimes we stole and mixed with elderberry wine nicked from the silent, dark sitting room). There was always a ginger-beer plant and in summer we drank milk beaten with eggs and sugar. When I stayed I read *Swallows and Amazons*, dreamt of catching a huge carp from lumps of floating bread, and listened to Radio Luxembourg before the parents complained that it was too late for that dreadful noise. Sometimes, when it was late, and it was to be hoped safe, we'd raid the larder and make beetroot sandwiches for a midnight feast, and we learned to make imitation espresso coffee by grinding instant coffee and sugar into a white paste, before adding hot water and a thick cream floated to the top of the cup.

In term-time there were other and different issues; like memorising last night's *Hancock's Half Hour*, or learning the lyrics of *All Shook Up*, and of course, on Saturday morning, during break, everyone crowded round a wireless to listen to Brian Matthews' *Saturday Club*. In fact, it was about the time of Buddy Holly's *That'll be the day*, when two profound events occurred in my life. The first was when my Mother gave away my faggots to my Uncle Len, and I can tell you I've never forgiven either of them! You see, faggots were very important to me.

It was always faggots and peas after *Dick Barton* on Thursdays. When the van came round I would stand in the rain while the fat man with a thin moustache and stained white coat filled my white pudding basin with faggots and peas, overflowing with thick gravy that I licked on the way back up the garden path. And swallowed a hot fingerful of sweet mushy peas before I closed the door.

We ate offal of all kinds in our house. Chitterlings for breakfast, roast stuffed heart for lunch, liver and bacon for supper. Sometimes golden fried sweetbreads with butter and capers, sometimes boiled pigs' trotters, hot and gelatinous, with salt and pepper and vinegar, and on cold winter days tripe in a creamy onion sauce with doorsteps of bread and butter. Hogs' puddings with fried laver bread; thick slices of fat bacon with field mushrooms (if my Uncle Len hadn't sold them first to the Red Lion Hotel!); crisp slices of black pudding marbled with diamonds of pork fat and grilled tomatoes.

Mealtimes were precisely timed affairs. However delicious Mum's own faggots were, you had to eat them before *Hancock's Half Hour* or *The Goon Show*. How could a boy concentrate on the two finest things in his life at the same time?

Some days the kitchen at home resembled an operating theatre from some farcical *Carry On* film. Clad in a huge apron and head band, the table bloody with spongy pink pigs' lights, a heart, liver, caul, a pig's head balefully peeking from behind a pile of onions, bunches of dried sage falling to the floor, Mother would scold me for leaving mud on the floor after I had picked the parsley from the bottom of the winter garden. The windows steamed up as she went to work with a knife and huge pots of steaming stock. During *Workers' Playtime* we ate bread and pickles in the middle of the surgery. And in the quiet afternoon I dried and offered for inspection a million bowls for brawn. We stirred and thickened, we licked and tasted. And that night I ate seven wonderful faggots, thickly wrapped with crisp fat caul. (The recipe – my Mum's – is on page 200. Turn to it at once and see that faggots have nothing to do with Brains or Wall's or whatever. [Though *The Eagle* used to carry a Wall's ice cream strip at that time they had not got on to faggots in those days. Ho-Ho!]) Fabulous aren't they? You can, if you are remotely sensitive, understand why, despite all my Mother's done for me, I still harbour this aching resentment after all these years about the meal she gave away. And even though each Christmas she makes me a box of brilliant faggots, individually frozen to eat at my leisure, I shall never forget the day Uncle Len ate my faggots and peas.

Right, the other dramatic event. . . . Quite simply, I cooked my first, dare I say professional, meal at Cobhay Farm. During half-term, for some inexplicable reason, Mrs Ratsey decided to go away for the day. Probably on some trifling excuse like visiting her ageing mother, or having dental treatment. Outrageous when you think of it, I mean who was going to cook the lunch for Mr Ratsey, the four sons and me?

Calmly I volunteered for the task. Predictably, the boys hooted with derision, but Mrs Ratsey merely interrogated me as if I were applying for a job. Somehow I convinced her I knew my onions, so to speak (sheer bravado in fact), and she departed and left me to it. Well, the roast spuds were a disaster because I didn't par-boil them before roasting, but the carrots, cabbage and roast parsnips were a triumph, and the beef was exquisitely rare and the fat golden and crispy. The blackberry and apple pie was divine (she'd told me how to make pastry, though I recall it was a little short) and the custard was lumpless, albeit a little thin.

Emboldened by this success – the boys ate every morsel and Mr Ratsey said 'Humph, I feel no pain' – I declared myself a cook and the next lot of trout we caught at the reservoir I cleaned, gutted and deep-fried in batter and made the chips. And remember, my dear gastronauts, frozen chips did not exist in those days – nor did Mazola oil.

Thanks to the Ratseys' influence I became a

very keen fisherman and was never happier than sitting on the bank watching a float. When we planned an early morning trip I'd go to sleep with a piece of string tied to my toe and hung out of my bedroom window, so my pal Lynn could tug it to wake me without disturbing the household.

It was dark as we free-wheeled down Town Hill on that crisp Somerset Sunday morning. I leaned into the steep left-hander at the bottom and pedalled madly to maintain speed along the flat. By Milverton the sun had risen and the mist, defeated, revealed soft hedges heavy with nuts and berries, and orchards thick with hard red apples that I sometimes scrumped.

Just the swish of our tyres on the empty road. The dawn chorus faded as abruptly as it had begun. Past the house where the old lady had once caught us pinching plums from the garden and into the lane that led to the lake.

We climbed off our bikes and propped them against a silver birch tree, unpacked our tackle and walked gingerly to the water's edge. Over the reeds which fringed the lake a huge fallen tree arched crazily across a patch of water lilies. A thicket of elder behind us, black with fruit, threatened to cause casting problems if we weren't careful. The water was still and the bank shelved away gradually into soft mud. We could see the stalks of the lilies for yards ahead till the water turned dark green.

A shoal of fry spattered the surface in panic as a pike lunged at them. Eight o'clock. I rigged the tackle, threaded a bright red worm on to the hook and cast. The antenna float bobbed, dipped and steadied itself in the shadow of the fallen tree. With an eye on the float I reached for my haversack and poured a mug of cocoa from my Thermos. Hot and sweet.

The float shot away. A minute later I landed a small perch with brilliant red stripes and put it in the keep net. Within an hour I had caught half a dozen – the biggest about fourteen ounces. And then nothing. The perch had gone off the feed. I rebaited with stale bread soaked to a paste and tried for some bottom-feeding fish. Tench or bream perhaps. But the sun was creeping across the water and they wouldn't feed under those conditions. The float was motionless. The morning and my spirits were ebbing fast. And I was hungry!

The sandwiches were in my saddle bag, or so I thought. But when I opened it there was nothing. I had left them behind. Lynn was cross because I had promised to bring them for both of us. All I had was a loaf of stale bread and a Thermos of cocoa. Not much for a growing lad. I stomped around a bit, then the solution dawned on me. I would cook the perch. Going home early was out of the question, so I despatched two of the fish, badly pricking my thumb on a dorsal spine in the process. I cut off their heads and fins and gutted them (there is a black ribbon that runs along the spine, which must be scraped out). I cleared a small patch of grass and laid a ring of stones of about fifteen inches in diameter. I had no paper to start the fire but there were plenty of dry twigs around, and soon sweet wood smoke was spiralling into the sky as I piled on larger pieces to get the glowing embers I needed for cooking.

On either side of the ring I put another stone so that I could prop my wooden spit above the fire to prevent it burning through while the fish was cooking. I sharpened the end of an ash branch, skewered a perch on to it and placed it over the fire. I turned it every few seconds – I was afraid of it burning – and as I had no idea

how long it would take I could not risk leaving it unattended for a second.

I did overcook it. But we munched every mouthful of the charred skin and dried flesh with relish. It was fabulous. The second fish was more successful; I got it crisp on the outside and moist within. To this day I swear it was better even than the perch *en papillote* that I ate in Lyons years later in a restaurant renowned for its perch dishes! Trouble was I was still hungry, yet I couldn't face the prospect of cleaning another fish – to be honest, I didn't really like the killing and was squeamish at the idea of doing it again. It was then that I had the inspirational idea of elderberry breadcakes, a hitherto unknown, and probably to this day little considered, gastronomic delight. I ripped out the heart of my stale loaf, soaked it in water, squeezed it into a paste and pushed in a dozen or so elderberries. I then flattened it in my hands to a sort of thick pancake and toasted it over the fire. I had browned one side when I remembered that I had seen some cobnuts in a hedge down the lane.

I took the cake off the fire and collected a handful of nuts, which weren't quite ripe, crunched them open with my teeth and stuffed them in with the elderberries and toasted the other side. I admit it was a bit soggy in the middle, but it tasted like heaven to a pair of hungry fifteen-year-olds.

That was the last time we went fishing together. Rock-'n'-roll and girlfriends erupted on to the scene. I sold my fishing rods to buy suede shoes and Chuck Berry LPs. I was in with the in crowd. Lynn was a prefect. And my family moved from Somerset to the city.

Growing Awareness

After *Lady Chatterley's Lover* had been cleared by the courts as okay reading material, even for 'servants and wives', I bought a trilby hat, a trench coat, learned to tie a bow-tie, knocked on the door of the *Bristol Evening Post* and asked for a job.

Incredibly, Richard Hawkins gave me a job as a reporter – much to the annoyance of the news editor who already had his hands full with other, in his eyes, useless protégés of the editor including Tom Stoppard, who sat at the back of the reporters' room in a black jacket and dark glasses, chain smoking. There was also another potential genius whose name I forget, but who achieved momentary fame when he won the 'name this aeroplane' competition by calling the strange machine Concorde. Of course, there were bound to be snags and finally the news editor's patience expired and he asked the editor to fire me.

In a tense showdown a compromise was reached, I became the editor's PA – dogsbody and wine carrier actually – and the news editor snorted triumphantly back to his desk, rid of at least one pest. As PA to the editor my contribution to the success of the paper was unremarkable; and as the paper continues to thrive to this day, I obviously inflicted no lasting damage. And although over the years my friendship with Hawkins has been, to say the very least, tenuous, I shall be eternally grateful to him for introducing me to food in general and to George Perry Smith's 'Hole in the Wall' in particular.

I should remind you that in the late 1950s and early 1960s restaurants as we know them today did not exist. There were no Albert Rouxs and the gastronomic getalong gang and Gault and Millaut in those days were probably flogging yellow pages or something. Fine, real restaurants were very few and far between. Of those that there were, George's 'Hole in the Wall' had to be one of the greatest, and even today, despite splendid advances in the cooking and understanding of food in Britain, I still would give my all to eat again the first meal that George cooked for me and to feel again that sense of sheer excitement and amazement that I experienced when I was barely eighteen. Of course, today's kids get to eat out early in life and are much more sophisticated, and probably wouldn't be fazed in the way I was. But for me it was just as stunning as the first rock-'n'-roll. I had known nothing like it before in my life. I was so naive I didn't even know who Elizabeth David was.

George was bearded and wore sandals, an open neck shirt and had the eyes of a prophet – he'd have been really good serving 'Last Suppers'. I think that women were crazy about him. The girls who served were like ladies in waiting at some ethereal banquet who took your order from memory. Pens and pads were out. I have loved waitresses of all ages and beauty ever since.

We sat at a plain polished table and one of those honey-tongued beauties brought the menus, written on two formica boards, the contents of which left me reeling with excitement, ignorance and embarrassment. Turn at once to page 14 to see the menu I saw.

Hawkins sat very still and upright at the table and studied the wine list long and hard, before ordering some Pouilly Fuissé and Gevrey Chambertin. For a man so passionate about food and wine he showed no emotion at all. I, on the other hand, was agog, but trying to be very cool about the whole thing. Such richness of choice left me indecisive, so Richard advised me to take the cold table (one of the few culinary creations that can truly be called legendary), then *Perdrix aux Choux*. This, I soon

INTRODUCTION

Cold Beginnings

Various hors d'œuvres	from 12/6
Jambon persillé	12/6
Jellied eels	10/6
Ceviche – a Mexican dish of marinated fish with a tomato and chilli sauce	11/6
Terrine of game with cream cheese, nuts and olives	12/6
Mussels with saffron	12/6
Peperoni Don Salvatore (anchovy and garlic sauce)	8/6

Hot Beginnings

Garbure savoyarde – game soup with cheese and celery croûtons	7/6
Fish soup with garlic croûtons and sauce rouille	8/6
Petites fondues à la bourguignonne	8/6
Mussels – marinière in garlic butter	15/6
Flamiche – a leek and cream tart, 20 minutes	9/6
Pheasant rissoles 'à la parisienne' with marsala and bouillon	13/6
Aubergine fritters with provençale sauce	9/6

Main Dishes

– usually –

Cold buffet: roast chicken, cider-baked ham, noix de veau à l'alsacienne, loin of pork with truffles	21/–
Fish 'plaki' – marinated in lemon and herbs, cooked with tomatoes and white wine	25/–
La queue de bœuf des vignerons – oxtail cooked with grapes and herbs	21/–

Pheasant braised with celery and port wine	30/–
Entrecote or rump steak 'à la bordelaise'	27/6
Pork noisettes with prunes and cream	21/–
Roast game, according to shopping and season, from:	
Pheasant, plain or 'à la cauchoise', 40 minutes	60/–
Saddle of hare with grapes and cream, 30 minutes	45/–
Wild duck (*underdone*) 'à la presse', with a bigarade sauce, 30 minutes	52/6
– sometimes –	
Cold buffet: lobster salad	35/– to 40/–
Scallops with bacon and white wine	16/6
Blanquette of veal – cooked with lemon and herbs, finished with egg and cream	21/–
Chicken roasted in tarragon butter, finished with brandy and cream	21/–
Goose, cooked 'à la poitevine' in tomatoes and white wine, served with chestnuts, bacon and sugared onions	30/–
Fillet steak baked in pastry with mushrooms and port wine, 30 minutes for two	60/–
Perdrix aux choux	30/–

Endings

Cheeses 5/– Home-made ices 7/6 and sorbets 5/– Cheesecake 6/6 St Emilion au chocolat 6/6 Candied oranges with curaçao and cream 8/6 Apple meringue pie with cream 6/6 Apples in Calvados 9/6 Coeur à la crème with pears in red wine 8/6

---

found out, was an aromatic pot of partridge stewed with cabbage and white wine. The cabbage tasted vinous and gamey, the partridge was succulent. I ate the lot and spooned the last drops of the juice from the pot. I looked up, distressed to find that Hawkins, his plate delicately half eaten, was staring, with hands folded as if in prayer, at the ceiling and chewing carefully. That uneasy feeling of being uncouth swept over me. I need not have worried, he was so absorbed in his dinner that I'm sure he was quite unaware of my presence, let alone my chomping, hasty gluttony.

Presently, another angel cleared the plates and then brought me a bowl of *St Emilion au chocolat*, a thick, smooth chocolate sauce poured over a little macaroon steeped in

Cognac and topped with thick cream. Hawkins, of course, had cheese and Bath Olivers, in order, he explained, to avoid wasting the remainder of the Chambertin.

It was many years before I felt able actually to talk to George Perry Smith and when I did I asked him how he learned to cook. 'Oh, I can't really cook,' he said, 'I just rely on Elizabeth David.' It was a bit like Moses coming down from the mountain with the tablets and saying okay chaps, this is what we've got to do. A typically modest remark from a culinary genius who should be knighted for his dedication to and influence on eating, drinking and cooking in Britain. Oh, by the way, my version of that first memorable meal I had with George is on page 150.

'My name is Corporal of Horse Clark, they call me the Black Mamba because I strike so fast. Nobody, repeat nobody calls me Nobby. Is that clear?'

Well, of course, it was clear to most of us and we contained our mirth, but the guy standing next to me, Rupert somebody or another, burst into fits of uncontrollable laughter. He might have got away with stifling his giggles had he not, in his frantic attempt to clasp his hand over his mouth, inadvertently knocked his hat off. Naturally enough, the sight of a Mons Officer Cadet School hat falling to the ground without a previous command being issued is to a drill sergeant viz Corporal of Horse Clark what a red rag is to a bull. With his face bristling and his pace-stick firmly right-angled under his arm, he stamped sideways like a computerised crab, along the rank and halted smartly in front of the offending hat and the tall cadet that stood above it. As his heels snapped together, without pausing for breath he plunged his pace-stick into the stomach of dear Rupert and exclaimed, 'Sir, there is a **** at the end of this stick.' Rupert, to his eternal credit and to my misfortune, because it was then that I started to giggle, squared his shoulders, stuck out his chest, even though the brightly polished brass point of the pace-stick was causing him some discomfort and said brightly, nay, not brightly, but in clear ringing tones, 'Not at this end Staff'.

In the way of fate it was not Rupert that ran ten times around the drill square with his rifle over his head, it was I for having laughed at a superior. This inadvertent fall from grace made me a marked man during my time at Mons Officer Cadet School. I was known as a wag, something that people like Corporal of Horse Clark, the Company Commander and indeed the Camp Commandant wholly despised. And despite the fact that I was an enthusiastic and dedicated student, I was always in trouble.

Like the time they planned a little night-time shooting exercise. This involved us crawling around in mud in the middle of the night. An old hand gave me a tip: 'Even though the time-table says that you return to barracks at 3 a.m., and the morning starts absolutely as normal at 7 a.m., be warned, because they will spring an unscheduled rifle inspection just before breakfast, and of course, you won't have cleaned it.' So I hit on a wizard idea. I shot into town, bought a pair of lady's tights and with the skilful use of some scissors made a sleeve that would fit over the breech of my rifle, thus keeping it clean should I fall into the mud, yet still allowing the easy fitting of the magazine. That evening, before the exercise, we were issued with two magazines, one containing live ammunition, one empty.

I decided to test my theory and, carefully pointing the rifle at my bed, snapped in the empty magazine and operated the mechanism of the gun to make sure the system would work. Unfortunately, I had chosen the wrong magazine and blasted a neat hole through the mattress. This naturally resulted in the most dire consequences. I was confined to camp for twenty-eight days, obliged to wear uniform each and every day, all day, and made to do extra drill parades as if I were a common mutineer. The worst of it was that I couldn't escape to the Hen and Chickens, an excellent hostelry some miles from the School which served wonderful game dishes, excellent wine and was generous with its measures of port. Needless to say, I took my punishment stoically and by working hard and diligently, gained the grudging respect of my instructors.

It was during this time that we were unexpectedly woken in the small hours of the morning and told to be ready for a map reading

16

exercise, for which full battle equipment would be worn. We were heavily laden in this kit and my room-mates scoffed at me when they saw me packing my little Primus stove into an already overfilled rucksack.

We assembled in the half-light of the winter dawn outside our wooden hut, under the bleak electric lights, rather like a bunch of dissidents waiting to be transported to Siberia. In a rare moment of compassion, or even dare I say it humanity, Corporal of Horse Clark, who had a head like a death mask and skin like a tortoise, hissed to me from the gap that passed as a mouth as he inspected my boots, my belt, my buckles and my blanco: 'Do well on this one, Sir, and you'll be all right.' Then he stamped off to the cadet next to me and came out with one of his immortal one-liners as he spat into the cadet's ear, 'Am I hurting you Sir?' 'No Sir,' replied the cadet. 'Well I should be because I'm standing on your hair.' I didn't even smile.

It was not a map reading exercise! They marched us to the railway station and took us to Dartmoor. Dartmoor in winter of all places! I love Dartmoor, I love Exmoor, and the Yorkshire moors, I really like winter too. Winter is a fabulous time. You wake up hot under the heavy blankets but your nose is cold. No sound comes through the frosted window. The stream that tinkles like distant church bells in summer is now silent and the cocks no longer crow. The soft Somerset slopes are thick with snow like old-fashioned plum puddings, fat and fruity under the white sauce. The slopes that years ago, blue with cold and tense with excitement, I tramped for hours with a spade, a handful of nets, a ferret and my Uncle Ken. On a good day, a dozen or more paunched rabbits would be hanging stiff from the crossbars of our bikes by noon, leaving frozen drops of blood scattered like rubies in the snow. We ate thick cheese sandwiches and pickled onions, and sipped scalding sweet tea from a flask.

I love winter and its very special food. You pick sprouts that are thick with frost and taste sweet and nutty. You mash swede with butter and black pepper, and mop up the sauce from a rabbit stew. You roast wild duck with glazed turnips, or marinate a boned leg of pork in wine and herbs. When roasted, it tastes like wild boar. Frost and cold does much for the flavour of food. Winter perch or pike are full of vigour and colour. Fresh perch cleaned and gutted, grilled over the embers of the Sunday fire, make a brilliant supper.

In winter you can stand on the touchline with a hip-flask and cheer the home team; and after the match, a mug of mulled wine in hand, you can tell them why they lost. You can trudge over the lowlands with a gun, or lie cold and cramped in a punt. You can cast into the winter waves on some desolate beach or skilfully lure great pike from the dark reaches of a winter river. Or you can curl up in front of the fire, sip a glass of port and dream of the good old days.

Some winters I would seek refuge at the dark Exmoor farmhouse of my friends, Ted and Molly. On winter weekends there was a gastronomic delight, despite the draughts and outside loo, because Molly was a cook who kept a larder with chutneys and preserves and, most important of all, bowls of lard, fat and dripping. I recall a meal that started with eel smoked in the huge chimney in the sitting room, washed down with sharp cider. After the eels came a wild rabbit stewed with homecured bacon, a crispy roast pig's head with succulent meat under the golden crackling, and a pigeon, roasted in fat collected from many earlier roasts, with a woodcock and a rook. There was an all-purpose gravy made from simmering a pot of game giblets and pig's trotters. All served with mountains of mashed swede and roasted parsnips – and more cider. For lunch next day she drew off pints from the stock pot and added pearl barley till it was cooked, then thickened this wonderful soup with some mashed swede left over from the night before.

Ted had been stalking the fast-running Exmoor stream with a rod and some lively pink worms, and returned with a dozen or so brilliant brown and vermilion dwarf trout, plump and full grown at about four inches, which we fried in bacon fat to follow the soup. Virtually everything that was eaten had been grown or caught with rod or gun – quite legitimately, of course (or so Ted said). I would feel a twinge of guilt for my city ways when he raised a glass to toast the meal, as he always did, with the words, 'The Lord will provide, and the meek can quite easily inherit the earth.'

Next time I see him I must ask about that large horned animal hanging in the outside larder. . . .

But I digress, back to the 'map reading' exercise. We got to Okehampton late that afternoon and they calmly said, 'All you have to do, gentlemen, is walk across the moor tonight and don't worry, because we are going to drive on ahead of you in some nice warm Land Rovers and be there to meet you in the morning.' We set off in groups of four. I was the leader of our little team and, although charged with the responsibility of accurate map reading, at least I didn't have to carry the radio, the rocket launcher or the barbed wire. By about the middle of the night Brooking Thomas had developed a couple of blisters and was beginning to chunter as well as getting less keen on carrying the barbed wire, but I was quite chuffed, because we made our first rendezvous ahead of schedule and in front of the other teams. So there was still plenty of rum to be poured into the vegetable soup that they had waiting for us before we set off again.

Despite the snow it was a pleasant night, very clear and moonlit; in fact, it was like walking on the moon. We marched on for three reasons; one because we had been told to, two we had been hyped up to win and three, when we reached the base camp there would be a whacking great hot breakfast. I mean it would be a breakfast of thick slices of streaky bacon, a bit salty with a thick rind. The fried bread would be cold or very fatty. The scrambled eggs would be made from powder and the tea would have mud in it, but it would taste fabulous.

We got to the base camp first and sat around waiting for the ration truck and the other parties to come in. I remember thinking it was odd that although we had all left from the same point, my platoon's little groups approached the camp from every point of the compass. The ration truck arrived with wonderful supplies, but it was not until it disappeared over the skyline that we realised they had not left us a cooker. So I cooked breakfast for twenty-six chaps on my Primus stove.

A full mug is better than a half empty crystal glass.

Isn't it strange how life goes round in circles? Shortly after I left the *Evening Post*, so did Richard Hawkins, and he bought a cherry farm in Provence. And so it's his fault again. Because one day, while camping on his farm during an horrific thunderstorm, I took shelter in what turned out to be an estate agent's office and bought a semi-derelict grocer's shop and converted it into a restaurant.

Foolishly or wisely, I shall never know, I moved to L'Isle-sur-la-Sorgue and fell in love with the magic of Provence. Early each morning I strolled the 250 yards or so from the restaurant to do the shopping. I was part of a dawn chorus of feeders and traders, united by the wonderful produce this region of France has to offer. Just opposite the grubby façade of the Café de France was a trestle table laden with wicker baskets of fresh herbs and garden greenery, still dripping and glistening with dew, such as: a tub of springy chives; a dilapidated can of crisp salad sprigs; and vivid bundles of fiery radishes.

And as I wandered to buy the day's ingredients, perhaps some fragrant garlic sausage from the butcher's, or some soft, creamy goats' cheese, I would see this little *tableau* take shape. Its creator was a robust, busy little madame, whose plumpness was contained beneath both overcoat and apron. As an artist her palette was perhaps limited, but it was nonetheless tinged with every colour of the rainbow. Green salad leaves were edged in red; dark green artichokes were veined purple and mauve like old men's noses and under-age kindergarten *frisée* was tipped with delicate, crisp yellow wisps. As the church clock opposite my friend Leo's café struck seven, she would be adding the final dabs of dandelion, the last brush strokes of sweet basil or spinach.

An hour's shopping later and it was time for breakfast. Strong coffee, sometimes splashed with a dash of rum, or perhaps a glass of wine. Leo's world smelled like him. Old. Summer or winter there was the whiff of Mazout, the oil used to fire the boiler. Sometimes it was just the lingering memory of colder days; at others a living, lung-penetrating pungency, layered with pastis and Gitanes. And when the summer waned and the stove wheezed into autumnal action, the café would become a place of plotting and guarded talk. The normally gregarious bar crowd would splinter into secretive little groups. They would huddle together with trusted friends and nod heads approvingly into the cautiously open mouths of ragged carrier bags. No stranger or rival ever got to see their contents.

But one September night *le patron* beckoned me furtively into his scruffy inner sanctum. The way Leo tilted his grey head and twinkled his eyes told me I was about to be party to something very special. Into the tiny, tatty kitchen I followed him, as he warily checked that no interloping snooper was tailing us into his dingy domain beyond the smoke-filled bar. Only after a quick peek behind the greying net curtain in the dividing door did he feel safe.

Reassured we were alone and unwatched, he delved through two decades of accumulated debris in the drawer of his kitchen table. From beneath the elastic bands, tangles of old string and misshapen blobs of wax which had once been candles, he unearthed a small knot of brown paper. Conspiratorially, he pressed it into my palm. 'Don't tell anyone,' he said. 'And don't open it now.' I had to wait until I got home to unravel the mystery, and the fist-sized brown paper twist. Inside were what looked like three well-bashed squash balls with a dull, black bloom. Leo had presented me with one of the gastronomic treats of the French year. The black gold at the end of every mushroom-hunter's rainbow. Truffles.

That night, as my benefactor went back behind the bar and the wizened old men went on whispering, I had a feast I shall never forget. I wrapped each coal-black truffle in caul and, after seasoning, wrapped it in foil. The silver parcels were laid to cook on the edge of my fire, and I rubbed garlic into the rough surface of some hard-grained brown bread. After half an hour my banquet was ready, the foil balls sizzling hot and the bread toasted and dripping with virgin Provençal oil. The hat-trick of truffles singed my fingers and left my heart soaring. I still dream about that heavenly medley of flavours as I dipped my garlicky croûton into a bowl of Châteauneuf-du-Pape from which I would slurp between each blissful, munching mouthful. Leo had indeed honoured me.

His café, with its high-ceilinged smokiness so full of truffle talk and suspicion every September, was always a good place to start the day. Whether inside at the red formica tables with crunchy nut shells underfoot, or outside on the dappled pavement terrace as the rising sun bathed the old ochre roofs in warmth and light. And then it was back to work, as others piled in to idle and to play cards, or sip Armagnac as they strained to peer through the grimy windows. From *le petit déjeuner* to tiffin was but a glug and a few Gauloise butts. If breakfast is important to the French, then lunch is a matter of life or death.

I remember sitting outside Leo's one lunchtime as the church clock across the road struck midday. As I sipped chilled Kir, waiting for my friend Pierre, the streets suddenly emptied and the shops shuttered in near synchronised unity. I soon learned that everything stops for lunch. Only the sun stays out. But not the purple-cheeked old men, the be-suited bank managers, the drivers of the deafening diggers and the man behind the wheel of the giant sixteen-wheeled Moroccan wine tanker. They waddle, shuffle, scuttle and lumber into the shade, and into a restaurant. Even the parking fines take a lunch break in Provence. A plaque on one wall announces a daily amnesty between the sacred hours of 12 to 2 p.m. But I doubt if even clamping could quell the chomping and ritual of the Provençal lunchbreak.

The streets had cleared, and still no sign of Pierre. We had arranged to visit a wonderful new restaurant he had stumbled upon which served *coq au vin* so divine it would be a crime to miss it. His enthusiasm had been breathless and I was swept along. The chef was such a perfectionist that he even killed his own animals to make sure the sauce would be thickened with only the very freshest blood.

The twenty-kilometre drive to the Hotel St Hubert would be more than rewarded, he had said. It would be paradise on a plate. Now I was restless; and hungry. Pierre was late and I could see our heavenly feast fading by the minute. At last a battered blue Renault bumped to a reluctant standstill near my feet. Pierre bounded out full of apologies and tales of broken cars and borrowed replacements. I leapt in and Pierre sped off on an engine-screaming drive, slicing through the blood-red rocks and the tilled red soil of Apt and Roussillon. The fruit which hangs from the neatly serried cherry trees on either side of the road are crystallised each year to dandify Christmas cakes from Cheam to Cheadle. How much nicer they looked *au naturel*.

Pierre raced nonchalantly in Frederique's complaining car, one elbow on the steering wheel as he lit a cigarette. A drowsy dog narrowly missed death, but then Frederique's car breathed its last. Dead. *'Merde,'* we spat in stereo. The vision of lunch was torturing us and our tummies were rumbling. Could we fix it perhaps? I prepared to tinker. With two broken cars under his belt, Pierre had a better idea. He strode on to the road and flagged down a bemused motorist.

'What's the problem?' asked the driver. 'The problem?' said Pierre, his hand already on the passenger door. 'The problem is we're late for . . . oh you mean the car. The **** car. Can you give us a lift? We'll worry about that heap of *merde* later.' It was all a matter of priorities, see.

And so we did get our lunch at the Hotel St Hubert (see Claud's recipe for Stuffed Rabbit on page 155) which stood elegant and over-shadowed by a medieval *château* in a modest hill village tinted the colour of soft nougat. Behind the dull green doors and sparkling windows, rosy-cheeked farmers spooned soup and ripped bread from crusty loaves as we dashed in.

Outside the restaurant their fields were empty, like the streets by Leo's café. The workers were munching their lunches elsewhere in impromptu refectories. Each year the *vignerons* set up long trestle tables in barns to cope with the feeding of the annual invasion of pickers. In chummy chaos and the camaraderie of the field they share cured ham, warm bread spread with Provençal *tapenade*, garlic sausage, black olives and, of course, wine.

To celebrate our safe arrival at the restaurant Pierre and I drank champagne and myrtleberry liqueur. We ate wild mushrooms and asparagus the size of Roman candles. Then there was boned rabbit, stuffed with its kidneys and served with broccoli purée, and of course, Pierre's heavenly *coq au vin*. It had been an eventful journey, but what a way to work up an appetite!

In winter, lunch in Provence might be plump, free-range ducks, gently simmered with turnips and baby carrots until the sauce was as black as the charred Charollais steaks, served bubbling with herb butter, or marooned in a lake of marrow-enriched shallot and Chambertin sauce. In spring it might be a fast-roasted duckling, whose dribbling juices would be briskly reduced with a flagon or few of good red wine. As the tender, pink-fleshed breasts and sauce were downed, the duckling legs were popped under a hot grill to be eaten as a second course with stewed peas and artichoke hearts.

The larder seemed full all year round, but winter was one of my favourite times. When the sky was still impossibly blue, but the pavement parasols had closed their wings and gone into hibernation. In winter the shutters were tight and berets were clamped on to heads with hands chilled blue as the mistral roared through the streets. I loved the wind screaming through the now empty town square. I loved watching the old priest, his cassock flapping like a storm-lashed sail, struggle across to the church. I loved warming my bones by Leo's smelly stove, with an everlasting cup of coffee and a quiet broken only by the gentle flick of my companions' cards.

Each year, on one special winter evening in L'Isle-sur-la-Sorgue, the afternoon stillness would darken to a deafening drunken revelry. It was the night of the *Grand Loto*, a game-winning game, for which the prizes were inevitably argued over. Trophies of scarlet-coated hares were festooned outside Leo's café with the black-pepper-speckled hams and dangling salami. A wild boar swung heavily in the freezing wind of the closing day, its hind leg nudging partridge and pheasant for the runners-up. These were the glistening, glinting prizes to be won. In a nearby shop other examples of the *traiteur*'s wares were displayed like a macabre multi-coloured still life. Still in death. A window crammed with the fruits of winter skies and scrub, the brown and cream-dotted thrushes, the emerald green brilliance of wild duck and the beige pink baldness of well-plucked quail.

Throughout the year the plump *boucher* and *madame boucher* conducted their business in a setting that looked like a cross between a Renaissance painting and a medieval torture chamber. Knives glinted. Purple spills of blood dripped from huge hanging carcasses and ashen-faced apprentices stooped under the weight of scrubbed pink pig slung over their shoulders. I like butchers' shops, watching the chop and fillet, the slice and flash of knife. The sawdust on the floor is thick and speckled with crimson. I can trace the outline of a perfect pork chop with my polished toe.

When the *Grand Loto* prizes of pâté, pigeon and pig had been handed out, I ended up a winner anyway. My friends Eva and René had prepared a rare regional treat for me. A *brochette des oiseaux Provençaux* – thrushes doused with olive oil and garlic. Eva was in charge. She sipped a pastis and smoothed her floral pinny, then laid the tiny birds to grill in the glowing embers of her hearth. René had just brought in a rabbit he bagged that afternoon. The larder was full. The ducks and chickens outside had been fed for the day. Now it was our turn. The *petits oiseaux* were reverentially laid to rest on crispy croûtons layered with foie gras. We swigged heartily some of the fragrant red wine from Mont Ventoux, spirits flying like birds. . . .

Twice a year, at Easter and in August, the village witnessed an avalanche of antiquity. Dealers from all over the south of France converged for the biggest antiques fair the south could boast. Lorries laden with precious china, furniture, paintings and delicate Dresden trundled down the dreadful *autoroute du soleil* and disgorged their tacky junk to be pecked at by vulturous traders.

At Easter I would sit out in the spring warmth under the shade of a plane tree and watch the throng grabbing and grasping. On my other side, in the dark green waters of the Sorgue, boys fished and ducks swam. And the streets would seethe. In the middle of buying and selling, a stubbly-faced stall-holder was frying golden-yolked eggs on a blackened camping stove. Under his fading canvas *bache* he slid the eggs on to an enamel plate and dropped a splash of vinegar into the fuming frying pan. The dark butter fizzed and he tipped it on to his sizzling eggs. The sight of him slugging red wine from a mug sent me off in search of refreshment.

I strolled down the pedestrian walkway, as heavy trucks groaning with melons thundered over the bridge and out of town. The footpath was really intended for the patrons of a gloomy hotel manned by black-jerkined waiters who hovered outside like crows at a funeral. The place was dead. Everyone was at the Café Bellevue. Pichelin's Bar, where the garrulous Guy Pichelin greeted me with a hearty thump on the back of my head. He puffed and dashed and called me 'General' and 'Old Cabbage', and gave me a belting kiss on both cheeks. A double-strength pastis was thrust into my hands. While he rolled back on to his worn heels, as brash as his wife was blonde, the bar filled.

He smiled the satisfied smile of a man who knows his place and purpose in life. While he serenaded incomers, his wife sweated and slaved in a cramped kitchen the size of a

22

cupboard. I choked on Guy's throat-clutching aperitif and he ran through the possibilities.

Spaghetti and chicken, maybe. Or fluffy pike quenelles and crayfish sauce. A towering mound of steaming salt cod with dazzlingly orange carrots.

Roast milk lamb with purée *Steak frites* or fragrant steamed clams with creamy garlic mayonnaise.

At the next table shaven-headed men with dusty neckerchiefs tempted me with their bowls of crisp green *salade composée*. Forks stabbed sprigs of springy *frisée* and curly endive and pierced ripe, red tomatoes, bitter black olives and plump anchovy fillets.

Or perhaps the *civet de porcelet?* That's best today, said Guy, and I knew there was little point arguing.

Earlier in the day I had bumped into the buxom Madame Pichelin in the crowded butcher's. She had been deliberating, with the deadly seriousness of a priest delivering the Holy Sacraments, over pink cutlets, loins and legs. After witnessing her perfectionist poking, prodding, sniffing and waving, I knew the pork she chose for her *civet* had to be superb. As I watched her, I had been quite happy to idle there a while, waiting for a pig's head to cook for tomorrow's lunch. I was absorbed with the butchery and already looking forward to the next day's dish, which I was going to roast in the baker's wood-burning oven.

When at last the slippered old man had shuffled out with his sliver of veal, and the stroppy high-heeled lady had teetered out with a plump, creamy leg of lamb, my head arrived. Horrors! The porker was earless! Your fault, shrugged the butcher, you should have specified. But what had happened to the ears, which I knew would be crispy and delicious when roasted?

'Ah,' said the butcher. 'All our ears go to the Spanish.' It turned out that a group of Hispanic travellers, who knew a good thing when they tasted it, had lodged first claim on all the piggy lobes. Unless they were specifically claimed by the head-hunter, they made a pig's ear of it. My loss, their gain.

At least I had the compensation of the Café Bellevue's rich *civet de porcelet* with chicory, and a healthy serving of Vinsobres. What a very silly name for such a very strong wine. Almost as silly as the size of Guy's bill. A morning's slaving and stirring for the price of a necktie.

You needed feeding up for the antiques fair. All that lifting and lugging had to be fuelled. The president of the fair, Albert Gassier, was not so much fuelled as overcharged. Bear-like and towering, he greeted you with a big hug and a slap on the back that made Guy Pichelin's feel like a gentle tap. His arms embraced a world of antiques and amigos. They could encompass a crowd, and once inside you knew you couldn't escape. There was no arguing with Albert. If he wanted to buy you a drink, you drank. Why worry if you also had to pay for it. And if he wanted to do you a good turn, you gulped and gratefully accepted.

One afternoon, shortly before the fair was about to start, he offered to do me a favour. 'Mucho dinero,' he promised, thumping my back. Behind his yellow formica counter Leo was listening carefully. What had I to do?

It was important work, he said. It was to make me a very rich man, he said. It had to do with bribes, building, bricks and barter. And he needed me to do the job. Even then he wouldn't explain. The agony was dragged out until nine that evening, when I arrived at Albert's office to discover his favour and my fate. I was to cook the barbecue for the duration of the antiques fair.

Albert had it all sussed out. There was no escape. My restaurant would close. I would make use of the huge fireplace he had built into the newly-constructed hangar at the bottom of his garden. I would merely feed the entire antique-dealing population from the south of France for a week, and he would take a modest agent's fee of 10 per cent.

Who could refuse? Even a sturdy Scotch couldn't send me to sleep that night. A million brochettes floated before my weeping eyes. Seering charcoal stabbed at my terror glands. What had I done?

Guessing wildly, I ordered what I thought should be enough supplies. The next day was a never-ending chain of dread and horror at what I was about to take on. Would half a ton of charcoal last one day or five? I didn't have a clue.

Albert's cavernous hall was housing a hundred and fifty extra stalls, and into it I ferried countless tables, chairs, flower tubs and trestles. The result was stark and stable-like. A sprinkling of scarlet geraniums softened the concrete and steel. It would have to do. As the crocodile of cursing dealers arrived, my adrenalin surged. They jostled and sniped, vying to set up the best stall. Could they have a few centimetres more, Monsieur Gassier? Could they shut up or get lost came the reply!

Meanwhile, I tried not to crack. Would the tin bath of salad be sufficient, or should I have made it a swimming pool? I had had sacks full of rolls and buckets of brochettes made to my exact specifications. But would the starving *brocanteurs* scream for more? With an hour to go Albert loomed into view, a chilling smile on the lips which gripped a Gauloise. 'Everything *ça va?*' '*Ça va.*' By noon it had to be.

It was over the top lads. Into battle and never mind the bullets and blue steaks! The Calor gas cooker roared, and the kebabs spat like wild cats. Cellophane ripped and paper plates flew like UFOs. When the last sizzling steak was wearily delivered to the two hundred and fiftieth trader, and the final retreat sounded, I knew I had triumphed. I had survived under fire. What's more, I had survived one of Albert Gassier's favours.

Never put off till tomorow the good meal you can have today

Years before I went to France I had run a small bistro in Bristol in the late 1960s. It was an elementary little place with about four tables that sat eight or nine people per table. It had an open kitchen, two or three old domestic gas stoves linked together, and a simple menu of freshly prepared dishes like stuffed peppers, moussaka, boeuf bourguignon, Hungarian goulash, kidneys in cream sauce and chicken Provençale. Good, honest so-called French food, and although we only sat about thirty-six people at one time, some evenings we would do as many as a hundred and twenty covers. Indeed, a queue usually formed outside the entrance before we opened at seven o'clock. I reckoned it was a really authentic little place, it was certainly incredibly popular, but niggling in my mind all the time was the feeling that I didn't really know what I was talking about. I didn't really know, for example, why a plain salad of tomatoes, chopped basil and olive oil was quite good in my bistro, but was absolutely stunning and indescribably delicious when served on a heavy white porcelain plate on the terrace of a workaday Provençal restaurant.

Why was it that despite people's apparent culinary awareness, they wouldn't eat in the unfussy way of the French, but would demand with their kidneys in cream sauce – a dish that really needed only some rice and then a green salad – sprouts, carrots, potatoes and French beans as well?

Anyway, to cut a long story short, I returned from France in 1980, enriched by my experiences there, inspired by the unassuming genius of Claud Arnaud and totally at ease with the fundamentals of cooking, be it the slowly simmered peasant *pot-au-feu*, or the immediacy of a butter-mounted sauce that became the hallmark of modern cooking, and decided to open a small restaurant once again.

I set off with gusto and vigour to produce small menus of freshly cooked dishes prepared from the freshest seasonal ingredients. In summer I would concentrate on fish, in spring there would be Welsh lamb, and if you ordered a leg of Welsh lamb it would be roasted for you then and there. In winter there would be game – pheasant, grouse, partridge, mallard, teal, blackcock and snipe. I took the trouble to get unpasteurised farmhouse French cheeses, offered fresh fruits and had a splendid wine list. People who loved food loved the restaurant, but unfortunately, and at the time I was unaware of this, partly because my interpretation of modern cooking relied upon the freshness of the ingredients and the simplicity of their preparation rather than on the more popular, but misguided ideas of *nouvelle cuisine*, and partly because, when, after ten years, people still wanted me to slap a plate of stuffed peppers or moussaka in front of them with a pleasant insult and a slap across the back, the restaurant was not the financial success that it needed to be to make life really cheerful.

It was well supported, much admired and loved, but people could only afford to come occasionally, unlike in my bistro days when some customers would come two or three times a week. And although my integrity as a cook was intact, or even beyond reproach, I had clearly misjudged the market. As a restaurateur I was like a river that never quite got to the sea, and I was slipping slowly but inexorably into the abyss of the financial also-ran.

But isn't it funny that when the storm clouds gather and blot out the sun, when the heart becomes as heavy as lead and you live in fear of that quiet man who stands at the bar with the black briefcase that contains yet another writ, isn't it funny how as Mr Micawber used to say, 'Something will turn up'.

I shall never forget the night. The first person to come into the restaurant was a bailiff with some very serious news – you know the man wants eleven dollar bills but you've only got ten – and the last person to leave was a slightly fat, bald, greedy, gluttonous, cheerful television producer called David Pritchard, who shortly before he nodded off into a dish of clams grilled with garlic butter, which he was enjoying as a post-dessert snack much as Gargantua might have enjoyed a roast suckling pig after a banquet which terminated with a mountain of steamed treacle pudding, said to me, 'Have you ever thought whether you would like to make a television programme?' And although I thought he was bragging, it in fact became a reality and thanks to that slightly plump, gourmet television producer with only slightly thinning hair, I was rescued from a certain financial holocaust.

Don't dine in restaurants with folk who spend more time with the bill, a pen and a pocket calculator than with a raspberry soufflé

THE IMPORTANCE OF HAPPY SHOPPING

Shopping is one of my favourite hobbies. Whether it is buying fishing tackle, books, records, clothes or presents for friends, I love it and it's great doing it impulsively.

Shopping for food is one of the most exciting things. Whether you are sifting spices through your fingers in Istanbul, haggling over a leg of kid in a Portuguese market, waltzing through Harrods' Food Hall, arguing with storeholders in a Provençal market, shopping in a Leeds market or pushing a trolley through Waitrose. Shopping is not only exciting, it's also very important. Whether you are the kind of person who chooses a recipe and sets out with a list of ingredients, though I think this is a frustrating way of doing things, or whether you set off with a basic idea of what you want and let yourself be led by what is seasonal and fresh, thoughtful shopping is one of the essentials of a successful meal.

Try to make food shopping a relaxed and happy occasion, don't do it in a hurry. Be prepared to visit different shops; find out where in your locality some enterprising market gardener or poultry farmer takes the trouble to produce organically grown vegetables, or free range fowls and meat.

Take the trouble to buy free range eggs, seek out the shop that sells good Jersey cream, take the time to make friends with your butcher so that, for example, you can get veal bones and calves' feet, which are so useful for making stocks with, or with your fishmonger. Tell him in advance that you will require some cut of meat or some unusual fish so that he can order it for you. Be prepared to touch, sniff and smell the produce that you are offered; be prepared to reject meat that looks old with yellow fat. Imagine that it is as important as any other of your activities: like having your hair done, choosing tickets for the theatre, or planning your holiday and take the same trouble over it.

Cooking is an art — but then so is eating.

Fish and Shellfish
Fresh fish should smell of the sea and seaweed and not be too fishy. Their eyes should be bright, alert and shiny and the gills bright red. The flesh should be firm and tight, not soggy, limp or flaky. In the case of a whole fish it must be stiff, rather like the difference between a freshly picked cucumber and one that you bought in desperation from the wrong kind of corner shop at 9 o'clock one evening. Never buy precooked shellfish, especially lobsters, crayfish and crabs, which must be alive and kicking and feel heavy. Don't buy things like mussels, clams and oysters unless their shells are tightly shut.

Poultry and Game
Wherever possible, buy your game with its fur or feathers on. This way you can see if it is young or old and whether it is one for lightly roasting or more suitable for slow stewing. Your poultry farmer can always then pluck and draw the beast in question.

With chicken and ducks you simply must buy fresh, free range birds, even if you have to travel miles to get them. Bear in mind that an old cockerel or hen no longer fit for laying makes a fine curry or casserole and the young, large ones are splendid for grilling or roasting.

If you use a frozen chicken, duck, or quail that has been battery reared for any of the recipes in this book I am delighted to tell you that it will taste disgusting, so don't buy them.

Beef
Experts argue over the merits of Charollais, a beast that always makes me think of pantomimes, and Angus, Hereford and Devon, et al. But the real problem with beef today is that it's being bred leaner, killed younger and is rarely properly hung.

It's important to find a butcher who clings to the old values of buying his beef on the hoof, slaughtering it and hanging it well. Good beef must be a deep vermilion, finely grained, firm and slightly marbled with fat. It should appear to be dry, not moist, and certainly should not be grainy and bright red. It should have creamy white fat which is not stained or tainted and you must avoid the sort of beef that has a waxy yellow fat around it, because that's very often not beef but an old cow.

Veal
The flesh of good veal should be white or very pale pink and although soft to the touch it should not be flabby, neither should it be moist nor weeping.

Lamb
There is no substitute for good English or Welsh lamb (even the French prefer ours to theirs, and that's saying something). The meat should be pale pink with finely grained flesh and creamy white fat, which indicates, of course, a young lamb.

If the meat is darker or reddish brown, then it's probably an older animal, usually called mutton, but real mutton, which is more difficult to obtain these days, is a very dark colour.

Pork
There are two schools of thought here. Sadly, to my mind, farmers are now breeding virtually fatless pork. For a good roast where you want crisp crackling, you need good, firm flesh with at least ½ inch (1 cm) pure white fat between the flesh and the skin. But, for say a grilled pork chop or a boned out loin of pork, you want a younger animal with finely grained flesh that is lightly marbled with fat and slightly moist to the touch.

Vegetables

If you are not fortunate enough to have a garden whence you can pluck, lift or pick your carefully grown fresh vegetables only minutes before you need to cook them, then do take care to buy vegetables which are in season and which haven't been left lying around in the shop until they have become sad and flabby. Choose, particularly in the case of peas, beans and carrots, the small, young ones. Remember that those huge vegetables that win prizes at the village fête do not automatically taste the best and make friends with your tummy! Don't be afraid to pick vegetables up and smell them. Search out locally grown vegetables where perhaps, as with celery, you may be fortunate enough to find sticks white and crisp with little bits of earth or soot around them, which will indicate that they have been grown in soil by someone who loved them rather than having been forced up under polythene in some undoubtedly exotic, but quite inappropriate, part of the world.

Always try to buy fresh herbs and it's pleasing to note that some supermarkets these days are taking the trouble to stock them.

Fruit

Dramatic scientific progress in methods of preserving, ripening and transporting fruit has led to the undesirable situation of greengrocers' shelves piled high with exotic-looking, but bland-tasting fruits from the four corners of the earth, regardless of the season.

No matter how temptingly displayed, fruits out of season are a waste of money. It is better to create a dessert of freshly picked plums, ripened to sweetness by the summer sun, than it is to have an exotic palette of thinly sliced fruits that have been force-grown, force-ripened and probably irradiated to stop them going bad.

Cheese

Cheese is such a significant part of a well-balanced meal that its selection, storing and serving merits the same attention to detail as any other part of the meal. It is better to have a small selection of authentic farmhouse cheeses, for example, an Irish Milleens, a Cornish Yarg, a properly matured Cheddar, or a classic French Roquefort or Reblochon, than a wide range of those pasteurised, cling-wrapped plastic-flavoured shapes of cheese that adorn so many of our supermarket shelves. Cheese should smell of cream or cows or goats, it should be tangy. Soft cheeses like Brie should feel spongy when you buy them and you must keep them in a cool place, not in the refrigerator. Always have your cheeses at room temperature before you eat them.

Choosing a good wine is as important as choosing a career — only more difficult.

TOOLS OF THE TRADE - SOME SUGGESTIONS

Gardeners are very proud of their tools. They take great care to choose the best trowel, or hoe, or the latest 'hovver or bovver' – a sort of food processor of the garden – but I reckon the tools of the kitchen are pretty neglected.

How often do you go into a shop to buy a knife and actually weigh up the merits of carbon steel versus those of stainless steel? Do you ask yourself whether the knife is properly bal-anced, or if it sits easily in your hand? You'd probably ask those sorts of questions if you were buying a pair of secateurs.

I could go on for pages about every piece of kitchen equipment from the perfect omelette pan or sauce separating jug, to gravy jugs, to woks, to sauteuse pans, to blenders and chop-pers, but instead I'll let the illustrations do the talking. . . .

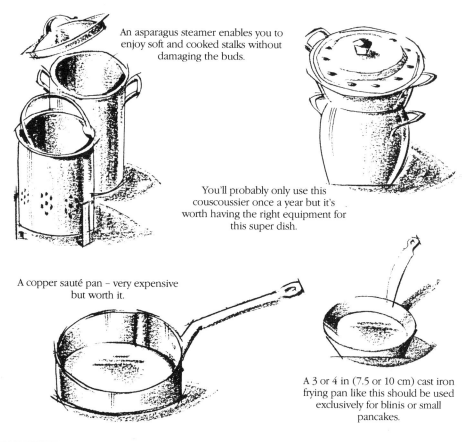

An asparagus steamer enables you to enjoy soft and cooked stalks without damaging the buds.

You'll probably only use this couscoussier once a year but it's worth having the right equipment for this super dish.

A copper sauté pan – very expensive but worth it.

A 3 or 4 in (7.5 or 10 cm) cast iron frying pan like this should be used exclusively for blinis or small pancakes.

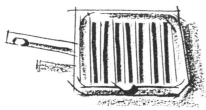

A grill pan like this (there's a Floyd one on the market) is indispensable for steak and chops.

I love kitchen utensils so buy the best-looking fondue set you can afford.

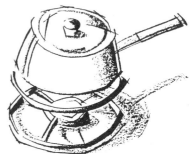

A sauce separator takes fat off the pan juices from a roasted dish. Very, very important.

A heat diffuser is useful for slow or gentle cooking.

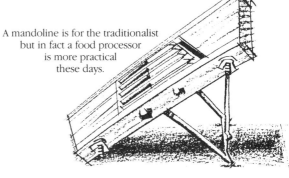

A mandoline is for the traditionalist but in fact a food processor is more practical these days.

If your kitchen is big enough to swing a cat get a salad shaker. A plastic rotary one is quite good to.

My Desert Island luxury item! A kitchen is merely a room without one.

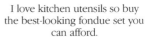

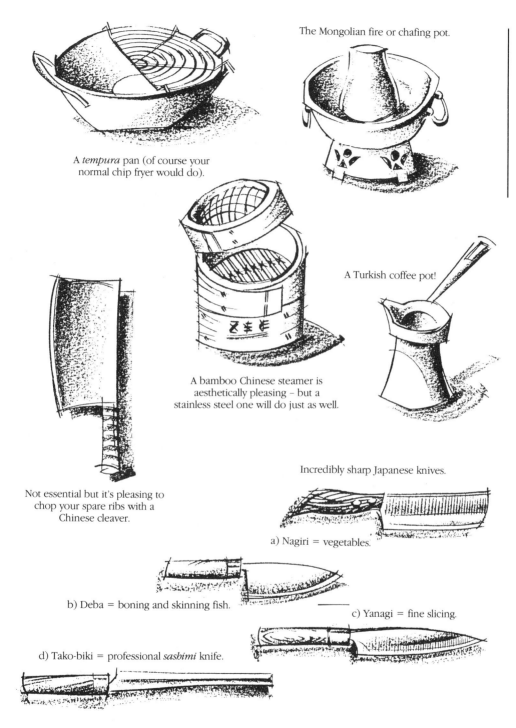

The Mongolian fire or chafing pot.

A *tempura* pan (of course your normal chip fryer would do).

A Turkish coffee pot!

A bamboo Chinese steamer is aesthetically pleasing – but a stainless steel one will do just as well.

Not essential but it's pleasing to chop your spare ribs with a Chinese cleaver.

Incredibly sharp Japanese knives.

a) Nagiri = vegetables.

b) Deba = boning and skinning fish.

c) Yanagi = fine slicing.

d) Tako-biki = professional *sashimi* knife.

A NOTE ON MEASUREMENTS

Although I and a team of culinary geniuses have checked every recipe in this book, please take all cooking times, temperatures and measurements with a pinch of salt! Ovens vary in performance, scales are sometimes incorrect and clocks go wrong. Remember that a dish is cooked when *you* are satisfied – not just because the recipe says so!

Imperial and metric measures are given in this book, so you can use whichever you prefer. But use only one or the other as the amounts are not always interchangeable.

Weights	
Ounces	Recommended conversion to nearest unit of 25 grams
1 oz	25 g
2 oz	50 g
3 oz	75 g
4 oz	100 g
5 oz	150 g
6 oz	175 g
7 oz	200 g
8 oz	225 g
9 oz	250 g
10 oz	275 g
11 oz	300 g
12 oz	350 g
13 oz	375 g
14 oz	400 g
15 oz	425 g
1 lb	450 g
1¼ lb	575 g
1½ lb	675 g
2 lb	900 g
3 lb	1.4 kg
4 lb	1.75 kg
5 lb	2.25 kg
6 lb	2.75 kg

Liquid measures	
Fluid ounces pints	Recommended millilitre conversion
¼ pint	150 ml
6 fl oz	175 ml
7 fl oz	200 ml
8 fl oz	250 ml
9 fl oz	275 ml
½ pint	300 ml
11 fl oz	325 ml
12 fl oz	350 ml
13 fl oz	375 ml
14 fl oz	400 ml
¾ pint	450 ml
16 fl oz	475 ml
17 fl oz	500 ml
18 fl oz	550 ml
19 fl oz	575 ml
1 pint	600 ml
1¼ pints	750 ml
1½ pints	900 ml
1¾ pints	1 litre
2 pints	1.2 litres

Oven temperatures

Temperature	Fahrenheit (°F)	Centigrade (°C)	Gas mark
Very cool	225	110	¼
	250	120	½
Cool	275	140	1
	300	150	2
Moderate	325	160	3
	350	180	4
Moderately hot	375	190	5
	400	200	6
Hot	425	220	7
	450	230	8
Very hot	475	240	9

Flour
All flour used in the recipes is plain unless otherwise stated.

Herbs
All herbs used in the recipes are fresh unless otherwise stated.

BASIC SAUCES RELISHES AND STOCKS

W hen you build a house you put it together in stages and layers and, if the foundations are solid and you buy the best bricks and don't take short cuts, you should end up with something rather splendid. Cooking is like that. Think of relishes and sauces as the decoration. You could go to the nearest mega-market and buy any old coloured paint, but after you've put all that care into building the house, it's worth mixing your own to get the right effect.

Sadly, we've lost the tradition of preserving and pickling and making real sauces and mayonnaise. They've been jilted in favour of things that come out of bottles and packets. So it's dead easy to say: 'I won't bother to make real mayonnaise.'

But, if you want to score over your friends, it's a crucial thing to do, just like bothering to dry your lettuce leaves for the salad so that the dressing isn't diluted, or tracking down a boiling fowl that's done time in the farmyard to make a *coq au vin*, instead of settling for a frozen chicken from the supermarket. It's all part of the love and devotion to detail that good food deserves.

Anyone can boil an egg, smother it in bottled salad cream and call it egg mayonnaise – even if it tastes like something that would be cast out of the works' canteen. But if you whizz up your own dressing with the best olive oil, lemon juice and wine vinegar you have something which will win compliments at a dinner party.

So, here is a random and entirely personal smattering of some really useful sauces and relishes to help you astonish your guests and separate you from the also-rans.

Mayonnaise

It is so easy to learn to make a mayonnaise, an aïoli or a hollandaise sauce, and they are so much better home-made than anything you can buy in a bottle, giving a lift to the humblest dish, such as eggs or salad.

MAKES ABOUT 2 PINTS (1.2 litres)

6 egg yolks, at room temperature
juice of 1 or 2 lemons
1¾ pints (1 litre) olive oil, at room
  temperature

1 tablespoon white wine vinegar
salt
freshly ground black pepper

Beat together the egg yolks and lemon juice in a bowl, using a wooden spoon or a whisk, until they are pale and thick. Add the oil, drop by drop at first, then in a thin stream, beating steadily all the time. Stir in the vinegar and season to taste with salt and pepper.

Alternatively, you can make the mayonnaise in two batches in a food processor or blender. Whizz together half the ingredients, except for the oil, for 30–40 seconds until the eggs are foaming. Dribble in half the oil while the motor is running. Taste and adjust the seasoning, then take out and repeat with the remaining ingredients.

Aïoli

MAKES ABOUT ¾ PINT (450 ml)

8 cloves of garlic
2 egg yolks
¾ pint (450 ml) olive oil

juice of 1 lemon
salt
freshly ground black pepper

The best way of making this is to pound the garlic in a pestle and mortar until it is reduced to a paste. Using a whisk, beat in the egg yolks. Then stir away madly while dribbling in the oil, until you have a thick, yellow mayonnaise. Finally, stir in the lemon juice and season to taste with salt and pepper.

Alternatively, put all the ingredients, except for the oil, into a food processor or blender for 30–40 seconds until the eggs are foaming. Dribble in the oil, slowly but evenly, while the motor is running. Taste and adjust the seasoning.

Use immediately; or, if left for a few hours in a refrigerator, whisk lightly before serving.

Wine Butter

MAKES ABOUT 4 OZ (100 g)

4 shallots, finely chopped
7 fl oz (200 ml) red wine
3 oz (75 g) butter, softened

juice of ½ lemon
salt
freshly ground black pepper

Put the shallots and wine in a pan, bring to the boil and simmer until the wine has reduced completely, leaving the shallots soft and full of flavour. Allow to cool. Whisk in the butter, then the lemon juice and season to taste with salt and pepper. Use or freeze for up to three months.

Clarified Butter

This is very simple to make. You just melt some unsalted butter over a low heat in a pan, skim off the scum that floats to the top and leave the remainder to rest. You will see a sort of milky mixture floating to the bottom. Carefully pour off or strain the clear liquid from the top, and that is clarified butter. You can save it in the refrigerator, if you like, and use it when required.

Rouille

There is nothing quite like a tureen of fish soup, with crusty bread spread with aïoli, grated cheese and a pot of fiery rouille to spice up the soup. Close your eyes and you might almost be in Provence.

SERVES 4

2 large cloves of garlic, finely chopped
stale bread, soaked in water and squeezed out
*   to the size of an egg*

2 red chilli peppers, seeded and chopped
2-3 tablespoons olive oil

Pound the garlic in a pestle and mortar until it is reduced to a paste – the quantity is too small for a food processor. Grind in the bread and chilli peppers until smooth. Finally, whisk in the oil until the mixture is smooth and shining.

Hollandaise Sauce

The sauce can be made with all lemon juice instead of lemon juice
and vinegar.

SERVES 4-6

4 oz (100 g) unsalted butter, softened
2 tablespoons lemon juice
2 tablespoons white wine vinegar
5 teaspoons water

3 egg yolks
salt
freshly ground white pepper

Cut the butter into about eight small pieces. Place the lemon juice, vinegar and 3 teaspoons of the water in a small pan and boil briskly until reduced to just 2 tablespoons. Stir in the remaining cold water and place in the top of a double boiler. Whisk in the egg yolks and cook gently, stirring constantly, over very lightly simmering water, until the mixture begins to thicken.

Add the butter, piece by piece, whisking well between each addition to melt and incorporate. When all the butter has been added the sauce should be shiny and thick enough to coat the back of a spoon. Season to taste with salt and pepper before serving.

Barbecue Sauce

This is an excellent sauce to serve with char-grilled pork or chicken; it is
also splendid with shellfish and good cold with things like vegetable
mousse.

MAKES ABOUT ½ PINT (300 ml)

2 cloves of garlic, finely chopped
½ teaspoon salt
½ teaspoon ground paprika
4 tablespoons clear honey

3 tablespoons tomato purée
4 tablespoons orange juice
4 tablespoons white or red wine vinegar
6 tablespoons soy sauce

Pound the garlic, salt and paprika in a pestle and mortar until reduced to a paste, then gradually stir in the remaining ingredients.

Alternatively, the quicker way is to whizz together all the ingredients in a food processor or blender.

Transfer the sauce to a pan, bring to the boil and simmer for 5–10 minutes.

Tomato Sauce

MAKES ABOUT ½ PINT (300 ml)

1 tablespoon olive oil
1 medium onion, finely chopped
2 cloves of garlic, chopped
14 oz (400 g) can tomatoes

1 teaspoon fresh or ½ teaspoon dried basil
1 tablespoon chopped parsley
1 level tablespoon sugar
lots of freshly ground black pepper

Heat the oil in a pan and fry the onion and garlic until soft. Add the remaining ingredients and cook over a low heat for 15 minutes. Purée the lot in a food processor or blender.

This sauce is equally delicious served either hot or cold.

Preserved Tomatoes

Have you ever wondered why spaghetti bolognese eaten in Italy tastes of sunshine – it's the super ripe tomatoes, bursting with sweetness. A tin of tomatoes simply won't do, but in summer you can come pretty close, with the ripest, freshest tomatoes you can find – so make sure you purée some using this recipe to keep for the long winter months.

MAKES 2 × 1 PINT (600 ml) BOTTLES

3 lb (1.4 kg) ripe, fat and sweet tomatoes,
*   quartered*
1 onion, peeled and left whole
1 clove of garlic, peeled and left whole

bouquet garni (thyme, bay leaf and parsley,
*   for example)*
salt
freshly ground black pepper

Put all the ingredients into a pan without water and cook over a low heat, stirring occasionally. After 45 minutes, remove the onion and bouquet garni and purée the tomatoes by straining through a fine sieve.

Pour the sauce into warm bottles (ideally 1 pint [600 ml] bottles fitted with a clamp top). Leave a headspace of about 1 inch (2.5 cm). Stopper the bottles, place them in a deep pan and cover with warm water. Bring the water to the boil over a medium heat and simmer for 30 minutes. Remove, cool, label and store.

Aromatic Oil

MAKES ABOUT 1¾ PINTS (1 litre)

30 black peppercorns
6 bay leaves
3 sprigs of tarragon
4 sprigs of thyme
4 red chilli peppers

4-5 sage leaves
½ teaspoon fennel seeds
20 coriander seeds
extra virgin olive oil

Pop all the herbs and spices into a 1¾ pint (1 litre) wine bottle. Fill with the oil and seal with a cork. Leave for two weeks before using.

A dash of this on a pizza is delicious.

Onion Chutney

MAKES ABOUT 2 LB (900 g)

4 tablespoons olive oil
3 lb (1.4 kg) onions, finely sliced
4 oz (100 g) caster sugar
½ pint (300 ml) white wine vinegar
4 whole cloves

2 bay leaves
1 teaspoon freshly ground black pepper
1 teaspoon salt
2 tablespoons tomato purée
large pinch of cayenne pepper

Heat the oil in a pan and sauté the onions until they are transparent. Add the remaining ingredients. Cover and cook gently for about 1 hour or until no excess liquid remains. Taste and adjust the seasoning, adding a little more sugar and salt or pepper as necessary. Continue cooking gently until the chutney is of a fairly thick consistency. Allow to cool.

Pour off any remaining oil. Spoon into preheated jars and cover with airtight, vinegar-proof tops (that is, metal or bakelite caps with a vinegar-proof lining; greaseproof paper and then a round of muslin dipped in melted paraffin wax or fat; preserving skin or vinegar-proof paper; or boiled corks covered with greaseproof paper tied down with string). Store in a cool, dry, dark place and leave to mature for two–three months before eating.

Pickled Damsons

These delicious little treats are made using only small, ripe damsons. My good chum Claud Arnaud uses yellow cherries from Apt instead – they are quite the best – and serves them with pots of Chicken Liver Mousse (see page 77 for recipe). I like to nibble these with a pre-dinner glass of Kir.

MAKES ABOUT 2 JARS

½ pint (300 ml) white wine vinegar
thinly pared rind of 1 small lemon
2 whole cloves
small piece of fresh root ginger

1 bay leaf
1 lb (450 g) sugar
2 lb (900 g) damsons, in perfect condition

Place the vinegar, lemon rind, cloves, ginger, bay leaf and sugar in a large pan. Heat gently to dissolve the sugar, then bring to the boil. Turn off the heat and leave until quite cold. Strain the spiced vinegar, discarding the spices and flavourings. Return the vinegar to the pan and bring to the boil.

Meanwhile, prick the damsons and place in a bowl. Pour over the boiling vinegar, cover and leave to stand for 5 days.

Strain the vinegar from the damsons, place in a pan and bring to the boil. Pour over the damsons, cover and leave to stand for a further 5 days. Strain the vinegar from the damsons, place in a pan and bring to the boil.

Pack the damsons into two medium-sized preserving jars. Pour over the boiling vinegar and cover at once. Cover with airtight, vinegar-proof tops (that is, a bakelite cap with vinegar-proof lining; a greaseproof paper disc and then a round of muslin dipped in melted fat; a piece of preserving skin or vinegar-proof paper; or a large, boiled cork, covered with a piece of greaseproof paper and tied down with string). Store in a cold, dry place and leave to mature for two–three months before eating.

Pickled Lemons or Limes

These are a North African favourite with chicken, lamb and fish.

MAKES 1 LARGE JAR

12 lemons or limes
salt

3 pints (1.75 litres) spiced vinegar – you can buy this ready-made

Wash the lemons or limes very well and, if the skin is thick, thinly pare away. Place in a large preserving jar, sprinkling each layer generously with salt. Cover and leave for 10 days, until the lemons or limes are well softened.

Remove the lemons or limes from the jar and

wipe away most of the salt. Return to the clean jar. Heat the spiced vinegar until boiling, then pour over the lemons or limes. Leave a little headroom at the top of the jar. Cover with one of the following: a bakelite cap with vinegar-proof lining; a greaseproof paper disc and then a round of muslin dipped in melted fat; a piece of preserving skin or vinegar-proof paper; or a large, boiled cork, covered with a piece of greaseproof paper and tied down with string. Store for about three months before using.

Mincemeat

This is a delicious, rich mincemeat that is simple to make and tastes so much nicer than the bought stuff. Once made and sealed it should be kept for two weeks before using, but it can be kept for up to a year in a cool place.

MAKES 3 LB (1.4 kg)

1 orange
2 lemons
10 oz (275 g) seeded or stoned raisins
6 oz (175 g) currants
6 oz (175 g) sultanas
4 oz (100 g) chopped mixed candied peel
2 oz (50 g) glacé cherries, quartered

10 oz (275 g) soft dark brown sugar
8 oz (225 g) shredded suet
2 oz (50 g) whole almonds, cut into slivers
3 teaspoons ground mixed spice
2 pinches of ground cinnamon
little freshly grated nutmeg
5 tablespoons brandy or whisky

Grate the orange and lemon zests into a large bowl, being careful not to add the pith. Squeeze out the juice and add to the bowl with the remaining ingredients. Cover with a cloth and leave to marinate overnight.

Mix thoroughly and pack the mincemeat into clean, dry jars. Cover with waxed discs, seal with dampened cellophane and elastic bands, label and store in a very cool place.

One of my favourite ways to use this is to line a Swiss roll tin with shortcrust pastry, fill with mincemeat adding a few sliced bananas, cover with another layer of pastry and bake. Dust with icing sugar and cut into wedges.

Stocks are things we make a big song and dance about in cookery books, but in the old days we made them as a matter of course, boiling up bones with a few root vegetables and herbs. Stocks are the foundation stone of good cooking and with a selection stored in ice cube trays or in little pots in the freezer, you are halfway to making rich casseroles and soups.

Obviously, stocks need bones so every time you have a leg of lamb on a Sunday or a roast goose for a celebration dinner, pop the leftovers into labelled bags in the freezer and save them for a mammoth stock-making session.

Veal Stock

This is the fundamental, pure and essential stock, which can be used on its own or to enrich other kinds of meat stock by substituting it for some or all of the water required in the recipe, depending on how rich you want the stock to be.

M A K E S   A B O U T   3 ½   P I N T S   (2 litres)

4½ lb (2 kg) veal bones
2 calves' feet, cut in half
4 oz (100 g) onions, chopped
7 oz (200 g) carrots, chopped
7 oz (200 g) mushrooms, chopped
1 large stick of celery, chopped

2 cloves of garlic, chopped
14 fl oz (400 ml) dry white wine
7 pints (4 litres) water
8 large tomatoes, skinned, seeded and chopped
large bouquet garni (parsley, bay leaf and
*   thyme, for example)*

Put the veal bones and calves' feet in a roasting tin and brown in a preheated oven, 400°F/ 200°C (gas mark 6), turning occasionally. Transfer the bones to a large pan. Using the same roasting tin, lightly cook the onions, carrots, mushrooms, celery and garlic over direct heat or in the oven until they are softened but not browned. Add the wine and continue cooking until most of it has reduced. Tip the vegetables into the pan with the bones, scraping the roasting tin to collect any bits stuck to the bottom.

Cover the bones and vegetables with the water. Bring to the boil, reduce the heat and simmer. Skim off any scum and grease from the surface two or three times during the first 30 minutes of the cooking time and from time to time afterwards.

Add the tomatoes and bouquet garni and continue to cook – just bubbling – over a low heat for at least 3 hours. Strain the stock through a very fine sieve, without forcing, and allow to cool completely.

Skim and store meat stocks in the refrigerator for up to 48 hours, or pour into ice cube trays or freezer tubs and freeze. Alternatively, freeze half and keep half back to make into a meat glaze.

Veal Glaze

Put the veal stock in a pan and boil rapidly to reduce by three-quarters until it is of a thick, syrupy consistency. Allow to cool. It will set like a jelly. You can use this glaze to make all sorts of sauces for steak, such as Red Wine or Chasseur, see pages 165–7.

All of the meat stocks that follow can be made into a glaze in the same way.

Beef Stock

MAKES ABOUT 5 PINTS (2.8 litres)

2 lb (900 g) shin or leg of beef
4 lb (1.75 kg) beef tail, shank or chuck
1 veal knuckle bone or 1 calf's foot (optional)
about 9 pints (5 litres) water
2 medium onions, stuck with whole cloves

1 head of garlic, unpeeled
4 carrots, chopped
bouquet garni (using leek and celery)
salt

Put all the meat and bones into a large pan and add enough of the water to cover by about 2 inches (5 cm). Bring slowly to the boil, and skim off any scum from the surface. Keep doing this, adding a little cold water occasionally, until no more scum rises to the surface.

Add the onions, garlic, carrots and bouquet garni and a little salt to taste. Bring the liquid to the boil again and skim. Reduce the heat, partially cover the pan and simmer for 5–8 hours. Strain the stock through a very fine sieve, without forcing, and allow to cool completely. Skim off any traces of fat from the top and use or freeze as required.

Lamb or Mutton Stock

Follow the recipe for Beef Stock (above), but substitute 6–7 lb (2.75–3 kg) lamb or mutton bones (including the shank and middle neck or scrag end) for the beef bones.

NOTE
Although stocks can happily be frozen for up to six months, it is best to keep them only for a few weeks and from time to time to have a rummage through your freezer and throw away things you are worried about.

Chicken Stock

MAKES ABOUT 6 PINTS (3.6 litres)

butter
4 carrots, finely chopped
2 firm leeks (white part only), finely chopped
1 stick of celery, finely chopped
few button mushrooms, finely chopped
4½ lb (2 kg) chicken carcasses (raw or cooked),
   feet, necks, wings etc (not giblets)

1 good-sized veal bone, preferably knuckle
2 onions, stuck with whole cloves
bouquet garni (parsley, bay leaf and thyme,
   for example)

Melt a little butter in a large pan and soften the carrots, leeks, celery and mushrooms. Add the chicken carcasses and the veal bone. Cover with cold water and bring to the boil. Reduce the heat and simmer for 20 minutes. Stir in the onions and bouquet garni and simmer gently for a further 2 hours. Strain the stock through a very fine sieve, without forcing, and leave to cool completely. Use or freeze as required or make half into a chicken glaze.

Game Stock

If the stock is required for making a light sauce, use white wine instead of red.

MAKES ABOUT 2¾ PINTS (1.6 litres)

oil
chopped leftover meat of any game such as
   duck, pigeon, pheasant etc, including
   chopped carcasses, necks and giblets
1 onion, chopped
1 carrot, chopped
1 pint (600 ml) good red wine

1 pint (600 ml) veal stock, see page 41
2 pints (1 litre) water
some juniper berries, crushed
bouquet garni (parsley, bay leaf and thyme,
   for example)

Heat a little oil in a pan and brown the leftover game pieces. Add the onion and carrot and cook until they are softened but not browned. Add the wine, veal stock, water, juniper berries and bouquet garni and simmer for at least 2 hours, frequently skimming off any scum from the surface. Strain the stock through a very fine sieve, without forcing, and leave to cool completely. Use or freeze as required or make half into game glaze.

Fish Stock

MAKES ABOUT 3 PINTS (1.75 litres)

4 lb (1.75 kg) fish trimmings (leftover bones,
*   skin, heads and tails)*
2 onions, chopped
2 carrots, chopped
2 leeks or celery leaves, chopped

bouquet garni (parsley, bay leaf and thyme,
*   for example)*
2 tablespoons white peppercorns
½ pint (300 ml) dry white wine
3½ pints (2 litres) water

Put all the ingredients in a large pan, bring to the boil then reduce the heat and simmer, covered, for not more than 30 minutes, or unpleasant flavours will come through. If the stock doesn't taste strong enough, you can cook it for a little longer to reduce it, until you are satisfied. Strain the stock through a very fine sieve, without forcing. Skim and store fish stocks in the refrigerator for up to 24 hours or freeze for up to 1 month.

Court Bouillon

This is a rather high-faluting name for what is basically a light vegetable stock for poaching any kind of fish or shellfish. After the fish has been cooked in the *court bouillon*, and given some of its flavour to the liquid, you can use it again as the base for a fish soup.

MAKES ABOUT 2 PINTS (1.2 litres)

1 large onion, stuck with whole cloves
2 carrots, sliced
1 large leek, cut into 4 pieces
bouquet garni (parsley, thyme and bay leaf,
*   for example)*

2 slices of lemon
1¼ pints (750 ml) water
1¼ pints (750 ml) dry white wine or dry cider
1 tablespoon white wine vinegar

Put all the ingredients into a large pan. Bring to the boil, reduce the heat and simmer for about 30 minutes. Strain the stock through a very fine sieve, without forcing. Allow to cool completely. Use or freeze as required.

These stocks really are worth doing!!

REAL SOUPS

Real soups are a bit like people – you can have hefty, jolly ones; cool, thin, elegant ones; and fiery, exotic, surprising ones. The trouble is that soups are an endangered species, which must be saved at all costs.

It seems absurd that we actually need cookery books to tell us how to make soups. In the past they were just 'there'. We automatically boiled up the bones from the Sunday roast to make stocks for soups and casseroles. In winter, soups were the ultimate in one-pot cooking: economical, rich, sustaining and brilliant. And, in summer, we'd pick a few vegetables from the garden, shred a piece of leftover chicken, or find some dried vermicelli in the store-cupboard to stretch the stock into excellent broth.

All that has changed and nowadays clever marketing men are constantly trying to persuade us to make 'fast' soups in mugs, or to heat up the contents of a can in minutes. Okay, I will admit that when the chips have been down and the spirit low there have been times when I've taken solace in a can of Mr Heinz's tomato liquid but the real joy of soup-making lies in the gentle bubbling of the enamel pot on the stove, filling the house with safe, comforting aromas.

I'd happily starve all day in anticipation of a bowl of friendly bean and cabbage soup for supper, accompanied by a hunk of tomato bread topped with slices of Cheddar cheese and toasted under the grill, a bottle of carefully chosen red wine, and the promise of a sticky pudding later.

Hungarian Fish Soup

The red bouillabaisse!

SERVES 6

3 lb (1.4 kg) of a variety of fish – herring,
   mackerel, white fish and eel if possible
1 large tomato
½ red pepper, seeded and chopped
1-2 whole chilli peppers

1 oz (25 g) paprika
1 small potato, diced
salt
1 onion, chopped
4 oz (100 g) vermicelli

Wash and gut the fish, cut them into pieces and place in a pan. Put in the whole tomato, pepper, chillies to taste, paprika, potato and salt. Fill up the pan with water and put in the onion. Bring to the boil, then reduce the heat to a simmer and cook for 40 minutes – though you may need to remove the fish earlier to prevent it from crumbling. When cooked, remove the fish if you haven't done so already, and strain the soup. Return the soup to the pan and add the vermicelli and the pieces of fish. Cook for a further 5–10 minutes or so until the vermicelli is tender.

PS If you don't like heads cut them off, but tie them in a muslin cloth and put in the soup during cooking to add more flavour – then discard.

Chicken Soup with Dahl

A really substantial soup best served as a meal in its own right – and for best results try to buy a boiling fowl, not a spring chicken.

SERVES 6

1¼ lb (550 g) calves' bones
1 onion, chopped
4 oz (100 g) white radishes, which look like
   carrots, chopped
4 oz (100 g) carrots, chopped
1 celery root, chopped
1 bay leaf
5 pints (2.8 litres) water
1 boiling fowl

4 oz (100 g) split peas or lentils
2 oz (50 g) long-grain rice
3 oz (75 g) lard
7 oz (200 g) button mushrooms, finely
   chopped
salt
freshly ground black pepper
2 egg yolks
½ pint (300 ml) soured cream

Put the calves' bones, vegetables and bay leaf in a large pan, add the water and simmer for 2 hours. Strain the liquid, discarding the bones, return to the pan and put the chicken in whole.

Cook for 1½–2 hours, or until the chicken is tender. Take the chicken out, remove the flesh from the carcass and cut it into pieces. Set aside and keep warm.

Cook the split peas or lentils in half of the vegetable soup for about ¾–1 hour until soft. Use the other half of the soup to cook the rice until tender – about 30 minutes. When the rice is cooked, purée the soup in a food processor or blender and add to the cooked split pea or lentil mixture.

Melt the lard in a frying pan and fry the mushrooms, adding salt and pepper to taste. Mix together the egg yolks and the soured cream in a tureen, put in the chicken pieces and cooked mushrooms and pour in the soup.

Hare Soup with Lentils and Madeira

Paul Gayler at Inigo Jones, London

As you would expect from an artist like Paul, a soup of pedigree and style. If you prepare this, I think you should make it the centrepiece of your meal. Needless to say, you do need a *fresh* hare, ordered in advance – and remember to ask your butcher to collect and save the blood as he is hanging the hare.

SERVES 4-6

1 hare, skin removed, cleaned, blood reserved
2 oz (50 g) carrots, finely chopped
3 shallots, finely chopped
white part of ½ leek, finely chopped
½ stick of celery, finely chopped
1 clove of garlic, finely chopped
1 bay leaf
thyme
whole cloves
salt

freshly ground black pepper
5 tablespoons (75 ml) dry white wine
¼ pint (150 ml) Madeira
4½ oz (125 g) butter
½ tablespoon tomato purée
2½ pints (1.4 litres) water
3½ oz (90 g) lentils, soaked for 12 hours and
    drained
5 tablespoons (75 ml) double cream
chopped chervil, to garnish

Place the skinned hare on a work surface. Take out the liver and remove the gall bladder. Turn the animal over, pulling one foreleg away from the body, and sever the connective tissue joining the leg to the body. Cut off the other foreleg the same way. Set aside. Remove the hindquarters by cutting across the body at a point where the hindquarters join the saddle. Separate the hindlegs by cutting lengthways through the hindquarters to one side of the backbone, then set aside. This leaves the saddle whole. Cut up the forelegs and hindquarters into small 1 inch (2.5 cm) pieces, place all in a bowl (not aluminium), and add the vegetables, including the garlic. Stir in the herbs, cloves and some salt and pepper and pour on the wine and half the Madeira. Leave to marinate for 12 hours. (Ideally, this should be done the day before making the soup.)

Lift out the hare from the marinade. Remove

the fillets from the saddle by freeing from the backbone with a sharp knife. Melt 2 oz (50 g) of the butter in a heavy-based pan and fry the hare pieces and the saddle bones. Add the reserved marinade and the tomato purée, then pour in the water and bring to the boil. Add the soaked lentils, cover, reduce the heat and cook very gently for 40–45 minutes. When cooked, pass the liquid first through a coarse sieve, then again through a fine sieve to remove any bone fragments from the hare.

Melt the remaining butter in a clean pan and fry the hare fillets for 8–10 minutes, keeping them nice and pink. Allow the meat to rest while you finish the soup. Beat the hare blood with a little water, add to the soup and simmer for 1–2 minutes on a gentle heat, pass through a fine sieve again and stir in the cream and the remaining Madeira.

Slice the hare fillets into neat medallions by cutting across the flesh to make rounds, arrange in a circle in the soup bowls, pour on the hot soup and garnish with a little chervil. Serve immediately.

Russian Soup

SERVES 6

2 oz (50 g) oil or lard
1 onion, finely chopped
2 carrots, diced
4 oz (100 g) white radishes or baby turnips, diced
2 oz (50 g) celery root, diced
10 oz (275 g) beef (cheapest), cubed
10 oz (275 g) pork (say belly of pork), cubed

salt
freshly ground black pepper
2 oz (50 g) flour
½ oz (15 g) ground paprika
1¼ lb (550 g) firm cabbage, sliced
¼ pint (150 ml) soured cream
2 egg yolks
chopped parsley or chives

Heat the oil or lard in a pan and fry the onion until softened. Add the carrots, radishes or turnips and celery root and continue to cook gently. Throw in the beef, cover and cook for 30 minutes, then add the pork. Season to taste with salt and pepper and cook, covered, until the meat is almost tender, adding a little warm water from time to time. When all the liquid has cooked away, add the flour and paprika and fry for a few minutes, stirring all the time. Cover with 3½ pints (2 litres) warm water and add the cabbage. Continue cooking on a low heat until the cabbage is tender – at least 1 hour.

Mix together the soured cream and egg yolks in a serving bowl and, stirring constantly, gradually add the soup. Sprinkle with the parsley or chives and serve with dumplings or noodles of your own choice.

Iced Borsch SALT 1

May I suggest a menu for lunch?
Iced Borsch
Aubergine Caviar
Tandoori Chicken
And I thought caviar came in jars till I tasted Smirnoff. Geddit?

S E R V E S , S A Y , 4

1 lb (450 g) raw beetroots
2 slices of pumpernickel bread
2 eating apples, sliced or diced
½ large cucumber, chopped
3 oz (75 g) spring onions, trimmed and
  chopped (including the green part)

2 hard-boiled eggs, chopped
salt
sugar
red wine vinegar or lemon juice, to taste
small quantity of soured cream
chopped dill, to taste

Boil the beetroots whole in their skins for about 1 hour, or until tender. Peel, grate finely and pour over about 1¾ pints (1 litre) boiling water. Add the pumpernickel bread and leave to infuse for 4 hours.

To make the soup, strain this liquid, add the apples, cucumber, onions and eggs. Season to taste with salt, sugar and vinegar or lemon juice. Chill and serve with soured cream and dill. A less sweet version may be made using boiled potatoes instead of apples.

Clear Borsch SALT 2

S E R V E S 4

8 oz (225 g) raw beetroots, plus 1 additional
  beetroot to liquidise into juice
2¼ pints (1.25 litres) good beef or other
  stock, see pages 41–3
1 teaspoon red wine vinegar or lemon juice,
  or to taste

1 teaspoon sugar
1 wineglass of medium-sweet white wine
  (optional)
cayenne pepper
small quantity of soured cream

Peel the beetroots, chop small and cook them slowly in the stock for about 1 hour. Strain and add the vinegar or lemon juice, sugar, wine, if using, and a little cayenne pepper to taste. Add the juice of the 1 additional uncooked beetroot to heighten the taste and colour of the borsch. Serve with a dollop of soured cream in each bowl.

Ukrainian Borsch SALT 3

You are now really back in the USSR.

S E R V E S   4 - 6

1 large raw beetroot, about 10 oz (275 g),
*   plus 1 additional small beetroot to liquidise*
*   into juice*
1 tablespoon red wine vinegar
1 oz (25 g) bacon fat
2 teaspoons sugar
2-3 tablespoons tomato purée or 2 tomatoes,
*   skinned and finely chopped*
1 oz (25 g) butter
2 onions, finely chopped
1 carrot, finely chopped
1 parsley root or ½ parsnip, finely chopped
¼ Dutch cabbage, about 10 oz (275 g),
*   chopped*

12 oz-1 lb (350-450 g) potatoes, cut into
*   chunks*
3 pints (1.75 litres) beef stock, see page 42
5-6 black peppercorns
3 whole allspice
3 bay leaves
up to 1 head of garlic, minced
chopped parsley
salt
small quantity of soured cream

Peel and chop the beetroot and put in a pan with the vinegar, a little of the bacon fat, the sugar and the tomato purée or chopped tomatoes. Cover and cook gently.

Meanwhile, melt the butter in a pan and slowly cook the onions, carrot and parsley root or parsnip. In another pan, simmer the cabbage and potatoes in the stock for 15 minutes. Add the beetroot, the onions, carrot and parsley or parsnip, the peppercorns, allspice and bay leaves, and cook for 10 minutes. Finish with the garlic, the remaining bacon fat and the chopped parsley. Leave to stand for 24 hours and reheat gently, or leave in a low oven for a good 8 hours.

Before serving, season with salt to taste and add the raw beetroot juice, which will heighten the soup's taste and colour. Fish out the bay leaves and serve with a dollop of soured cream in each bowl.

Another Iced Borsch

This is a cold beetroot soup that is based on a mixture of soured cream diluted with *kvas* (beetroot water) or water.

SERVES ABOUT 4

1 lb (450 g) young raw beetroots with leaves
½ large cucumber
1¾ pints (1 litre) chilled liquid, made up of
  half soured cream and half soda water
3 oz (75 g) spring onions, trimmed and
  chopped
2 hard-boiled eggs, chopped

6 oz (175 g) peeled shrimps
½ lemon, sliced
salt
freshly ground black pepper
sugar, to taste
chopped dill, to taste

Peel the beetroots and cook them whole in a little salted water, adding the finely chopped leaves after about 20 minutes. Simmer for another 10 minutes, then drain. Dice the beetroots and cucumber. Mix together the chilled liquids to make the soup base and add all the vegetables, the eggs, shrimps and lemon. Season to taste with salt and pepper and a little sugar if liked. Sprinkle with dill. Chill again and serve in a large bowl with an ice cube to keep it cool.

PS Yes, I know there are four borsch recipes but I happen to really like borsch. So there.

Celeriac and Apple Soup

Christopher Oakes at Oakes Restaurant, Stroud

A delicate soup with pleasing subtle flavours, which is ideal for a summer lunch.

SERVES 8

2-3 oz (50-75 g) butter
1 head of celeriac, peeled and chopped into
  cubes
5 Granny Smith apples, peeled and chopped
  into cubes

4 pints (2.25 litres) chicken stock, see page 43
salt
freshly ground black pepper
¼ pint (150 ml) double cream
celery leaves and diced apple, to garnish

Melt the butter in a heavy-based pan. Sweat the celeriac and apples without colouring for 5 minutes, or until soft. Add the stock and bring up to the boil. Reduce the heat and simmer slowly for 30–45 minutes. Purée the soup by processing it briefly in a food processor or blender.

Pass the purée through a sieve. Return the mixture to the pan and reheat; if it is too thick add more chicken stock. Season to taste with salt and pepper. Swirl in the cream and garnish with the celery leaves and diced apple.

Celery, Apple and Tomato Soup

Colin White at Whites, Cricklade

A soft summer soup that reminds me, for some strange reason, of palettes of the delicate emulsion you see in the TV ads. But don't be put off – it tastes great!

SERVES 6

3 oz (75 g) butter
8 oz (225 g) onions or leeks, chopped
8 oz (225 g) carrots, chopped
2 lb (1 kg) celery, chopped
3 pints (1.75 litres) chicken or veal stock, see page 43 or 41
2 lb (1 kg) very ripe tomatoes, chopped
1 lb (450 g) Bramley apples, peeled and chopped

salt
freshly ground black pepper

For the garnish:
2 eating apples, chopped
croûtons
double cream (optional)

Melt the butter in a large pan and gently soften the onions or leeks, carrots and celery for 15 minutes or so, with the lid on. Add the stock, tomatoes, apples and season to taste with salt and pepper. Simmer gently for 30 minutes.

Purée the soup in a food processor or blender, then pass the purée through a sieve. Return the soup to the pan and reheat. Check the seasoning and serve garnished with pieces of chopped apple and croûtons and a little cream, if liked.

Curried Parsnip Soup

Clive Imber at Michael's Brasserie, Newcastle upon Tyne

SERVES 4

2 oz (50 g) butter
1 onion, finely chopped
2 lb (1 kg) parsnips, peeled and chopped
1 heaped tablespoon mild curry powder
1 pint (600 ml) chicken stock, see page 43

salt
freshly ground black pepper
juice of ½ lemon
2 egg yolks
¼ pint (150 ml) double cream

Melt the butter in a large pan and sweat the onion for 2 minutes. Add the parsnips and cook for about 5 minutes, or until softened. Stir in the curry powder and stock. Bring to the boil, reduce the heat and simmer for 15–20 minutes, or until the parsnips are tender.

Purée the soup in a food processor or blender and return it to a clean pan. Season to taste with salt and pepper, add the lemon juice and reheat the soup until hot but not boiling. Whisk together the egg yolks and cream and gradually stir into the soup. Serve hot.

Stilton Soup

Clive Imber at Michael's Brasserie, Newcastle upon Tyne

SERVES 4-6

2 oz (50 g) butter
1 onion, diced
1 clove of garlic, chopped
2 sticks of celery, chopped
2 tablespoons flour
¼ pint (150 ml) dry cider
1½ pints (900 ml) chicken stock, see page 43
½ pint (300 ml) milk

8 oz (225 g) Stilton cheese, crumbled
4 tablespoons double cream
salt
freshly ground black pepper
pinch of cayenne pepper
pinch of freshly grated nutmeg
1 eating apple, diced, to garnish
celery leaves, to garnish

Melt the butter in a pan and sweat the onion, garlic and celery until soft. Stir in the flour and add the cider, stock and milk. Bring to the boil and simmer for 10 minutes.

Strain, then purée the sieved vegetables with the cheese in a food processor or blender.

Return the purée to a clean pan and stir in the cream. Season to taste with salt, pepper, cayenne and nutmeg.

Reheat until hot but not boiling and serve garnished with the diced apple and celery leaves.

REAL SOUPS

Bean and Cabbage Soup

An economical and filling soup for cold winter days – you could enrich it by adding pieces of leftover chicken or goose and so on. A great pot of this on bonfire night would go down well.

SERVES 6

2 oz (50 g) lard, or better still, goose or duck dripping
4 onions, finely chopped
4 cloves of garlic, crushed
1 small hard white cabbage, core and stalks removed, finely sliced
11 oz (300 g) dried white haricot beans, soaked overnight and drained

about 4 pints (2.25 litres) water
1 sprig of thyme
1 bay leaf
salt
freshly ground black pepper

Melt the fat in a large pan and gently fry the onions and garlic until soft, but not browned. Now add all the other ingredients, cover and simmer gently for at least 2 hours. It may be necessary to add a little more water. The soup is ready when the beans have started to disintegrate. Check the seasoning, remove and discard the bay leaf and serve.

Chickpea Soup

SERVES 4-6

8 oz (225 g) chickpeas, soaked overnight and drained
2½ pints (1.4 litres) clear stock, that is chicken or veal, see page 43 or 41
8 oz (225 g) bacon, diced
1 medium onion, chopped

1-2 cloves of garlic, crushed
8 oz (225 g) can tomatoes, roughly chopped
1 tablespoon chilli powder
salt

Put the chickpeas in a large pan with the stock. Bring to the boil, reduce the heat to a simmer and cook for 10 minutes.

Meanwhile, fry the bacon, without additional fat, until crisp. Remove from the pan and pour off any excess fat. Sauté the onion and garlic in the bacon fat until softened – about 5 minutes. Finally, add the tomatoes, the bacon, chilli and salt to taste. Transfer the pan's contents to the chickpeas and stock, cover and cook gently for 1½-1¾ hours, or until the chickpeas are tender. Serve piping hot.

Black Bean Soup

SERVES 8

1½ oz (40 g) butter
2 onions, chopped
2 cloves of garlic, crushed
3 sticks of celery, chopped
bouquet garni (parsley, thyme and bay leaf,
    for example)
2–3 lb (900 g–1.4 kg) beef bones
1 ham bone (optional)
2½ pints (1.4 litres) chicken stock, see
    page 43
6 black peppercorns

1 teaspoon salt
1 lb (450 g) dried black beans, soaked
    overnight and drained
1¾ pints (1 litre) water
2 tablespoons lemon juice
¼ pint (150 ml) Madeira or brandy

For the garnish:
1 lemon, very thinly sliced
2 hard-boiled eggs, chopped
2 tablespoons parsley, finely chopped

Melt the butter in a large pan and sauté the onions, garlic and celery until softened, but not browned. Add the bouquet garni, beef bones, ham bone if using, stock, peppercorns, salt, beans and water. Bring to the boil, then reduce the heat, skim the surface and simmer very gently for 4 hours, or until the beans mash easily against the side of the pan.

Remove and discard the beef and ham bones and the bouquet garni. Purée the soup by processing it briefly in a food processor or blender. Add the lemon juice and Madeira or brandy, and if the soup is too thick, a little extra hot stock. Return the mixture to the pan, reheat and check the seasoning. Serve garnished with lemon slices and sprinkled with the hard-boiled eggs and parsley.

Yum Yum!

Vegetable Soup

This soup has no meat stock – so the vegetables must be fresh and of good quality to realise the true vegetable flavour.

SERVES 6

2 lb (900 g) mixed vegetables, such as celery, onions, swede, carrots and potatoes, peeled and roughly chopped
salt

freshly ground black pepper
10 thin slices of white bread
5 oz (150 g) Gruyère or Emmenthal cheese, grated

Put all the vegetables into a large pan with enough boiling water to cover and season to taste with salt and pepper. Simmer the soup for 30 minutes, or until the vegetables are soft. Mash the vegetables with a fork, stir well and pour the soup into an ovenproof casserole. Float the bread slices on top, sprinkle with the cheese and brown in a preheated hot oven until golden and bubbly.

Monica Poelchaud's Summer Vegetable Soup

This is a classic Vauclusienne summer soup – it's not dissimilar to minestrone, but the addition of the basil, garlic and olive oil is what makes it so special.

SERVES 6

olive oil
2-3 cloves of garlic, chopped
12 oz (350 g) tomatoes, skinned, seeded and chopped
3 pints (1.75 litres) water
2 oz (50 g) dried white haricot beans, soaked overnight and drained
8 oz (225 g) broad beans or peas, shelled

2 small potatoes, peeled and chopped
8 oz (225 g) courgettes, peeled and chopped
8 oz (225 g) green beans, topped and tailed
1 sprig of basil, chopped
1 handful of thin cellophane rice noodles
salt
freshly ground black pepper
Emmenthal or Parmesan cheese, grated

Heat 1 tablespoon oil in a large pan and fry 1 clove of the garlic. Add the tomatoes and water. Bring to the boil and add the haricots and broad beans or peas. After 15 minutes add the potatoes, courgettes and green beans. Simmer for a further 25 minutes.

Meanwhile, pound together the basil and remaining garlic with a little olive oil in a pestle and mortar, or in a blender, until you have a smooth, thick paste. Stir in a cupful of slightly cooled soup liquid. Add to the rest of the soup. Throw in the noodles. Season to taste with salt and pepper and cook for about 5–10 minutes, or until the pasta is tender. Serve with grated Emmenthal or Parmesan cheese. You can make more of the basil and garlic mixture if you wish and serve it separately so the diners can add more if they like it – which they should.

PS In my view, you can't have too much basil in this soup and you can add another dash of olive oil at the last minute.

Manhattan Clam Chowder

SERVES 6-8

4 oz (100 g) salt pork or bacon
24 hard-shelled clams, or mussels or cockles if clams are not available, scraped and cleaned, see page 125
2½ pints (1.4 litres) boiling water
1 medium onion, finely diced
2 large sticks of celery, finely diced
12 oz (350 g) tomatoes, skinned and chopped

2 dessertspoons parsley, chopped
1 bay leaf
1 teaspoon Worcestershire sauce
pinch of cayenne pepper
14–16 oz (400–450 g) large potatoes, diced
salt
freshly ground black pepper

Wash the salt pork, if using, to remove excess salt and pat dry. Dice the pork or bacon and fry in a large pan until the fat runs out and the pieces are nearly crisp. Lift out the pork or bacon from the pan and set aside. Keep the fat in the pan for cooking the vegetables later.

Place the prepared shellfish in a large pan with the boiling water. Boil for about 5–10 minutes, until the shells open. Lift out the clams, mussels or cockles, reserving the liquid, and discard any that remain shut. Cut the flesh from the shells and chop it roughly. Strain the liquid through a fine sieve to remove any sand.

Add the onion and celery to the pork or bacon fat in the pan and sauté for about 5 minutes, until softened. Return the salt pork or bacon, chopped shellfish and strained cooking liquid to the pan with the tomatoes, parsley, bay leaf, Worcestershire sauce and cayenne pepper. Cover and simmer over a low heat for 2–3 hours. About 30 minutes before the end of the cooking time, add the potatoes to the pan. Just before serving, discard the bay leaf and check the seasoning. Serve piping hot.

Corn Chowder

Simple soups like this only work if you use fresh ingredients. In this case
the corn. Although it's easy to open a tin, the essential taste will
be missing.

S E R V E S   6 - 8

½ oz (15 g) butter

4 oz (100 g) bacon, diced

2 medium onions, finely diced

3 medium potatoes, peeled and diced

¾ pint (450 ml) chicken stock, see page 43

3-4 sweetcorn cobs or 12 oz (350 g) kernels

1¾ pints (1 litre) milk

½ pint (300 ml) double cream

salt

freshly ground black pepper

Melt the butter in a large pan and fry the bacon until crisp. Remove from the pan and reserve. Add the onions to the fat and sauté gently until golden – about 5 minutes. Add the potatoes and the stock, cover and cook for 15–20 minutes, until the potatoes are soft.

Strip the kernels from the corn cobs, add to the pan and cook for a further 5–10 minutes, or until the corn is tender. Finally, stir in the milk and cream, season to taste with salt and pepper and reheat the soup until hot but not boiling. Serve hot with the reserved bacon pieces scattered over the top of the soup.

SOME BEGINNINGS

My philosophy on eating is that – to mix a metaphor – you mustn't overegg the omelette. Since eating is supposed to be a joyous experience, you don't want to overdose on too much of a good thing – so if you're serving a three-course meal, make one an extravaganza and keep the rest simple.

It's all about balance. Very often an Ogen melon in season, or the heart of a crisp lettuce with some good olive oil, wine vinegar and basil, can knock spots off a tricky soufflé. A dinner party should be approached like a theatrical production. The starter can be the warm-up act for the main attraction, or a real show-stopping number to wow them from the off.

This selection of goodies should cover both options – they are also superb one-man shows if you're looking for a quick snackette.

Salad of Endive Lettuce with Steamed Red Mullet and Coriander Dressing

Shaun Hill at Gidleigh Park, Chagford

Not only delicious to eat but you can have fun arranging it artistically on white plates – just like the very talented Shaun does at his restaurant on remote Dartmoor.

SERVES, SAY, 4, DEPENDING ON THE SIZE OF THE FISH

2 medium-sized red mullet
salad leaves (curly endive, lamb's lettuce, for example)
1 small red onion, sliced very thinly into rings

For the dressing:
¼ pint (150 ml) walnut oil

2 cloves of garlic, bruised
2 sprigs of thyme
¼ teaspoon black peppercorns, crushed
4 firm, ripe tomatoes, skinned, seeded and diced
salt
freshly ground black pepper

Scale and fillet the red mullet, taking care that all small bones are removed. Steam the fish for 5 minutes, or until just cooked. Allow to cool.

To make the dressing, warm the oil in a pan with the garlic, thyme and the peppercorns. Allow to cool, then remove and discard the garlic and add the tomatoes. Season to taste with a little salt and black pepper.

Serve the mullet with an accompaniment of salad leaves, spoon over the dressing and scatter with the red onion rings.

Shaun – hope you don't mind me adapting your recipe a bit. It's still good. KF

Herring Salad

The classic French starter – never found in posh restaurants but always in Routiers and the like. Use it as a starter or double up the quantities and make a meal of it on a hot day with fresh bread and some iced lager.

S E R V E S   4

10 oz (275 g) can herrings (they sometimes
*   come in plastic sachets, which are*
*   acceptable), drained, cut into 1 inch*
*   (2.5 cm) long pieces*
1 lb (450 g) cold, boiled potatoes, cut into
*   ¼ inch (7 mm) thick slices*

1 large sweet onion, cut into very thin rings
1 apple, peeled, cored and thinly sliced
2 tablespoons olive oil
1 tablespoon finely chopped chives
salt
freshly ground black pepper

Throw all the ingredients into a salad bowl, turn once or twice, chill and serve.

Fennel and Lemon Salad

A tangy salad, the sharp creamy lemon dressing blending harmoniously with the distinctive flavour of fennel. Lovely to serve also as a side salad with fish or with a curry of meat or fish.

S E R V E S   A B O U T   4

1 large fennel bulb
1 lemon
1 dessertspoon chopped parsley

For the dressing:
1 tablespoon lemon juice

2 tablespoons olive oil
2 tablespoons double cream
1 dessertspoon sugar
salt
freshly ground black pepper

Wash and finely slice the fennel, discarding any tough outer leaves. Place in a pan of boiling water and simmer for 1 minute. Drain and refresh under cold running water.

Pare the rind from half the lemon, being careful to avoid the white pith, and cut into very fine shreds. Blanch the shreds in boiling water for 1 minute and refresh. Cut away the pith from the lemon and slice the flesh. Cut into pieces and mix with the fennel, parsley and lemon rind.

Mix together the ingredients for the dressing, pour over the salad and toss well. Serve immediately.

Dandelion and Bacon Salad

Known as 'piss in the bed' in France, this bitter salad is superb when freshly prepared and eaten at once.

SERVES 6

10 oz (275 g) young dandelion plants (which you must pick yourself from the fields – not, I hope, your lawn)
5 oz (150 g) lean smoked bacon, finely chopped
3½ oz (90 g) very fat streaky bacon, chopped
1 small onion, finely minced

2 oz (50 g) warm croûtons

For the dressing:
3 tablespoons white wine vinegar
1 tablespoon groundnut oil
pinch of sea salt
freshly ground black pepper

Wash the dandelion plants thoroughly, drain well and dry gently with absorbent kitchen paper. Cut each plant into four. Fry both bacons together, without additional fat, until brown and crispy.

Mix together all the ingredients for the dressing. In a large bowl toss the leaves and onion in the dressing, add the hot fried bacon and warm croûtons and any fat from the pan. Serve immediately.

A Provençal Cheese Salad

SERVES 4

1½ lb (675 g) tomatoes, some very ripe, some a little green, thinly sliced
¾ wineglass of extra virgin olive oil
dash of white wine vinegar
3 tablespoons chopped basil

2 teaspoons caster sugar
salt
freshly ground black pepper
4 oz (100 g) Mozzarella cheese, cut into ¼ inch (7 mm) cubes

Mix the ingredients carefully with your fingers and refrigerate for a couple of hours – then toss gently again. In Apt on market days I used to lunch on thin slices of peppery sausage, fol-lowed by a bowl of this with bread and big glasses of iced rosé! It's terrific. But please use only the best ingredients – don't, whatever you do, use dried basil or nasty cheese.

A Greek Salad

SERVES 4

1 small head of curly endive
1 small head of Cos lettuce
1 cucumber
2 large tomatoes
6 oz (175 g) stoned black olives
4 oz (100 g) Feta cheese, crumbled
2 oz (50 g) can anchovy fillets, drained
    (optional)
2 spring onions, trimmed and chopped

2 tablespoons capers

For the dressing:
4 fl oz (100 ml) olive or vegetable oil
3 tablespoons red wine vinegar
1 teaspoon dried oregano
½ teaspoon salt
large pinch of freshly ground black pepper

Wash the endive and lettuce thoroughly, drain well and dry gently with absorbent kitchen paper. Shred the leaves and put them in a large salad bowl.

Wipe the cucumber, pare off alternating strips of the skin and slice the flesh thinly. Cut the tomatoes into small wedges. Add the cucumber slices, tomato wedges, olives, cheese, anchovy fillets if using, spring onions and capers to the salad bowl.

Mix together all the ingredients for the dressing, pour over the salad and toss until well mixed. Serve immediately.

Greek Mushrooms

This was for seventeen years one of the most popular starters I ever served in my restaurants but the fresh coriander, not parsley, is essential.

SERVES 4-6

1 lb (450 g) small button mushrooms
salt
freshly ground black pepper
4 tablespoons olive oil
1 tablespoon sherry vinegar

1 tablespoon coriander seeds, coarsely crushed
1 bay leaf
½ lemon, cut into very, very thin slices
1 tablespoon chopped coriander
8 oz (227 g) can tomatoes and their juice

Wash and dry the mushrooms. Season with salt and pepper. Heat the oil and vinegar in a pan with the coriander seeds. When hot drop in everything else including the mushrooms and cook wildly for 5–6 minutes.

Lift out the mushrooms and boil the sauce rapidly to reduce by half. Pour it back over the mushrooms. Cover, chill for ages and eat them later. Remove and discard the bay leaf before serving.

Another Greek Salad

The crumbly white Feta cheese used in these Greek salads is available
from delicatessens and good supermarkets but it's the chopped mint that
makes the difference – fresh of course!

SERVES 4 OR SO

1 crisp lettuce
½ cucumber
4 ripe tomatoes
1 large sweet onion, roughly chopped
8 oz (225 g) Feta cheese, diced
4 oz (100 g) black olives, stoned and
  quartered
1 bunch of mint, coarsely chopped

For the dressing:
4 tablespoons olive oil
juice of ½ lemon
pinch of sugar
salt
freshly ground black pepper

Wash the lettuce thoroughly, drain well and dry
gently with absorbent kitchen paper. Separate
the leaves and use to line a salad bowl. Cut the
cucumber into quarters lengthways, reassemble
and slice. Cut the tomatoes into eighths.

To make the dressing, mix together the oil,
lemon juice, sugar and salt and pepper. Toss
all the other ingredients in the dressing and
pile into the middle of the lettuce. Serve
immediately.

An Italian Salad

A robust salad that goes down well with lots of red wine – a good starter
for filling hungry people!

SERVES 3-4

4 oz (100 g) short-cut macaroni or small
  pasta shells
4 oz (100 g) green peas, cooked
2 oz (50 g) lean ham, chopped or sliced
2 oz (50 g) salami, chopped or sliced
2 oz (50 g) mortadella, chopped or sliced

2 oz (50 g) black olives, stoned
1 teaspoon French mustard
¼ pint (150 ml) mayonnaise, see page 34
salt
freshly ground black pepper

Cook the pasta in boiling salted water until it is
al dente, drain and refresh very well under cold
running water. Allow to drain thoroughly, then

mix with the remaining ingredients. Season to
taste with salt and pepper. Serve immediately.

Avocado Salad

Personally, I hate avocados but this little dish made for me by a little 'dish' has captivated my heart. It is avocado vinaigrette with a difference.

SERVES 4

2 tablespoons green pepper, seeded and finely
   chopped
2 tablespoons finely chopped spring onion
6 black olives, stoned and shredded
1 teaspoon finely chopped parsley
2 ripe avocado pears

For the dressing:
salt
freshly ground black pepper
1½ tablespoons white wine vinegar
5 tablespoons olive oil
squeeze of lemon juice
caster sugar

Drop the green pepper into boiling water, cook for 1 minute, then drain and rinse well with cold water.

To make the dressing, mix a large pinch of salt and black pepper with the vinegar and whisk in the oil. Sharpen with the lemon juice and add a little sugar to taste. Add all the other ingredients, except the avocado, to this dressing and mix well.

Just before serving, split the avocados in half and remove the stones. Fill each half with the dressing. Serve immediately.

Pears Stuffed with Goat's Cheese

This makes a refreshing start to a meal.

SERVES 4

4 oz (100 g) fresh goat's cheese
4 or so tablespoons good double cream
1 teaspoon finely chopped mint

1 teaspoon finely chopped chives
8 small ripe pears, peeled
juice of ½ lemon

Mix together the goat's cheese and cream and beat to a smooth, soft paste. Stir in the mint and chives.

Just before serving, use the mixture to fill halves of peeled pear, piling it into the hollow left when the core has been removed. Brush the pears with the lemon juice to prevent them turning brown.

Tomatoes in Soured Cream Dressing

SERVES 4-6

1–2 lb (450–900 g) tomatoes, thinly sliced

For the dressing:
4 tablespoons soured cream
2 tablespoons white wine or cider vinegar

salt
freshly ground black pepper
pinch of sugar
dill or grated horseradish (optional)
chopped spring onion, to garnish

Mix together all the ingredients for the dressing and pour over the tomatoes. Top with a little chopped spring onion and freshly ground black pepper.

Coat the tomatoes immediately before serving, otherwise their juice will dilute the dressing and make the dish look watery.

Sweet and Sour Cucumber

A lovely combination of dill and cucumber, which really freshens the palate before a fine main course.

SERVES 4

1 cucumber
½ teaspoon salt
2 tablespoons sugar
1 tablespoon boiling water
½ teaspoon freshly ground black pepper

6 tablespoons white wine vinegar
2 tablespoons chopped dill (when fresh dill is unobtainable infuse 1 tablespoon dill seeds in the boiling water for a few minutes and strain, reserving the water)

Peel the cucumber and slice it finely. Sprinkle with the salt and leave it pressed between two plates in the refrigerator for 30 minutes.

Dissolve the sugar in the water. When cold mix with the black pepper, vinegar and dill. Drain any liquid from the cucumber, place in a dish and pour over the dressing.

Asparagus Salad

Tony Marshall at Dukes Hotel, London

S E R V E S   2

12 asparagus spears
small knob of butter
6 sprigs of thyme
12 oz (350 g) mangetout peas, topped and
  tailed
2 eating apples
chives
4 oz (100 g) haricots verts, topped and tailed
mustard and cress

2 tomatoes, skinned, seeded and cut into
  ½ inch (1 cm) long strips

For the dressing:
2 oz (50 g) blackcurrant vinegar
1 egg yolk
½ pint (300 ml) olive oil
salt
freshly ground black pepper

Peel the top third of each stem of asparagus thinly. Cut away about 1 inch (2.5 cm) of the woody stems and tie in a bundle. Cook, tips uppermost, in boiling salted water with the butter and thyme for about 15–20 minutes, until tender, according to thickness. Place immediately in iced water to prevent over-cooking.

Blanch the mangetouts in boiling water and refresh under cold running water. Cut twelve into large diamonds and cut the rest into ½ inch (1 cm) lengths. Peel and quarter the apples, remove the cores and square off the ends. Cut into thin ½ inch (1 cm) lengths. This should be left until the last minute to prevent the apple discolouring.

To make the dressing, whisk the vinegar into the egg yolk and slowly add the oil, beating all the time. Season with salt and pepper.

Arrange the mangetout diamonds symmetrically, like the spokes of a wheel, around two dinner plates, leaving plenty of room at the centre for the main salad. Cut the asparagus spears into 2 inch (5 cm) lengths and place a spear between each mangetout diamond. Place a ½ inch (1 cm) chive leaf in each of the gaps, also radiating outwards. Chop the asparagus stalks into thin rounds. Toss the apples, beans, mustard and cress, chopped asparagus stalks, chopped mangetouts and tomatoes in the dressing. Drain and pile them into the centre of the plates.

A bit pernickety perhaps but it looks good.

Asparagus Soufflé with Maltese Sauce

Allan Holland at Mallory Court, Bishops Tachbrook

You have to admit that Allan knows his onions, I mean asparagus.

S E R V E S   4

6 oz (175 g) asparagus, weighed after peeling
    and trimming
2½ oz (65 g) butter
1 tablespoon chopped shallot
1½ oz (40 g) flour
½ pint (300 ml) milk
salt
freshly ground black pepper
freshly grated nutmeg
cayenne pepper
4 eggs, separated

2 oz (50 g) Gruyère or Emmenthal cheese,
    grated
grated Parmesan cheese

For the sauce:
thinly cut peel of 1 orange, blood if possible
3 egg yolks
1 tablespoon lemon juice
6 tablespoons blood orange juice
6 oz (175 g) butter, melted
salt

Peel the top third of each stem of asparagus thinly. Cut away about 1 inch (2.5 cm) of the woody stems and tie in a bundle. Cook, tips uppermost, in boiling salted water with a small knob of the butter for 15–20 minutes, until tender, according to thickness. Drain and cut into small pieces.

Melt 1 tablespoon of the butter in a pan and cook the shallot for a moment, before adding the asparagus. Stir while the moisture evaporates, then lift out the shallot and asparagus and put to one side. Add the remaining butter, heat to melt, then stir in the flour and cook for 1 minute. Meanwhile, bring the milk to the boil. Remove the *roux* from the heat, mix in the milk, then return to the heat and cook for 1 minute. Stir in the shallot and asparagus and season to taste with salt, pepper, nutmeg and cayenne pepper. Beat in the egg yolks, one at a time, and half the Gruyère or Emmenthal cheese.

Whisk the egg whites with a pinch of salt until they hold stiff peaks. Fold one-third of the whites into the asparagus mixture. Pour the mixture back on to the remaining egg white and gently fold in. Do not overmix. Butter four small soufflé dishes, about 4 inches (10 cm) in diameter and 2½ inches (6 cm) deep. Butter the soufflé dishes and sprinkle with a little Parmesan cheese. Divide the asparagus mixture between the dishes. Sprinkle the remaining Gruyère or Emmenthal cheese on top. Place on a baking sheet and bake in a preheated oven, 400°F/200°C (gas mark 6), for 15–20 minutes.

While the soufflés are baking, make the sauce. Shred the orange peel into thin julienne strips (thinner than matchstick strips). Cook in boiling water for about 2 minutes until tender. Drain, rinse under cold running water and set aside. Put the egg yolks into a small pan and whisk, adding the lemon juice and 2 tablespoons of the orange juice. Place over a gentle heat or in a *bain-marie* and whisk until the eggs are pale and lighter in colour. Remove from the heat and very gradually whisk in the warm melted butter. Season to taste with salt and the remaining orange juice.

Serve the soufflés straight from the oven accompanied by the Maltese Sauce.

Fresh Broad Beans and Bacon

A snack from the Garden of Eden.

S E R V E S 4

2 lb (900 g) fresh broad beans from your
garden - which you were tending when the
guests unexpectedly arrived
dash of olive oil
1 clove of garlic, chopped

at least 8 oz (225 g) back bacon, diced into
1 inch (2.5 cm) pieces
freshly ground black pepper
bowl of freshly grated cheese

Shell the beans, keeping the young and tender pods intact but stringing both sides. Blanch them for 3 minutes in boiling salted water.

Meanwhile, heat your largest frying pan and add the oil, garlic, bacon and the drained beans. Mill over lots of black pepper and fry gently until the bacon is cooked and the beans are tender. Serve with the grated cheese.

PS Broad beans don't come from freezer chests.

Braised Leeks Vinaigrette

Only if you use very young leeks will you taste the supreme flavours. And for those of you who think leeks aren't smart enough for serious consideration - go back to the avocado and prawns with pink sauce!

S E R V E S 6

6 medium leeks
¾ pint (450 ml) chicken or veal stock, see
page 43 or 41
lettuce leaves, washed and dried

For the marinade:
½ small green pepper, seeded and finely
chopped

3 oz (75 g) can pimientos, drained and
chopped
¼ pint (150 ml) white wine vinegar
2 fl oz (50 ml) vegetable oil
1 teaspoon sugar
1 teaspoon salt
1 teaspoon dry mustard
½ teaspoon freshly ground black pepper

Wash the leeks in cold water and trim away the root end. Bring the chicken or veal stock to the boil, add the leeks and cook them for about 8–10 minutes, or until just tender, but still firm.

Meanwhile, mix together all the ingredients for the marinade in a large shallow dish. Drain the leeks and arrange in a single layer in the dish, turning to coat well. Cover and chill for several hours, turning the leeks occasionally.

To serve, line each plate with lettuce leaves, place a leek on each one and spoon over some marinade.

Aubergine Caviar

Eat this with hot toast and a wedge of lemon. And a glass of iced vodka.

SERVES 6

5 medium aubergines
4-5 tablespoons olive oil
6 onions, grated

6 tomatoes, skinned and chopped
salt
freshly ground black pepper

Bake the aubergines in a preheated oven, 375°F/190°C (gas mark 5), for about 30–40 minutes, or until black. Allow to cool, then cut the aubergines in half, from top to bottom, and scoop out the tender pulpy flesh.

Heat the oil in a pan and gently sauté the onions until they are transparent. Add the baked aubergine pulp and tomatoes and stir the mixture over a low heat for 1–2 minutes. Season to taste with salt and pepper and turn into a serving dish.

Chill well and serve very cold.

Beetroot Caviar

It tastes really fine and does not cost £40 an ounce.

SERVES 2

1 medium raw or cooked beetroot
½ tablespoon sugar
2 tablespoons vegetable oil

grated rind and juice of ½ lemon
pinch of salt

If using raw beetroot, wash and cook it whole in its skin in plenty of water for about 1 hour, until tender. Rinse in cold water and peel. Chop the beetroot into small pieces and put it through a mincer. Add the remaining ingredients, turn the mixture into a pan and stir over a low heat for 5–10 minutes.

Chill and serve with black bread and butter.

These "caviares" make super drinks snacks.

Salt Cod Tarts

An appetiser with a difference, this recipe will make about eighteen small, individual tartlets and take quite a long time to prepare, but it's really worth it.

S E R V E S   6

For the shortcrust pastry:
6 oz (175 g) plain flour
3 oz (75 g) butter, diced
1 oz (25 g) shortening
2 tablespoons cold water, to mix

For the *brandade* mixture:
12 oz (350 g) dried salt cod - about 1 side to give 8 oz (225 g) cooked
court bouillon, *see page 44*

3 oz (75 g) fresh white breadcrumbs
3 tablespoons lemon juice
3 fl oz (75 ml) olive oil
½ clove of garlic, crushed with salt
7 fl oz (200 ml) thick mayonnaise, see page 34

about 18 black olives, to garnish
mustard and cress leaves, to garnish

Soak the salt cod in cold water overnight, drain and rinse well.

To make the pastry, sift the flour into a large bowl. Rub in the fat, using your fingertips, a food processor, or a pastry blender, until the mixture looks like very fine breadcrumbs. Add the cold water and press the mixture together to form a dough. Chill. Roll the pastry out on a lightly floured surface to about ⅛–¼ inch (4–7 mm) in thickness and use to line eighteen small, individual tartlet tins. Line the tins with greaseproof paper, weight with baking beans and bake 'blind' in a preheated oven, 400°F/200°C (gas mark 6), for 10–15 minutes until

cooked. Remove the beans and paper and allow to cool.

Put the fish in a pan, cover with *court bouillon* and poach for about 20 minutes, until just tender. Leave to cool in the liquid, then drain and remove the skin and any bone. Soak the breadcrumbs in the lemon juice and oil. Crush and pound the fish with the garlic and soaked breadcrumbs and work in by degrees sufficient mayonnaise to give a smooth cream. Fill the pastry cases with the *brandade* and garnish each with a sliced black olive and mustard and cress leaves. Serve cold.

Quiche Divan

Juan Martin at Sharrow Bay Hotel, Ullswater

SERVES 2-3

1 quantity of shortcrust pastry, see page 71
3 eggs
½ pint (300 ml) double cream
6 cooked broccoli pieces (stalks and flowers)
3 oz (75 g) Gruyère cheese, grated

3 oz (75 g) cooked chicken meat, chopped
salt
freshly ground black pepper
knob of butter

Roll the pastry out on a lightly floured surface and use to line an 8 inch (20 cm) flan or quiche dish. Line with greaseproof paper, weight with baking beans and bake 'blind' in a preheated oven, 400°F/200°C (gas mark 6), for 10 minutes. Remove the beans and paper and reduce the oven temperature to 350°F/180°C (gas mark 4).

Beat the eggs, then add the cream and beat again. Place the broccoli in the par-cooked pastry case. Cover with the cheese and chopped chicken. Pour over the egg mixture and season to taste with salt and pepper. Dot with a little butter. Place on a baking sheet, return to the oven and bake for 30-40 minutes, or until the filling has set. Cool a little before serving.

Hot Onion Tarts

They say that only in Alsace will you find a good onion tart – where they vary from a kind of pizza to a high-sided quiche. But this one is the business.

SERVES 4

1 quantity of shortcrust pastry, see page 71,
  or 1 × 7½ oz (212 g) frozen puff pastry,
  thawed, depending on your taste
2 oz (50 g) butter
2 large onions, finely sliced

2 large eggs (size 1 or 2)
4 tablespoons double cream
salt
freshly ground black pepper
8 anchovy fillets

Roll out the pastry on a lightly floured surface to about ⅛–¼ inch (4-7 mm) in thickness and use to line four 3 inch (7.5 cm) tartlet tins. Prick the bases with a fork.

Melt the butter in a frying pan and throw in the onion slices, turning them until they are soft and transparent.

Beat together the eggs and cream and season to taste with salt and pepper. Mix in the onions and fill the pastry cases. Bake in a preheated oven, 425°F/220°C (gas mark 7), for about 15 minutes or until set.

Decorate with the anchovy fillets and eat the tarts before they deflate.

Stuffed Onions

SERVES 3

3 large Spanish onions
2-3 tablespoons cooked long-grain rice or
bulghur wheat
1-2 eggs, beaten (optional)
1 lb (450 g) minced lamb
up to 1 head of garlic, minced
1 tablespoon each chopped coriander, parsley,
basil

2 tablespoons thyme
3 teaspoons chopped mint
salt
freshly ground black pepper
slices of apple, quince, apricot, onion and
prunes
court bouillon, *see page 44*

Blanch the onions, unpeeled, in boiling water for 2 minutes. Cut a lid off the top of each and take out the centre, leaving three or four layers of flesh to form the case to be filled. Chop the centres finely.

Mix together the rice or wheat, chopped onions, eggs if using, meat, garlic and herbs. Season to taste with salt and pepper and stuff the onions with the mixture.

Put them in a pan or flameproof casserole and fill the spaces between the onions with slices of apple, quince, apricot, onion and prunes. Add sufficient *bouillon* to half-cover and cook for about 20–30 minutes, or until tender.

Serve hot with the fruit, *bouillon* from the pan and natural yoghurt or cold without the *bouillon*.

Stuffed Vine Leaves

Everybody in the Eastern Med does vine leaves – your average Egyptian housewife or male cook would not buy a recipe book to learn how. But in case you live in Nuneaton or Newlyn, this is how they do it.

SERVES 4 - 6

8 oz (225 g) fresh or preserved vine leaves
5 oz (150 g) long-grain rice
1 lb (450 g) minced lamb or beef
1 onion, finely chopped
3 tablespoons chopped parsley

¼ teaspoon freshly ground black pepper
2 teaspoons tomato purée
3 tablespoons melted butter
2 cloves of garlic, cut into slivers
juice of 1 lemon

If you are using fresh vine leaves, plunge the leaves in boiling water for a few seconds. As soon as they change colour and go limp, remove them carefully and drain. If you are using vine leaves that have been canned or bottled in brine, you will need to pour it off and draw out the excess salt. To do so, cover the leaves with boiling water and let them sit for 20 minutes. Drain, then soak them in cold water and drain again.

Line a baking pan with vine leaves to prevent the stuffed leaves sticking. Meanwhile, cook the rice in boiling salted water for 5 minutes, then drain. Mix it with the meat, onion, parsley, black pepper, tomato purée and half the butter.

To stuff a leaf, lay it flat, vein side up, with its stem pointing towards you. Remove the stem with a small, sharp knife. Place about a tablespoon of filling for a large leaf or half for a smaller one in a sausage shape near the stem

edge. Fold this edge up over the filling, then fold the two sides in and roll up from the bottom into a tight cylinder shape.

As you stuff the leaves, lay them in the pan, packing them closely so they don't unravel. Continue stuffing the leaves in this way until all the filling is used. Insert slivers of garlic between the rolls and sprinkle with the rest of the melted butter and the lemon juice. Pour in about 8 fl oz (250 ml) water – enough almost to cover the leaves. Cover with foil and cook in a preheated oven, 325°F/160°C (gas mark 3), for about 1½ hours, until the meat is cooked. It may be necessary to add more water during cooking if too much evaporates.

To serve, arrange the leaves on a large platter, accompanied by natural yoghurt or a cold yoghurt sauce, which is just natural yoghurt seasoned and flavoured with salt and pepper, grated onion and some chopped herbs.

SOME BEGINNINGS

Cream Cheese and Tomato Jelly Ring

When you make a time-consuming starter like this, be sure to have a simple main course – such as charcoal-grilled lamb chops. And don't forget you can make this the day before a dinner party!

SERVES 6-8

2 × 1 lb (450 g) cans Italian tomatoes and
    their juice
1 onion, sliced
1 bay leaf
1 pint (600 ml) chicken stock, see page 43
1 tablespoon tomato purée
6 black peppercorns
pinch of salt
pinch of sugar
1 oz (25 g) powdered gelatine soaked in
    ¼ pint (150 ml) chicken stock or water
1 bunch of watercress, trimmed

For the cheese mixture:
12 oz (350 g) cream cheese
2 green peppers, blanched, seeded and
    chopped
1 tablespoon chopped chives
salt
freshly ground black pepper
8 fl oz (250 ml) single cream
1 tablespoon powdered gelatine soaked in 4
    tablespoons dry white wine

Turn the tomatoes into a pan with the onion, bay leaf, stock, tomato purée and peppercorns. Season with salt and sugar and simmer for 10 minutes. Pass the mixture through a sieve and allow to cool.

Heat the soaked gelatine gently in a pan until it has dissolved completely and stir into the tomato mixture.

While cooling, prepare the cheese layer. Beat the cream cheese with the peppers and chives. Season to taste with salt and pepper and stir in the cream. Dissolve the gelatine by slowly heating in the wine, then stir carefully into the cheese mixture.

As the tomato jelly begins to thicken, pour about half of it into a 2½ pint (1.4 litre) wetted ring mould and, when just set, spread the cheese layer on top. Smooth with a knife. Gently pour on the remaining tomato mixture. Cover with clingfilm and chill until set, about 2–3 hours.

To serve, dip the mould briefly into hot water and turn out. Fill the centre with watercress.

Red Pepper Mousse

I first ate this in a restaurant in Orange (Vaucluse) in 1970 – many years before what came to be known as *nouvelle cuisine* arrived in Britain. Mousses have since become the curse of modern cooking, but this dish well iced and prepared with care can give you a taste of the sun and tickle your fancy.

S E R V E S 4 - 6

1 oz (25 g) sachet of aspic jelly powder
¼ pint (150 ml) water
2 large ripe red peppers
1 tablespoon tomato purée
pinch of thyme
dash of chilli sauce

5 tablespoons double cream
salt
freshly ground black pepper
4 egg whites, stiffly beaten
Tomato Sauce, to serve, see page 37

Make up ¼ pint (150 ml) aspic jelly with the water according to the instructions on the packet, except make it to double strength.

Cook the peppers in boiling salted water for 20 minutes or so, until tender. Drain, cut out the seeds and chop into small pieces.

Put everything except the egg whites and

Tomato Sauce into a food processor or blender and whizz for a few seconds. Allow to cool.

Just before the purée sets, fold in the egg whites, mixing thoroughly. Check the seasoning and pour into wineglasses or ramekins. Chill well. Serve with a spoonful of cold Tomato Sauce.

Another Pepper Mousse

Shaun Hill at Gidleigh Park, Chagford

This time by one of England's best cooks. More complicated than mine. What do you think?

S E R V E S 6

3 medium red peppers
10 oz (275 g) veal fillet
juice of 3 lemons
5 cloves of garlic
1½ teaspoons ground paprika
2 eggs

2 tablespoons olive oil
¼ oz (7 g) powdered gelatine
¼ pint (150 ml) double cream
salt
freshly ground black pepper

Skin the peppers by dropping them in hot oil for a few seconds, then peeling. Purée the peppers, veal fillet, lemon juice, garlic and paprika in a food processor or blender. Whisk in the eggs, oil and gelatine dissolved in a little hot water. Chill until almost set, about 1–2 hours.

Whisk in the cream and season to taste with salt and pepper. Pour into a medium oiled terrine or ovenproof dish. Place the terrine in a roasting tin filled with a little water. Cover with foil and bake in a preheated oven, 325°F/160°C (gas mark 3), for about 40 minutes until just set. Allow to cool. Turn out on to a serving dish and slice thinly to serve.

Chicken Liver Mousse

This is best made in individual ramekins that you tip out on to white plates, which have been covered with chilled tom. sauce. Then delicately decorate with a sprig of endive lettuce. Thin slices of hot toast are essential and sweet white wine well chilled is great with it.

SERVES 10

1 lb (450 g) chicken livers
2 oz (50 g) butter
½ onion, finely chopped
1 clove of garlic, chopped
1 teaspoon chopped thyme
1 measure of brandy
1 teaspoon chopped parsley
1 tablespoon tomato purée

salt
freshly ground black pepper
1 oz (25 g) sachet of aspic jelly powder
8 fl oz (250 ml) boiling water
¼ pint (150 ml) double cream
5 egg whites, stiffly beaten
Tomato Sauce, to serve, see page 37

Wash the chicken livers, removing any strings or bitter green bits, and dry well on absorbent kitchen paper.

Melt the butter in a pan until it is foaming and fry the livers with the onion, garlic and thyme for 10 minutes. Warm the brandy, pour over and flame it. Add the parsley and tomato purée and season to taste with salt and pepper. Cook for a further 5 minutes. Allow to cool.

Meanwhile, make up the aspic with the water according to the packet instructions. Leave to cool.

When the liver mixture has cooled, purée it in a food processor or blender. Add the aspic and cream and leave until it begins to set. Fold in the egg whites, then spoon the mixture into one large dish or individual pots and chill until set, about 1–2 hours.

Serve with cold Tomato Sauce.

Chicken Livers and Fresh Marjoram

Juan Martin at Sharrow Bay Hotel, Ullswater

A clever example of the inventive cooking taking place in Britain today.
If fresh marjoram is not available, then dried marjoram will not do, so add
some chopped parsley.

SERVES 4-6

1½ oz (40 g) butter
2 shallots or 1 small onion, chopped
2 oz (50 g) bacon, rind removed and chopped
4 oz (100 g) mushrooms, sliced
1 oz (25 g) flour

¾ pint (450 ml) double cream
salt
freshly ground black pepper
2 tablespoons chopped marjoram
1 lb (450 g) chicken livers

Melt half of the butter in a pan and sauté the shallots or onion, bacon and mushrooms until tender. Mix in the flour, then add the cream, stirring constantly. Bring up to boiling point and remove from the heat. Season to taste with salt and pepper and add the marjoram.

Wash the chicken livers, removing any strings or bitter green bits, and dry well on absorbent kitchen paper. Heat a pan until hot, add the remaining butter and livers and cook to seal, according to how pink you like them, about 2–3 minutes. Add the sauce and serve.

Kipper Pâté

Clive Imber at Michael's Brasserie, Newcastle upon Tyne

SERVES 4

10 oz (275 g) cooked Craster kippers (like
*   many people from Northumbria, Clive*
*   reckons that Craster kippers are the best in*
*   the world)*

2 oz (50 g) butter, softened
lemon juice, to taste
pinch of cayenne pepper
2–3 tablespoons double cream

Remove the skin and bones from the kippers and flake the flesh. Pass it through a fine sieve to remove any small bones. Place in a food processor or blender with the butter, lemon juice, cayenne and cream. Purée until the mixture is smooth. Pour into one serving dish or individual pots and chill for 3–4 hours until firm.

To serve, shape into quenelles, using two dessertspoons dipped in warm water. Scoop out a dessertspoon of the pâté mixture and smooth it into a neat egg shape with the other spoon. Serve with a small salad and fresh toast.

Salmon Pâté with Watercress Mousse

This is a very attractive layered pâté that should be sliced on a large plate with a small portion of the watercress mousse, and served by a hired waiter while you sit under your walnut tree in the garden. You can dream, I suppose.

SERVES 4-6

*1½ lb (700 g) brill fillets (plaice or sole can
    also be used)*
2 eggs, beaten
2½ fl oz (65 ml) double cream
1 lb (450 g) salmon steak

For the panada:
2½ oz (65 g) flour
7½ fl oz (215 ml) milk
2 oz (50 g) butter
salt

freshly ground black pepper
ground mace

For the watercress mousse:
2 bunches of watercress
¼ pint (150 ml) mayonnaise, see page 34
¼ pint (150 ml) double cream, whipped
dash of Tabasco sauce
dash of cayenne pepper
dash of lemon juice

To make the panada, sift the flour on to a piece of paper. Bring the milk to the boil with the butter. Remove from the heat, then tip in the flour all at once and beat by hand or in a blender until smooth. Season well with salt, pepper and a little mace and allow to cool.

Skin and bone the brill and process in a food processor or blender with the panada until smooth. Add the beaten eggs and cream. Check the seasoning and whizz again for a few seconds. If you do not have a food processor or blender, pound the fish well in a bowl before adding the other ingredients.

Remove the skin and bone from the salmon. Pound the flesh, season and shape into a roll about 8 inches (20 cm) long. Place half the white fish mixture in the bottom of a greased 2 lb (900 g) loaf tin, lay the salmon in the middle and cover with the remaining white fish cream. Smooth the top and tap the tin firmly on the table to remove any air. Cover with buttered foil. Place inside a terrine or roasting tin half-filled with water and pop in a preheated oven, 350°F/180°C (gas mark 4), for 45 minutes, or until firm to the touch. Remove from the oven, place a 1–2 lb (450–900 g) weight on top and leave until cold.

To make the watercress mousse, wash and pick over the watercress, keeping as much stalk as possible. Dry well with absorbent kitchen paper. Place in a food processor, chop finely and then add the remaining ingredients. Whizz for a few seconds until well mixed. Alternatively, chop the watercress very finely before stirring in the other ingredients.

Herby Chicken Pâté

This is a very tasty pâté, which is good served with crusty French bread and a glass of wine as a snack. Better still, serve with a green salad or fresh garden peas as a summer lunch.

SERVES 6 FOR A STARTER
OR 4 FOR LUNCH

3½ lb (1.5 kg) chicken, with giblets
½ onion, unpeeled
½ lemon
1 oz (25 g) butter
salt
freshly ground black pepper
1 bunch of watercress, trimmed

6 small sprigs of tarragon
3 large eggs
¼ pint (150 ml) double cream
3 extra chicken livers
6 rashers of streaky bacon, rind removed
sprigs of watercress and tarragon, to garnish

Roast the chicken the day before you wish to make the pâté, then you can use the lovely jellied juices. Place the onion inside the chicken. Squeeze the lemon over the bird and pop the lemon 'shell' into the cavity. Rub half the butter over the chicken and place the remainder in the cavity. Season well with salt and pepper and cover with foil. Roast in a preheated oven, 375°F/190°C (gas mark 5), for 1½ hours, removing the foil halfway through the cooking time and basting well at this stage. Turn off the oven but leave the bird inside for a further 30 minutes. Remove from the oven, drain off the liquid and reserve.

To make the pâté, place the watercress, tarragon, eggs and cream in a food processor or blender and whizz until it forms a thick, green cream. If you do not have a food processor or blender, chop the watercress and tarragon finely before mixing with the eggs and cream.

Remove the lemon shell from inside the bird and discard. Peel the onion and carve off the breasts in complete sections. Pull away all the remaining flesh from the carcass, discarding the skin. Put the onion and flesh, except for the breast meat, through a mincer, using a fine blade, or process in a food processor until it

forms a smooth paste. Mix thoroughly with the herby cream. Season well.

Wash the chicken livers, including the one that came with the giblets, and remove any strings or bitter green bits. Chop each liver into about four pieces. Skin the breasts and chop roughly across the grain. Scrape the fat from the jellied juices, retaining a tablespoonful for frying. Gently melt the 'jelly' in a pan. Fry the liver pieces in the reserved fat, just enough to seal on all sides so they do not discolour the finished pâté. Stir them into the pâté mixture with the frying fat and the chopped breast.

Stretch the bacon by pressing it against a board with the back of a knife. Use the bacon to line a buttered pâté dish or 2 lb (900 g) loaf tin, laying them neatly and closely together. Carefully pour in the pâté mixture, smooth the top and cover with buttered foil. Place inside a roasting tin half-filled with water. Bake in a preheated oven, 325°F/160°C (gas mark 3), until set. The time taken will depend on the dish used but it will probably be 1½ hours. Remove from the oven, cool, weight and chill.

To serve, dip briefly in hot water, to loosen the fat, and turn out on to a serving dish. Garnish with a sprig of watercress and tarragon.

Country Pâté

This is the kind of pâté you should make at least once a month – when cooked it keeps in the fridge for some time and is always there to use as a starter or a snack for unexpected visitors rather than reaching into the deep freeze for a supermarket pizza!

You can decide on the coarseness of the pâté yourself as to how finely you mince the meats. Like all pâtés, make it at least 24 hours in advance to allow the flavours time to develop.

SERVES 4-6

4 oz (100 g) streaky bacon, rind removed
1 lb (450 g) pie veal, minced
2 oz (50 g) pig's liver, minced
1 onion, finely chopped
generous pinch each of ground cinnamon,
    ground cloves and ground ginger

dash of Tabasco sauce
1 tablespoon finely chopped parsley
1½ teaspoons salt
freshly ground black pepper
1 teaspoon Worcestershire sauce
2 tablespoons brandy

Stretch the bacon by pressing it against a board with the back of a knife. Use the bacon to line a buttered 1 lb (450 g) loaf tin or terrine neatly and closely. Mix together all the other ingredients thoroughly. Carefully put the pâté mixture into the tin or terrine, so as not to disturb the bacon, and press gently. Cover with buttered foil. Place inside a roasting tin half-filled with hot water and bake in a preheated oven, 325°F/160°C (gas mark 3), for 1 hour or until set. When cooked, cover with a 2 lb (900 g) weight and chill for 24 hours.

Specially good with a dollop of onion chutney

Liver Pâté

Depending on the flavour required you can use either pig's or calves' liver. Pig's liver will give a very well flavoured and rich pâté, whereas calves' will give a more delicate flavour. Depends on your mood, and your pocket.

S E R V E S   6

1½ lb (675 g) pig's or calves' liver
10 oz (275 g) streaky bacon, the fattier the
    better, rind removed
3 tablespoons double cream
1 dessertspoon anchovy essence

For the sauce:
½ pint (300 ml) milk
½ small onion

8 black peppercorns
1 bay leaf
blade of mace
1 oz (25 g) butter
1 tablespoon flour
pinch of ground mace
salt
freshly ground black pepper

Place the milk in a pan with the onion, peppercorns, bay leaf and blade of mace. Bring to the boil, remove from the heat and let it stand while you do the next bit.

Remove any tubes and skin from the liver. Cut away any bony bits from the bacon. Put the liver and 6 oz (175 g) of the bacon through a mincer or process in a food processor.

To make the sauce, melt the butter in a pan, add the flour and cook for 1 minute without browning. Remove from the heat and gradually add the strained milk. Beat well; if it looks lumpy, whisk it. Return to the heat and bring to the boil, stirring constantly. Boil for 2 minutes, remove from the heat, add the ground mace and season with salt and pepper. Allow to cool.

When the sauce has cooled, stir in the liver mixture, cream and anchovy essence. Use the remaining bacon to line a buttered terrine, leaving the ends draped over the sides to lap over the top of the pâté. The mixture should be smooth – if it is not, process in a food processor or pass through a sieve. Pour the mixture carefully into the terrine, fold over the bacon ends and cover with buttered foil. Place inside a roasting tin half-filled with water. Bake in a preheated oven, 350°F/180°C (gas mark 4), for 50 minutes. When cooked cover with a 2 lb (900 g) weight and chill for 24 hours. If you wish to keep the pâté longer, cover the top with a little clarified butter, see page 35, and keep in a cool place.

Terrine of Pork

I think terrines should not be made for specific meals but treated as part
of a well stocked larder for you to eat as and when you want.

SERVES 4-6

1 lb (450 g) pork fillet
8 oz (225 g) streaky bacon, rind removed

For the stuffing:
1 oz (25 g) butter
1 small onion, finely chopped
4 oz (100 g) mushrooms, chopped
1 tablespoon chopped mixed herbs

4 oz (100 g) lamb's or calves' liver, minced
4 oz (100 g) pork, minced
2 oz (50 g) fresh white breadcrumbs
2 tablespoons brandy
12 pistachio nuts, blanched and halved
salt
freshly ground black pepper

Cut the pork fillet in half lengthways and beat with a rolling pin to flatten. Use the bacon to line a buttered 2 lb (900 g) or medium terrine or loaf tin.

To make the stuffing, melt the butter in a pan and soften the onion. Add the mushrooms and cook briskly for 4 minutes. Stir in the herbs, then tip the mixture on to a plate to cool down. When cooled, add the minced liver, pork, breadcrumbs, brandy and pistachio nuts. Season to taste with plenty of salt and pepper.

Put one-third of the stuffing mixture into a

prepared tin and cover neatly with half the pork fillet. Tip another third of the stuffing on top of the pork and cover with another layer of pork fillet. Top with the remaining stuffing mixture. If any bacon is left over or overhanging the tin, fold it over neatly. Cover with buttered foil and place inside a roasting tin half-filled with water. Bake in a preheated oven, 325°F/160°C (gas mark 3), for 1–1½ hours, or until firm. Remove from the oven, place a 2 lb (900 g) weight on top and chill for at least 24 hours.

NOTE

When possible always use a hand mincer for terrines as processors can reduce the meat to a pulp.
Always use or improvise a *bain-marie* when possible.
If your terrine is not big enough to take the amount, cook two loads and freeze one.

Turkey Terrine with Chestnuts

This is a layered pâté, using the dark and white meats of the turkey. Serve as a starter or for a light lunch with a glass of wine and toasted French bread.

You will need to start making this terrine three days before it is required.

EACH HALF SERVES 6
FOR A LIGHT LUNCH OR 8 AS A STARTER

For the meat:
1½ lb (675 g) white turkey meat
8 oz (225 g) belly of pork
1 lb (450 g) dark turkey meat
1½ oz (40 g) butter
8 oz (225 g) streaky bacon, rind removed

For the marinade:
½ pint (300 ml) dry white wine
4 fl oz (100 ml) port
2 tablespoons olive oil
1 carrot, sliced
½ onion, sliced
8 black peppercorns
1 bay leaf

1 sprig of thyme
1 sprig of parsley

For the stuffing:
½ onion, finely chopped
1 oz (25 g) chicken or turkey liver, finely chopped
2 oz (50 g) mushrooms, finely chopped
8 oz (225 g) chestnut purée
2 oz (50 g) streaky bacon, finely chopped
4 oz (100 g) fresh white breadcrumbs
1 tablespoon chopped parsley
salt
freshly ground black pepper
1 oz (25 g) butter, melted

Mix together all the marinade ingredients in a large bowl (not aluminium). Cut the white turkey meat and the pork into small cubes and place in the marinade. Add the dark turkey meat in one piece, coat well, cover and chill for at least 24 hours.

To make the stuffing, mix together all the ingredients and bind with the melted butter.

Remove the meat from the marinade. Put the white turkey meat, pork and butter through the mincer or process in a food processor. Slice the dark turkey meat very thinly.

Use the bacon to line a buttered 3 lb (1.4 kg) loaf tin or terrine. Carefully put in half the minced meat mixture and smooth with a knife. Then lay half the dark meat slices neatly on top. Spoon in the stuffing mixture and smooth. Cover with the remaining turkey slices and top with the other half of the minced meat mixture. If any bacon is overhanging the sides, fold over the top. Cover with buttered foil and place in a roasting tin half-filled with water. Pop into a preheated oven, 300°F/150°C (gas mark 2), for a couple of hours. When cooked, cover with a 2 lb (900 g) weight and chill before serving. Then cut it in half – eat one lot at once and freeze the other piece for a rainy day.

Hare Terrine

Again, this is cooking for the larder – do it some time when you're not busy.

S E R V E S   6

1 oven-ready hare, jointed and boned
8 oz (225 g) pork sausagemeat
1 small onion, grated
2 egg yolks
1 small carrot, grated
4 oz (100 g) seedless raisins

2 tablespoons game or chicken stock, see page 43
salt
freshly ground black pepper
8 oz (225 g) streaky bacon, rind removed

Cut the best pieces of hare meat into neat fillets and put the rest through a mincer. Mix the minced hare with all the remaining ingredients, except the bacon.

Line a 1 lb (450 g) buttered terrine with overlapping bacon rashers, leaving at least 2 inches (5 cm) hanging over each side. Fill with alternate layers of minced hare mixture and pieces of hare meat. Fold the bacon over the top, cover with buttered foil and place in a roasting tin half-filled with water. Bake in a preheated oven, 350°F/180°C (gas mark 4), for 1¼ hours. Pour off the excess fat. Weight and chill.

To serve, cut into thick slices.

Another Simple Terrine

S E R V E S   4 - 6

1 lb (450 g) belly of pork, finely chopped
8 oz (225 g) pig's liver, minced
12 oz (350 g) veal, minced
2 cloves of garlic, crushed
6 black peppercorns, crushed
4 juniper berries, crushed
pinch of ground mace
salt

freshly ground black pepper
generous wineglass of dry white wine
generous splash of brandy
4 oz (100 g) sheet of pork fat or 4 oz (100 g) slice of speck (cured pork fat), half cut into ½ inch (1 cm) thick strips and the other half into small cubes

Mix together all the ingredients, except the strips of fat, and chill for a couple of hours.

Scrape into a buttered medium terrine and lay the strips of fat over the top. Cover with buttered foil and place inside a roasting tin half-filled with water. Bake in a preheated oven, 300°F/150°C (gas mark 2), for about 1½ hours. Remove from the oven, place a 2 lb (900 g) weight on top and allow to cool for 24 hours before eating.

Garlic and Goose Liver Sausage

Ramon Farthing at Calcot Manor, Tetbury

S E R V E S 4

For the marinade:
2 chicken breasts, diced
6 chicken livers
8 oz (225 g) beef fillet trimmings
1 onion, chopped
1 clove of garlic, chopped
few sprigs of thyme
parsley trimmings
Madeira

Remaining ingredients:
½ pint (300 ml) veal glaze, see page 42

4 egg yolks
3 oz (75 g) brioche crumbs or fresh white
*   breadcrumbs*
4 oz (100 g) goose liver (optional)
chopped parsley
salt
freshly ground black pepper
8 inch (20 cm) square of clean caul fat

oil and butter for frying

Mix together all the ingredients for the marinade in a large bowl (not aluminium) and moisten with Madeira. Leave to marinate for 12 hours. Purée in a food processor or blender, then pass through a fine sieve.

Boil the veal glaze rapidly in a pan to reduce it by one-third, allow to cool and mix it into the sausage mixture. Stir in the egg yolks and brioche crumbs or breadcrumbs. Finely dice the goose liver, if using, and place in the freezer until firm. Stir it into the sausage mixture, add the parsley and season to taste with salt and pepper. Allow the mixture to rest for 1–2 hours.

Fit a piping bag with a plain ¼ inch (7 mm) nozzle and fill with the sausage mixture. Lay out the 8 inch (20 cm) square of caul fat and pipe the sausage mixture in a straight line along one edge of the caul. Roll up the caul into a sausage shape. Twist the ends gently in opposite directions to tighten. Secure each end with a small piece of string and form a small knot. Place in the refrigerator for about 1–2 hours to rest.

To cook, simply heat together a little oil and butter in a frying pan until nut brown. Seal the sausage on all sides and continue to cook over a moderate heat for about 20 minutes, turning frequently, until it is golden brown all over.

Serve the sausage, sliced and still warm, on a bed of picked salad leaves dressed with a light vinaigrette.

LIGHT DISHES FOR BUSY GASTRONAUTS

CHAPTER 4

You may notice a rather strong Italian bias in this chapter. I make no apology for that because, when it comes to inventing the kind of one-plate dishes which are delicious as light and simple lunches or suppers, but are also splendid enough to be expanded into the main course for a dinner party – the Italians get it right.

After all, they say the pizza was invented by an Italian baker who was feeling a bit peckish, but since it was too early to go home to dinner, took a ball of leftover dough, flattened it out, popped on a bit of anchovy, cheese and tomato, and baked it as a snack. The rest, as they say, is history.

Ratatouille Omelette

Allan Holland at Mallory Court, Bishops Tachbrook

S E R V E S 4

8 large eggs
4 tablespoons cold water
2 oz (50 g) butter
8 fl oz (250 ml) double cream
8 oz (225 g) Gruyère cheese, grated

For the ratatouille:
2 aubergines, sliced
2 courgettes, sliced
salt
2 fl oz (50 ml) olive oil
1 onion, sliced
2 large red peppers, seeded and cut into strips
1 clove of garlic, chopped
2 large tomatoes, skinned and chopped
freshly ground black pepper

To make the ratatouille, put the aubergines and courgettes in a bowl, sprinkle with salt and leave for an hour or so to drain. Pat dry with absorbent kitchen paper. Heat the olive oil in a heavy-based shallow pan and cook the onion gently until soft. Add the aubergines, courgettes, peppers and garlic, cover the pan and cook for about 20 minutes. Add the tomatoes and season to taste with salt and pepper. Cook for a further 20 minutes or so, until the vegetables are soft but not mushy. Keep warm.

Break the eggs into a bowl and add the cold water. Whisk lightly with a fork, but do not overbeat – the eggs should just be broken down. Heat an omelette pan and add a quarter of the butter. When it begins to turn brown, add a quarter of the egg mixture to the pan and immediately whisk the eggs with a fork for a few seconds until the base of the omelette begins to set. As soon as it is set over the base, spoon a quarter of the ratatouille along the middle and fold over. Turn out on to a plate, pour over a quarter of the double cream and cover with a quarter of the grated cheese. Glaze for 1–2 minutes under a preheated very hot grill. Use the remaining egg mixture and ratatouille in the same way to make four omelettes. Serve as they are cooked.

Classic Pipérade

Whatever you do, don't call this scrambled eggs in the Basque Country,
because they're fiercely proud of this dish and quite rightly so.

SERVES 4

oil and butter

2 red and 1 green pepper, seeded and chopped

4 ripe tomatoes, skinned, seeded and chopped

1 clove of garlic, finely chopped

½ red chilli pepper (or piment d'espellete –
  see below) or a pinch of ground paprika

chopped thyme

chopped parsley

1 bay leaf

salt

freshly ground black pepper

1 teaspoon caster sugar – the secret ingredient
  given to me by Mimi in Biarritz

6 eggs

4 slices of Bayonne ham or any cured ham
  (Parma, for example) or good bacon

Heat together some oil and butter in a frying pan and cook the peppers, tomatoes, garlic plus all the spices and seasonings (including the sugar), until they are very soft. Beat the eggs with a little cold water and stir them in as for scrambled eggs. Fish out the bay leaf.

Meanwhile, fry the slices of ham or bacon and serve with the pipérade mixture.

PS Espellete is a small town in the Basque Country that is the centre of France's red pepper powder industry. The locals and the cognoscenti wouldn't dream of using any other type.

Bacon and Eggs in Red Wine

Trust the French to pour cold wine over bacon and eggs. Trust the French
to turn it into a triumph. As Fats Waller used to say, 'I love my liquid ham
and eggs'. Understand?

SERVES 4-6

2 tablespoons oil
2 oz (50 g) butter
2 slices of bacon per person, cubed
1 onion, chopped
1 clove of garlic, chopped
bouquet garni (bay leaf, parsley and thyme,
  for example)

1¾ pints (1 litre) red wine
2 eggs per person
slices of bread fried in pork or goose fat
knob of butter (optional)
freshly ground black pepper (optional)

Heat together the oil and butter in a pan and fry the bacon. Add the onion, garlic, bouquet garni and wine. Boil rapidly for 15-20 minutes, until the sauce thickens a little and is well reduced.

Strain the sauce and return it with the bacon to the pan. Simmer the sauce very gently so that it is barely moving. Break the eggs in a cup and slide in one at a time. Poach for 2½-3 minutes until the white is set and the yolk is semi-liquid.

Serve on slices of bread fried in pork or goose fat. Spoon over the sauce and bacon cubes. If the sauce tastes too strongly of wine, beat in a knob of butter and plenty of pepper.

Bow Tie Salad

This makes a different lunch salad or first course.

VARY THE QUANTITIES DEPENDING ON
THE NUMBER YOU ARE SERVING

butter
noisettes of lamb (allow 2 per person)
bow tie pasta
grated Parmesan cheese
olive oil

Italian parsley, large leaved variety, or an
  interesting lettuce
black olives, stoned and halved
sherry wine vinegar

Melt a little butter in a frying pan and brown the noisettes on both sides. Then cook gently until tender, about 15-20 minutes. If you are cooking for three or four people, it is better to roast the noisettes in one piece and slice when the meat has rested. Roast in a preheated hot oven, 425°F/220°C (gas mark 7), for 20-30 minutes, according to taste, from pink to medium.

Cook the pasta in a pan of boiling salted water until it is just tender but still firm, *al dente*. The time depends on whether it is fresh or dried. Drain quickly and toss in some grated Parmesan cheese and a little olive oil.

Arrange the pasta on a bed of washed and dried parsley or lettuce. Lay the thin slices of warm noisettes and the olives on top. Sprinkle over a little vinegar and serve.

Tagliatelle Alfredo

Like so many simple dishes, immediacy is everything – don't muck about keeping the tagliatelle warm while you serve something else.

S E R V E S 4

8 oz (225 g) dried tagliatelle or 1 lb (450 g)
  home-made noodles
2 oz (50 g) butter, melted
1 oz (25 g) Parmesan cheese, grated

2 tablespoons creamy milk
salt
freshly ground black pepper
grated Parmesan cheese, to serve

Cook the dried tagliatelle or noodles in a large pan of boiling salted water for about 6 minutes (but cook fresh for 2–3 minutes), until it is just tender but still firm, *al dente*.

Meanwhile, mix the butter with the cheese and milk in a heated serving dish and season to taste with salt and pepper. Drain the noodles thoroughly and add to the cheese mixture. Toss well until the noodles are coated. Serve immediately with a little extra grated cheese.

Spaghetti alla Carbonara

S E R V E S 4 - 6

1 lb (450 g) dried spaghetti
4 oz (100 g) streaky bacon, rind removed
  and chopped
4 eggs

2 tablespoons single cream
2 oz (50 g) Parmesan cheese, grated
freshly ground black pepper

Cook the spaghetti in a large pan of boiling salted water for about 12 minutes, until it is just tender but still firm, *al dente*.

Meanwhile, fry the bacon until crisp. Beat the eggs in a bowl and add the cream and half the cheese. Season with black pepper.

Drain the cooked spaghetti and return it to the pan. Quickly stir in the bacon. Add the eggs at once and toss well together. (The heat of the spaghetti will be enough to cook the eggs.) Serve immediately, sprinkled with the remaining cheese.

Monique Conil's Fresh Pasta

Simplicity is all in this dish.

SERVES 6-8

2 lb (900 g) fresh spaghetti or 12 oz (350 g)
    dried fettucine or tagliatelle – fresh is best if
    you can get it, but it must be fresh
1 large handful of basil, chopped

¼ pint (150 ml) olive oil – at least
freshly ground black pepper
grated Parmesan cheese

Cook the pasta in masses of boiling salted water until it is just tender but still firm, *al dente*. The time depends on the type of pasta – about 8 minutes for fresh and 12 minutes for dried, but do not overcook it. Drain at once and rinse under the hot tap to remove any starch or stickiness. Shake until it's really dry.

Meanwhile, mix the basil and the oil in a large bowl. Add the pasta and toss thoroughly with plenty of black pepper. Sprinkle with Parmesan cheese and serve immediately.

You then might enjoy a slice or two of Bayonne ham briefly fried and served with a few fresh broad beans, tossed lightly in the fat that you have cooked the ham in. A splendid summer lunch.

Pasta with Clams

SERVES 4-6

4 tablespoons olive oil
1 clove of garlic, crushed
30-40 medium-sized fresh clams, scraped and
    cleaned
2 tablespoons dry white wine

1 oz (25 g) parsley, chopped
1 tablespoon chopped basil
½ teaspoon salt
1½ lb (675 g) fresh linguine or spaghetti
green or purple basil, to garnish

Heat the oil in a pan and fry the garlic until tender. Add the prepared clams, wine, parsley, basil and salt and cook for 10 minutes, stirring occasionally.

Meanwhile, cook the pasta in a large pan of boiling salted water for about 2-3 minutes, until it is tender but still firm, *al dente*.

Lift out the clams from the sauce and remove them from their shells, reserving a few in their shells for the garnish. Return the shelled clams to the pan and, as soon as the pasta is cooked, drain and mix with the sauce.

To serve, scatter over the reserved clams and garnish with the basil.

All pasta sauces will be brilliant if you use only fresh, fresh ingredients.
This is not always possible I know, but please try.

Tomato Sauce

S E R V E S   6 - 8
(M A K E S   A B O U T   1 ½   P I N T S   [900 ml])

2 tablespoons vegetable oil
1 onion, chopped
1 clove of garlic, crushed
2 × 15 oz (425 g) cans tomatoes or very ripe
fresh ones
5 oz (150 g) can tomato purée

2 teaspoons brown sugar
2 tablespoons chopped parsley
1 teaspoon chopped oregano
1 teaspoon salt
pinch of freshly ground black pepper
1 bay leaf

Heat the oil in a pan and fry the onion and garlic for 10 minutes, stirring frequently.

Add the remaining ingredients and bring the mixture to the boil. Reduce the heat, partially cover the pan and cook for 30 minutes. Remove and discard the bay leaf.

Pesto Sauce

S E R V E S   4 - 6

5 tablespoons olive oil
1 clove of garlic, quartered
4 tablespoons chopped basil, or more if liked
1 teaspoon salt

4 tablespoons chopped parsley
¼ teaspoon freshly grated nutmeg
1 oz (25 g) Parmesan cheese, grated

To make the sauce by hand, pound 2 tablespoons of the oil, the garlic and basil in a mortar, then gradually beat in the remaining oil. Add the salt, parsley and nutmeg and pound until reduced to a paste. Finally, stir in the cheese.

Alternatively, if you're busy, whizz all the ingredients in a food processor or blender until well mixed.

Bolognese Sauce

This poor old sauce is so often misused in so-called Italian restaurants to drown imperfectly cooked, stale pasta. The true purpose, however, should be to enhance the flavour of really fresh, beautifully cooked pasta, so use bolognese sauce sparingly.

S E R V E S   4 - 6

knob of butter
2 oz (50 g) bacon, rind removed and chopped
1 small onion, chopped
1 carrot, chopped
1 stick of celery, chopped
8 oz (225 g) minced beef

4 oz (100 g) chicken livers, chopped
1 tablespoon tomato purée
¼ pint (150 ml) dry white wine
½ pint (300 ml) beef stock, see page 42
salt
freshly ground black pepper

Melt the butter in a large pan and fry the bacon for 2–3 minutes. Add the onion, carrot and celery and fry for 5 minutes until they are just browned. Add the minced beef and brown lightly, then stir in the chicken livers and cook for a further 3 minutes. Add the tomato purée and wine and simmer for a few minutes more. Pour in the beef stock and season to taste with salt and pepper. Bring up to the boil, reduce the heat and simmer for 30–40 minutes, until the meat is tender.

Home-made Pasta Dough for Ravioli

Depending on my mood, I alternate between preferring dry and fresh pasta. Sometimes I really enjoy the dried stuff, particularly spaghetti, but when it comes to ravioli – and lasagne too, for that matter – I think you'll be staggered by the extra quality you can achieve with fresh pasta.

S E R V E S   4   (M A K E S   1 L B   [450 g]   D O U G H)

9–10 oz (250–275 g) strong plain flour
5 tablespoons water
2 eggs, beaten

1 egg yolk
1 tablespoon olive or vegetable oil
1 teaspoon salt

To make the pasta by hand, sift 4 oz (100 g) of the flour into a large bowl. Make a well in the centre and add the remaining ingredients. Gradually work the flour into the liquids, until they are well mixed. Stir in enough of the remaining flour to make a soft and manageable dough. Alternatively, to make in a food processor, place the flour in the processor. Mix the water with the eggs, egg yolk, oil and salt. Add to the flour with the motor running, in a steady stream, and process until a soft dough has formed, about 10 seconds.

Turn the dough on to a lightly floured surface and knead for about 10 minutes until smooth, firm and no longer sticky. Wrap in waxed paper and leave to rest for about 30 minutes before shaping as required.

Ravioli

SERVES 4-6

cheese, meat or spinach filling, see below
1 quantity of Home-made Pasta Dough, see
  page 94

1½ pints (900 ml) Tomato Sauce, see page 93
1 tablespoon vegetable oil
1 oz (25 g) Parmesan cheese, grated

Make the filling first: do not roll out the pasta until you are ready to make the ravioli. Cut the pasta dough into four pieces. Roll out one piece very thinly on a lightly floured surface to a 15 × 6 inch (38 × 15 cm) rectangle and cut it crossways into five 6 × 3 inch (15 × 7.5 cm) strips.

Spread some filling over half the surface of a pasta strip to within ¼ inch (7 mm) of the edges. Fold the dough over the filling, bring the edges together neatly and press them firmly together with a fork dipped in flour. Spread in a single layer on floured tea towels. Repeat with the remaining pasta and filling and leave them to dry for 30 minutes.

Meanwhile, heat through the Tomato Sauce.

Add a few of the ravioli and the oil to a large pan of boiling salted water and cook them for 10 minutes, or until the pasta is just tender but still firm. Drain well and keep hot while you cook the remaining ravioli. Arrange them in a heated serving dish. Spoon over the Tomato Sauce and sprinkle with the grated Parmesan cheese.

For cheese filling:

Mix well 8 oz (225 g) Ricotta, cream or curd cheese with 3 tablespoons chopped parsley, 2 tablespoons grated Parmesan cheese, 1 egg white, ¼ teaspoon salt and a pinch of freshly ground black pepper.

For meat filling:

Cook 8 oz (225 g) minced beef with 2 oz (50 g) onion, finely chopped, and 1 clove of garlic, finely chopped, until the meat is browned. Remove from the heat, spoon off the juices and mix in thoroughly 1 beaten egg, ½ oz (15 g) chopped parsley, 2 tablespoons grated Parmesan cheese and ½ level teaspoon salt.

For spinach filling:

Thaw and drain well 8 oz (225 g) frozen spinach and mix in 1½ oz (40 g) grated Parmesan cheese, 2 beaten egg yolks, ½ oz (15 g) butter, ¼ teaspoon salt, a few turns of freshly ground black pepper and a pinch of freshly grated nutmeg.

Veal Lasagne

SERVES 4-6

1½ lb (675 g) boned shoulder of veal
1 tablespoon vegetable oil
6 oz (175 g) lasagne
2 oz (50 g) butter or margarine
1 large onion, finely chopped
1 oz (25 g) flour
1 pint (600 ml) milk

3 tablespoons medium sherry
2 teaspoons salt
pinch of white pepper
pinch of freshly grated nutmeg
2 oz (50 g) Parmesan cheese, grated
chopped parsley, to garnish

Cut the veal into ½ inch (1 cm) cubes, trim and discard the fat. Heat the oil in a large frying pan, add the veal and cook it until it is lightly browned, stirring occasionally.

Meanwhile, cook the lasagne in a large pan of boiling salted water until it is just tender but still firm. Drain well. Melt the butter or margarine in a large pan and cook the onion gently for 5 minutes, or until soft but not coloured, stirring occasionally. Stir in the flour until well mixed. Gradually add the milk and continue cooking until thickened, stirring constantly.

Remove the cooked veal from the frying pan

with a slotted spoon and stir it into the sauce with the sherry, salt, pepper and nutmeg. Arrange one-third of the lasagne sheets lengthways in a large greased ovenproof dish and top with half the meat mixture. Repeat the layers and finish with a layer of lasagne. Cover tightly with foil and bake in a preheated oven, 350°F/ 180°C (gas mark 4), for 30 minutes.

Remove from the oven, sprinkle with the cheese and bake, uncovered, for a further 15 minutes, or until lightly browned. Sprinkle with parsley and leave to stand for 10 minutes before serving.

Use very thin sheets of pasta and avoid overlapping to stop the dish from being too stodgy.

Ukrainian Borsch (page 50)

Salad of Endive Lettuce with Steamed Red Mullet and Coriander Dressing (page 60)

Braised Leeks Vinaigrette (page 69)

Salt Cod Tarts (page 71)

Ratatouille Omelette (page 88)

Three en papillote dishes, from left to right: *Trout with Dill (page 107); Prawns with Pernod and Mushrooms (page 108); Mediterranean Sea Bass with Pine Kernels (page 107)*

Oriental Fish in Filo Pastry (page 112)

Breast of Duck with Ginger, Mango and Spring Onions (pages 141–2)

Rabbit with Prunes (page 156)

Raised Winter Pie (page 157)

Steak with Red Wine Sauce and Beef Marrow (pages 164–5)

Mutton Pasties (pages 189–90)

Pork with Apple and Calvados (page 192)

Cassoulet (page 194)

Boiled Bacon with Pease Pudding (page 196)

A Traditional Recipe for Blini

This mixture makes about twelve blini, which are probably best eaten with chopped hard-boiled eggs and soured cream and/or melted butter. Like English crumpets, they are also excellent just with butter and may be kept warm in the oven. Chopped herring, lumpfish cod roe and soured cream are other traditional accompaniments. They look nice garnished with some slivers of red onion too.

MAKES 12

4 fl oz (100 ml) milk or water and another
   ½ pint (300 ml) water
2 teaspoons dried yeast
sugar, to taste
12 oz (350 g) buckwheat flour

½ teaspoon salt
1 egg, separated
whipped cream, to taste (optional)
butter or butter and oil for frying

Warm 4 fl oz (100 ml) milk or water slightly and add the yeast and sugar. Set the mixture aside for about 10–15 minutes, or until the yeast has dissolved and the mixture begins to foam and bubble slightly.

Make a well in half the flour, pour in the dissolved yeast mixture and ½ pint (300 ml) water and draw in the flour. Beat the mixture with a wooden spoon until smooth. Cover the bowl with a tea towel or place inside a polythene bag and leave to rise for 1–2 hours, or until doubled in size, in a warm place.

Add the salt, the egg yolk and the remaining flour, beating well. Cover the bowl with a tea towel and leave to rise again for another 1–2 hours. Just before cooking, fold in the stiffly beaten egg white and a spoonful of whipped cream, if using, for extra lightness and crumbliness. The mixture may be quite thick.

To cook the blini, use a small, heavy-based frying pan and heat it gently for a few minutes before you are ready to start. Use butter or butter and oil, and reckon, especially the first time, to throw away the first few pancakes until you get the heat and the amount of fat and batter quite right. A 4–5 inch (10–13 cm) pan will need about 2 tablespoons of the mixture, depending on its thickness, for each pancake. Cook for about 4 minutes on each side, turning with a spatula. Blini do not toss. Re-oil the pan after each one is cooked. If you have a set of blini pans (which are difficult to find in this country) they may also be slipped into a hot oven to cook, which is the traditional method.

LIGHT DISHES

Stuffed Pancakes

These tiny pasties, which are usually eaten with clear meat, chicken or mushroom broth or a *borshchok*, are made with a raised dough (see below). Cut out the dough in small circles in which you can enclose the filling in a semi-circle or canoe shape. Seal the edges carefully with a little milk. Either brush with egg and bake in a moderate to hot oven for about 10 minutes until golden brown, or fry them uncoated in deep fat.

SERVES PLENTY

For the raised dough:
2-3 teaspoons dried yeast
pinch of sugar
5 tablespoons warm water
1 lb (450 g) plain flour, sifted
2½ oz (65 g) butter, softened
pinch of salt
8 tablespoons milk
2 eggs, beaten

For the meat filling:
1 tablespoon oil or butter
1 onion, chopped
8 oz (225 g) minced beef, veal or chicken
chopped herbs, to taste
freshly grated nutmeg
salt
freshly ground black pepper
2 tablespoons beef glaze, finely chopped, see page 42
1 egg, to bind

To make the dough, dissolve the yeast and sugar in the warm water. Sprinkle in 1 teaspoon of the flour and set the mixture aside in a warm place for 15 minutes until frothy. Pour the yeast mixture into a bowl and mix in the flour, butter, salt, milk and eggs and knead to a smooth dough. Cover the bowl with a tea towel and leave to rise for about 1–2 hours, until doubled in size.

Meanwhile, make the filling. Heat the oil or butter in a pan and lightly fry the onion. Add the meat and cook for 5 minutes, until browned. Transfer the mixture to a bowl and season to taste with the herbs, nutmeg and salt and pepper. Allow to cool. When the mixture is absolutely cold, add the jellied glaze and egg. Use the filling straightaway; turn out the dough on to a lightly floured surface, knead again and use to make the pasties as described above.

A Typical Fondue – My Favourite

Great fun, fondues, because all you have to do is prepare the ingredients as the guests do all the work of actually cooking them. Everyone can then sit around the fire or out on the terrace, drinking and talking and prolonging the meal. Most people keep the basic ingredients somewhere in the kitchen, so fondues are perfect emergency dishes when long lost friends show up unexpectedly.
And, of course, you can have great fun collecting fondue sets – I've got three.

SERVES 4

1 clove of garlic
10½ oz (290 g) Emmenthal cheese
9 oz (250 g) Gruyère cheese
½ pint (300 ml) dry white wine
1 tablespoon lemon juice
3 teaspoons cornflour

1 fl oz (25 ml) Kirsch
2 tablespoons finely chopped herbs (parsley, chives and chervil, for example)
freshly ground black pepper
cubes of bread for dipping in the fondue

Cut the garlic clove and rub it around the fondue dish. Cut the cheese into small dice that will melt evenly and put into the dish with the wine, lemon juice and the cornflour mixed with the Kirsch. Bubble it up gently, whisking constantly, until the mixture is smooth and creamy. Stir in the herbs and season to taste with pepper.

Serve with cubes of bread to dip into the fondue.

British Fondue

SERVES 4

2 oz (50 g) butter
½ pint (300 ml) dry cider
1 fl oz (25 ml) Cognac
14 oz (400 g) Stilton cheese
10 oz (275 g) Brie, without skin

pinch of celery salt
pinch of freshly grated nutmeg
freshly ground black pepper
cubes of bread for dipping in the fondue

Melt the butter in a fondue dish, add the cider and Cognac and bring to the boil. Reduce the heat and whisk in the cheeses, cut into small dice, until it is all mixed smoothly together. Season with the celery salt, nutmeg and pepper.

Serve with cubes of bread for dipping in the fondue.

Cider Fondue

SERVES 4

1 clove of garlic
½ pint (300 ml) dry cider or unsweetened
  grape juice
1¼ lb (550 g) Gruyère cheese, grated
1 dessertspoon cornflour

3 dessertspoons lemon juice
1 dessertspoon ground sweet paprika
pinch or two of freshly grated nutmeg
cubes of bread for dipping in the fondue

Cut the garlic clove and rub it around the fondue dish to give the fondue a delicate hint of garlic. Pour in the cider or grape juice and bring to the boil. Add the cheese and cornflour mixed with the lemon juice. Reduce the heat and whisk the mixture from time to time until it's all deliciously gooey. Season with the paprika and nutmeg.

Serve with cubes of bread for dipping in the fondue.

Meat lovers can of course fry little chunks of beef or lamb or pork in hot oil — and serve with a variety of cold sauces — tartare — mustard — mayonnaise blue cheese etc etc etc.

MY FAVOURITE FISH AND SHELLFISH

The good thing about fish is the almost infinite variety of tastes and textures it provides, from slivers of raw tuna fish with Japanese green mustard to thick fillets of North Sea cod dipped in batter and fried in dripping. Also, pauper and millionaire alike can gather mussels from the sea-shore, or clamber over the rocks at low tide probing the nooks and crannies for crabs, or wade in a rock pool with a net to gather shrimps. Fish is exciting for the cook as you can steam, fry, stew, poach, bake, cure, salt and pickle away to your heart's content. You can be outrageously lavish with lobsters, scallops and caviar; or you can be economic and skilful with the friendly herring or the humble sprat. You can stretch your skills and knowledge to make soufflés or to cook *en papillote* or you can rest easy on your laurels with a simple fillet of fresh plaice lightly fried in butter.

I love fish and I've eaten everything from anchovies to parrot-fish to shark, but one of the best meals ever was in the unlikely setting of a desolate beach on the Bristol Channel one very cold and over-cast March afternoon. The tide was out and the fine black mud glinted away to the far horizon of Wales as if a giant had unrolled a sheet of aluminium foil from the smooth grey pebbles on the beach across the Channel and curved it up to meet the leaden sky. A bitter wind played with the flotsam left by the tide. Plastic oil cans, lemonade bottles and Coke tins danced across the pebbles as if kicked by a kid dawdling home from school. Several hundred yards from the shore at the extreme edge of the water stood a row of black posts stark against the silver mud. Hung between the posts were ragged nets, like a derelict tennis court.

Brendon Sellick is a fisherman. He has no boat or rod. Just a sledge. Each day at low tide he walks across the mud to the nets pushing his wooden sledge, loaded with a basket and two razor sharp knives. Like an Eskimo he half lies on the sledge and, kicking out his feet, glides across the mud at a rate that would have amazed Captain Scott. Except today he was taking me. At every step I got stuck in the mud, which sucked and pulled at my waders. He'd told me to wear short rubber boots with waterproof leggings over them bound tight with rows of elastic bands. Advice I had chosen to ignore. And now we were making very slow progress indeed. Finally, we arrived at the nets. It was easier walking here and we set about untangling the fish trapped in the nets. Brendon said we must work swiftly because, when the tide turned, it came in with such rapidity you couldn't outrun it across the mud.

We collected fourteen codling and two skate. An average day for him, he said, was about sixty pounds weight of fish in all. And very fresh. We struggled back to the beach and lit a fire of driftwood in a circle of stones and while I cooked two cod fillets in butter over the fire Brendon told me that even if he won the pools, he'd still cross the mud each tide for the fish. As his family had for four genera-tions and he has done for the last forty years. The fish was sweet and we drank cider and ate doorsteps of crusty bread thick with butter. He was responsible only to the tide, he said. He was free and, who knows, tomorrow there may be a salmon in the net. And whatever the weather it was worth getting up and hacking across the mud to find out. As the man said: 'Give a man a fish and he will live for a day: teach him to fish and he will live for ever.'

Anyway, that's enough of that; it's time to toddle off to the fishmon-ger and get cooking. Or, as the other man said, 'Get out of that bed and rattle those pots and pans'.

"Fish is my favourite dish" — Fats Waller.

Fillet of Tweed Salmon with Watercress Sauce

Clive Imber at Michael's Brasserie, Newcastle upon Tyne

S E R V E S 4

4 bunches of watercress
1 oz (25 g) butter
2 oz (50 g) shallots, chopped
4 boneless fresh salmon fillets, weighing
about 7 oz (200 g) each

salt
freshly ground black pepper
8 fl oz (250 ml) dry white wine
8 fl oz (250 ml) fish stock, see page 44
4 fl oz (100 ml) double cream

Wash and pick over the watercress. Discard the stalks. Put the watercress in a pan of boiling water and blanch for 1 minute. Drain, refresh under cold running water and drain again. Purée in a food processor or blender until smooth. Set aside.

Lightly butter a roasting tin and cover the base with the shallots. Place the salmon on top and season with salt and pepper to taste. Pour in the wine and fish stock. Cover with foil or a butter wrapper and cook in a preheated oven, 325°F/160°C (gas mark 3), for about 8–10 minutes, depending on the thickness of the fish – do not overcook. Lift out the salmon, cover with the foil or wrapper and keep warm.

Pour the juices and stock into a clean pan and boil briskly until reduced to ¼ pint (150 ml). Add the cream, bring to a simmer, and cook until the sauce has a thin coating consistency. Just before serving, add the watercress purée (if you add it too early it will discolour and lose its lovely green appearance). Check and adjust the seasoning if necessary.

To serve, arrange the salmon on warmed plates and pour over the sauce.

Gravlax

SERVES 4-6

2-3 lb (900 g-1.4 kg) piece middle-cut fresh
    salmon, boned and cut into two pieces
    lengthways
large handful of dill
4 tablespoons coarse sea salt
2 tablespoons caster sugar
2 tablespoons crushed black peppercorns

For the mustard sauce:
2 tablespoons made German mustard
1 egg yolk
1 tablespoon caster sugar
2 tablespoons white wine vinegar
7 tablespoons sunflower oil
1 tablespoon chopped dill
salt
freshly ground black pepper
lemon wedges, to garnish

Place one of the salmon fillets, skin-side down, in a large dish (not aluminium). Sprinkle over the dill, salt, sugar and black peppercorns. Place the second fish fillet, skin-side up, on top. Cover with a wooden chopping board (wrapped in foil if liked) and weight heavily to press the salmon fillets firmly together. Place in the refrigerator and chill for at least 72 hours. Turn the fish over every 12 hours and, as you do so, spoon the juices that have oozed from the fish over the whole – rather like basting a turkey.

To make the mustard sauce, mix the mustard with the egg yolk, sugar and vinegar. Slowly add the oil, whisking all the time until well mixed. Add the dill and season with salt and pepper to taste.

To serve, carve the gravlax into slices, discarding the skin. Accompany with a little of the mustard sauce and garnish with some lemon wedges.

Parcels of Smoked Salmon with Yoghurt Cream Sauce

Allan Holland at Mallory Court, Bishops Tachbrook

Make this in small quantities as a starter and larger for a lunch or supper
main dish.

SERVES 4

8 slices of smoked salmon
sprigs of dill and chopped tomato flesh, to
    garnish

For the mousse:
3 oz (75 g) smoked salmon trimmings
1 oz (25 g) smoked trout fillet
¼ pint (150 ml) double cream

For the sauce:
¼ pint (150 ml) double cream
¼ pint (150 ml) low-fat natural yoghurt
juice of 1 lemon
sugar, to taste (optional)
salt
freshly ground black pepper

To make the mousse, purée the salmon trimmings and smoked trout in a food processor or blender, then rub through a very fine sieve. Place the purée in a bowl and set over crushed ice. Using a wooden spoon, gradually beat in the cream until the mixture has the consistency of a light mousse.

To make the sauce, carefully mix together the cream, yoghurt and lemon juice. Add a little

sugar if you want some extra sweetness and season to taste with salt and pepper.

Place a spoonful of mousse in the centre of each slice of smoked salmon and fold over to form a neat parcel. Pour some of the sauce on to four individual plates and arrange two parcels on each. Garnish with the dill and a little chopped tomato.

En papillote is a high-powered name for the simple business of baking the freshest of fish and the subtlest of fresh herbs, wrapped in a parcel of foil or greaseproof paper, to seal in the flavours.

Salmon with Vermouth en Papillote

SERVES 4

4 medium salmon fillets, skinned
1½ oz (40 g) butter, softened
grated rind and juice of 1 lemon
handful of herb sprigs (lemon balm, chervil and parsley, for example)

4 tablespoons dry Vermouth
salt
freshly ground black pepper

Cut four hearts out of foil or greaseproof paper large enough to enclose the fish fillets with space to spare around the edges.

Place each salmon fillet on one half of the foil or paper heart and dot with the softened butter. Sprinkle with the lemon rind and juice and scatter over a good quantity of herb sprigs. Drizzle over the Vermouth and season with salt and pepper to taste. Fold over the remaining

half to enclose – so that you end up with a semi-oval shape. Pleat the edges to seal securely.

Place on a baking sheet and cook in a preheated oven, 350°F/180°C (gas mark 4), for 12–15 minutes, or until the packets are well puffed up and the fish is just tender. Serve immediately.

Sole with Mushrooms and Caper Butter en Papillote

SERVES 4

1 small shallot, finely chopped
2 oz (50 g) butter
4 teaspoons chopped capers
salt

freshly ground black pepper
4–8 sole fillets (depending on size), skinned
2 oz (50 g) mushrooms, sliced

Mix the shallot with the butter, capers and salt and pepper to taste. If using eight small sole fillets then sandwich the pairs together with half of the caper butter.

Cut four hearts out of foil or greaseproof paper large enough to enclose the fish fillets with space to spare around the edges.

Place the sole fillets on one half of the foil or paper hearts. Dot with all (in the case of large fillets) or the remaining half of the caper butter. Scatter over the mushrooms and fold over the remaining half to enclose. Pleat the edges to seal securely.

Place on a baking sheet and cook in a preheated oven, 350°F/180°C (gas mark 4), for 15–20 minutes. Serve immediately.

Mediterranean Sea Bass with Pine Kernels en Papillote

SERVES 4

4 oz (100 g) pine kernels, toasted
2 oz (50 g) can anchovy fillets in oil, drained
2 tablespoons chopped parsley
1 tablespoon chopped basil leaves
grated rind and juice of ½ lemon

1½–2 lb (675–900 g) filleted sea bass,
  skinned and diced
2 tablespoons fruity olive oil
salt
freshly ground black pepper

Pound half of the pine kernels with half of the anchovy fillets to a smooth paste. Add the parsley, basil, lemon rind and lemon juice and pound again until well mixed.

Cut four hearts out of foil or greaseproof paper large enough to enclose a quarter of the diced fish pieces with space to spare around the edges.

Toss the fish pieces in the herb and anchovy mixture, then divide evenly and place each portion on one half of the foil or paper hearts. Top with the remaining pine kernels and anchovy fillets, coarsely chopped. Drizzle with the olive oil and season with salt and pepper to taste. Fold over the remaining half to enclose. Pleat the edges to seal securely.

Place on a baking sheet and cook in a preheated oven, 350°F/180°C (gas mark 4), for 15–20 minutes, or until the packets are puffed up and the fish is tender. Serve immediately.

Trout with Dill en Papillote

SERVES 4

1½ oz (40 g) butter
2 tablespoons chopped dill
salt

freshly ground black pepper
4 trout, filleted
4 oz (100 g) smoked salmon or trout

Cut four hearts out of foil or greaseproof paper large enough to enclose the fish fillets with space to spare around the edges.

Mix the butter with the dill and salt and pepper to taste. Sandwich the trout fillets together into four pairs with the dill butter. Cut the smoked salmon or trout into thin strips and loosely wrap, diagonally, around the fish fillets to give a striped effect.

Place each fillet on one half of the foil or paper heart and fold over the remaining half to enclose. Pleat the edges to seal securely.

Place on a baking sheet and cook in a preheated oven, 350°F/180°C (gas mark 4), for 20 minutes, or until the packets are well puffed up and the fish is just tender. Serve immediately.

Crayfish or Prawns with Pernod and Mushrooms en Papillote

8 tablespoons chopped wild or button
  mushrooms
3 tablespoons double cream
2-3 teaspoons Pernod
salt

freshly ground black pepper
16-20 crayfish or king prawns (depending on
  size), shelled
2 tablespoons chopped parsley

Mix the mushrooms with the cream, Pernod and salt and pepper to taste.

Cut four hearts out of foil or greaseproof paper large enough to enclose four to five large shelled crayfish or prawns with space to spare around the edges.

Divide and place the crayfish or prawns on one half of the foil or paper hearts. Top with an equal quantity of the mushroom mixture and sprinkle with the parsley. Fold over the remaining half to enclose. Pleat the edges to seal securely.

Place on a baking sheet and cook in a preheated oven, 350°F/180°C (gas mark 4), for 15-20 minutes. Serve immediately.

Red Mullet en Papillote

4 medium red mullet, cleaned and scaled
2 shallots, finely chopped
4 tablespoons chopped coriander
juice of 1 lemon

2 tablespoons fruity olive oil
salt
freshly ground black pepper

Cut four hearts out of foil or greaseproof paper large enough to enclose the fish with space to spare around the edges.

Stuff the fish cavities with half of the shallots and coriander. Slash the fish skin in a lattice design. Place each fish on one half of the foil or paper heart. Sprinkle with the remaining shallots, coriander, lemon juice, oil and salt and pepper to taste. Fold over the remaining half to enclose. Pleat the edges to seal securely.

Place on a baking sheet and cook in a preheated oven, 350°F/180°C (gas mark 4), for 20 minutes, or until the packets are well puffed up and the fish is just tender. Serve immediately.

Variation

French-style Mullet en Papillote: Prepare the fish as above but do not stuff or top with the onion and coriander. Top with a slice of smoked pork and bacon, drizzle if necessary with a little oil and season with salt and pepper. Cook as above.

Well I think that's the fish in paper section wrapped up! Excuse the pun. PLEASE. xxxx

FISH AND SHELLFISH

109

Monkfish Roasted with Garlic

SERVES 4

about 2¼ lb (1 kg) tail of monkfish
2 heads of plump garlic, as fresh as possible
2 tablespoons olive oil
salt
freshly ground black pepper
¼ teaspoon thyme leaves

¼ teaspoon fennel seeds
juice of 1 lemon
1 bay leaf
1 large red pepper, blanched, cored and
   seeded, and cut into strips
8 fl oz (250 ml) double cream

Skin the fish carefully, leaving no trace of the thin membrane under the skin, and remove the central bone. Wash and pat dry. Tie up with string like a piece of meat.

Peel two cloves of the garlic and cut into thin slices. Make some incisions in the fish with the point of a sharp knife and push in the sliced garlic.

Heat 1 tablespoon of the oil in a frying pan and brown the fish on all sides for about 5 minutes. Lift out the fish, season with salt, pepper, thyme, fennel and lemon juice and put into a roasting tin along with the remaining oil.

Arrange the rest of the unpeeled garlic head, separated into cloves, around the dish, put the bay leaf under the fish and cook in a preheated oven, 425°F/220°C (gas mark 7), for about 20 minutes. Five minutes before the end of the cooking time, pop the pepper strips into the roasting tin and stir the cream into the juices.

Arrange the fish, garlic and pepper on a serving dish and strain over the creamy sauce, removing the bay leaf. Carve the fish in thin slices.

Serve with grilled tomatoes and chive butter. The roast garlic is, of course, to be eaten.

Tuna with Mustard Sauce

Fresh tuna, like shark or swordfish, has a meat-like texture, is very filling and tastes best (I think) grilled over a wood fire. However, you can still make this recipe using a normal grill. In Spain and France you see a huge whole tuna – the size of a small bomb – laid out on a trestle table in the fish markets.

SERVES 4

2 cloves of garlic, crushed
4 slices of fresh tuna
1 tablespoon olive oil
salt

4 fl oz (100 ml) double cream
2 oz (50 g) butter, diced
2 tablespoons strong made mustard
freshly ground black pepper

Rub the garlic into the fish slices and brush them with oil on both sides. Place in a grill pan and cook under a preheated low to moderate grill for about 15 minutes, turning every 5 minutes. Sprinkle the fish with salt every so often.

While the tuna is cooking, heat the cream in a small pan and whisk in the butter, piece by piece, to thicken the cream. Add the mustard and salt and pepper to taste and continue to cook, whisking, over a low heat for a further 2–3 minutes. Strain the sauce through a fine sieve over the fish to serve.

Smoked Trout and Cucumber Soufflé

There is no mystery to soufflés – they are delightful things, just don't make them when everyone piles in after a day at the races. Save them for a quiet time when you can potter about in a relaxed way in the kitchen.

SERVES 4-6

2 oz (50 g) butter
2 oz (50 g) flour
1 pint (600 ml) milk
finely grated rind of 1 lemon
salt

freshly ground black pepper
3 eggs, separated
½ cucumber, very finely chopped
1 lb (450 g) smoked trout fillets, flaked
2 tablespoons chopped chives

Grease a 2½ pint (1.4 litre) soufflé dish and prepare by making a paper collar of double thickness greaseproof paper, which should stand about 1 inch (2.5 cm) above the rim.

Melt the butter in a heavy-based pan. Add the flour and cook for 1 minute. Gradually add the milk, mixing well. Bring to the boil, stirring constantly, and cook until smooth and thickened. Add the lemon rind and salt and pepper to taste.

Beat the egg yolks lightly and add a little of the hot sauce. Return the mixture to the remaining sauce with the cucumber, smoked trout and half of the chives and allow to cool for a few minutes until warm.

Whisk the egg whites until they hold stiff peaks. Fold into the soufflé mixture with a metal spoon. Pour into the prepared soufflé dish and sprinkle with the remaining chives.

Bake in a preheated oven, 400°F/200°C (gas mark 6), for about 40–45 minutes, or until well risen, golden and firm to the touch (but still creamy inside). Remove the paper collar and serve immediately.

Lobster Soufflé

SERVES 2-3

3 tablespoons grated Parmesan cheese
1 oz (25 g) butter
1 oz (25 g) flour
½ pint (300 ml) milk
1 teaspoon tomato purée
1 teaspoon dry mustard powder
dash of Tabasco sauce

salt
freshly ground black pepper
3 egg yolks
8 oz (225 g) cooked lobster, flaked or chopped
4 egg whites

Grease an 8 inch (20 cm) soufflé dish and sprinkle with 1 tablespoon of the Parmesan cheese to coat. Prepare by making a paper collar of double thickness greaseproof paper, which should stand about 1 inch (2.5 cm) above the rim.

Melt the butter in a heavy-based pan. Add the flour and cook for 1 minute. Gradually add the milk, mixing well. Bring to the boil, stirring constantly, and cook until smooth and thickened. Add the tomato purée, mustard powder, Tabasco sauce and salt and pepper to taste.

Beat the egg yolks lightly and add a little of the hot sauce. Return the mixture to the remaining sauce with the lobster and allow to cool for a few minutes.

Whisk the egg whites until they hold stiff peaks. Fold into the soufflé mixture with a metal spoon. Pour into the prepared soufflé dish and sprinkle with the remaining Parmesan cheese.

Bake in a preheated oven, 350°F/180°C (gas mark 4), for about 35 minutes, or until well risen and firm to the touch (but still creamy inside). Remove the paper collar and serve immediately.

Oriental Fish in Filo Pastry

This is much the same principle as the papillote, except you can eat the wrapping.

SERVES 4

4 sheets frozen filo pastry, thawed
sesame oil
4 cod or halibut steaks, boned and skinned
1 small piece fresh root ginger, finely chopped
2 oz (50 g) peeled prawns
2 tablespoons yellow bean or soy sauce

pinch of Chinese five spice powder
2 spring onions, trimmed and thinly sliced
salt
freshly ground black pepper
sesame seeds, to sprinkle

Brush one-half of each piece of filo pastry with a little sesame oil and fold over to enclose. Place a cod or halibut steak on top of each folded piece of pastry. Mix the ginger with the prawns, yellow bean or soy sauce, Chinese five spice powder, spring onions and salt and pepper to taste. Spoon equally over the fish steaks.

Carefully enclose the fish by gripping each piece of pastry by the corners, tucking in the sides and giving the parcel a half-turn twist to secure. The corners can then be folded back to produce a decorative effect. Brush with sesame oil and sprinkle with sesame seeds.

Place on an oiled baking sheet and bake in a preheated oven, 350°F/180°C (gas mark 4), for 20 minutes, or until crisp, golden and the fish is cooked. Serve immediately.

Variations

Salmon and watercress in filo pastry: prepare as above but use 4 salmon steaks and a topping of 4 tablespoons soured cream mixed with 1 bunch of finely chopped watercress, the grated rind of ½ lemon and salt and pepper to taste. Use sunflower oil or melted butter to brush the pastry and do not sprinkle with sesame seeds.

Prawns and scallops in filo pastry: mix 4 oz (100 g) queen scallops, 6 oz (175 g) shelled prawns, 2 oz (50 g) cooked button mushrooms, 2 tablespoons chopped watercress with ¼ pint (150 ml) coating sauce. Add seasoning to taste and divide between the pastry sheets as

above. Use sunflower oil or melted butter to brush the pastry and do not sprinkle with sesame seeds.

Coral island monkfish in filo pastry: flavour 7 fl oz (200 ml) wine-based coating sauce with 1 teaspoon tomato purée, 1 oz (25 g) chopped creamed coconut, 1 tablespoon chopped parsley and salt and pepper to taste. Fold in 1 lb (450 g) diced monkfish with a little chopped smoked bacon (optional). Divide between the pastry sheets as above. Use a fruity olive oil or melted butter to brush the pastry and do not sprinkle with sesame seeds.

Stir-fried Fish with Spring Onions and Ginger

SERVES 2

1 fish (mullet or bream, for example),
* weighing 1½ lb (675 g)*
1 teaspoon salt
2 tablespoons flour
3 tablespoons vegetable oil
3-4 spring onions, trimmed and cut into 1
* inch (2.5 cm) lengths*
2-3 slices of fresh root ginger, shredded
coriander leaves, to garnish

For the sauce:
2 tablespoons soy sauce
2 tablespoons medium or dry sherry
¼ pint (150 ml) chicken stock, see page 43, or
* water*
freshly ground black pepper

Scale, clean and gut the fish thoroughly. Remove the fins but keep on the head and tail. With a sharp knife slash both sides of the fish diagonally at ¼ inch (7 mm) intervals as far as the bone. Rub the fish inside and out with the salt, then coat with flour from head to tail.

Heat the oil in a large wok or frying pan until very hot. Reduce the heat a little and fry the fish for about 2 minutes on each side, or until golden and crisp, turning the fish carefully.

Using a slotted spoon, lift out from the pan.

Mix together all the ingredients for the sauce. Increase the heat and add the spring onions and ginger to the oil in the pan. Stir-fry for a few seconds, then stir in the sauce mixture and return the fish to the pan.

Simmer for a few minutes, then carefully transfer the fish to a warmed serving dish and pour over the sauce. Garnish with the coriander leaves.

A wok by keilh Floyd

Don't forget to buy a wok stand

Cod Fillets with a Saffron Butter Sauce

Clive Imber at Michael's Brasserie, Newcastle upon Tyne

A Dickensian observer once said: 'The cod is surely better than the
salmon. It's just a question of fashion.' Or words to that effect. Quite right.

SERVES 4

4 large cod fillets, weighing about 8–10 oz
   (225–275 g) each
salt
freshly ground black pepper
¼ pint (150 ml) fish stock, see page 44
¼ pint (150 ml) dry white wine

2 tablespoons double cream
2 good pinches of powdered saffron
8 oz (225 g) unsalted butter, chilled and
   diced
4 tomatoes, skinned, seeded and diced
1 oz (25 g) chopped chives

Place the cod fillets on a lightly buttered baking tray. Season the fillets with salt and pepper. Cook lightly under a preheated grill for about 6–10 minutes, until they are just cooked – the time depends entirely on the thickness of the fillets. Remove and keep warm.

Put the stock and wine into a pan and boil rapidly over a high heat until they are reduced by three-quarters. Add the cream and saffron.

Bring back to the boil and simmer for 2–3 minutes. Reduce the heat to very low and gradually add the butter, piece by piece, whisking constantly until it is well mixed. Do not allow the sauce to boil. Add the tomatoes and chives and check the seasoning.

To serve, place the cod on warmed plates and spoon over the sauce.

Creamed Salt Cod

You will find this super dish on menus throughout Provence – you can
buy it ready prepared from traiteurs. Many families have it as a celebration supper on Christmas Eve before they go to midnight mass.

SERVES 6

2 lb (900 g) plump salt cod
1¾ pints (1 litre) extra virgin olive oil
¼ pint (150 ml) double cream

juice of 1 lemon
3 cloves of garlic, crushed
1 tablespoon chopped parsley

Soak the salt cod in cold water overnight, drain and rinse well to get rid of the salt. Put the fish

in a pan, cover with cold water and poach gently for about 30 minutes, until cooked. Lift out the fish and carefully remove all the skin and every bit of bone. Put the fish through a mincer and mince it very finely – a food processor or blender is too fierce to use.

Put the minced cod in a pan over a low heat. In another pan, slightly warm the olive oil. Slowly add, alternately, a dash of the oil and a dash of the cream to the cod, stirring constantly with a wooden spoon – three hands would help. Keep stirring like mad until the mixture thickens and looks like creamy mashed potato. Be careful not to overheat the mixture or it will separate.

Add the lemon juice, garlic and parsley, still stirring constantly, then tip into a warmed serving dish and serve immediately.

Baked Curried Fish

SERVES 4

2 lb (900 g) firm white fish fillets, skinned and boned, such as haddock, cod or monkfish
2 tablespoons vegetable oil
3 large onions, sliced
2 chilli peppers or 1 teaspoon cayenne pepper

3 cloves of garlic
4 tomatoes or 6 oz (175 g) tomato purée
4 fl oz (100 ml) white wine vinegar
½ teaspoon ground cardamom
½ teaspoon ground cumin
½ teaspoon salt

Wash the fish and pat dry. Lay the fillets in an ovenproof baking dish. Heat the oil and fry the onion slices until transparent. Arrange over the fish.

Process the remaining ingredients in a food processor or blender until smooth, or crush the chillies and garlic in a pestle and mortar and mash the tomatoes with a fork before mixing with the other ingredients. Pour the mixture over the fish, cover and bake in a preheated oven, 350°F/180°C (gas mark 4), for about 30 minutes, until the fish is just cooked.

"Out of Africa Ho!ho!"

Grilled Sea Bass or Bream

Bass is absolutely my favourite fish – also, sadly, one of the most expensive. But a large, fresh one grilled, preferably over a charcoal grill, so that the skin is crisp and the flesh moist, is an experience not to be missed. It's a bit tricky getting fennel stalks in Britain but you'll sometimes find them growing in hedgerows so you should collect a few (without ripping the countryside to pieces, of course) in readiness for the feast.

SERVES 6

*3 lb (1.4 kg) sea bass or bream, cleaned and
  scaled
1 teaspoon coarse sea salt
freshly ground black pepper
olive oil*

*bundle of dried fennel stalks, equivalent in
  size to the fish
2 wineglasses of Armagnac or* eau de vie
3 lemons, halved

With a sharp knife, make diagonal slashes along both sides of the fish and rub the salt into the cuts and skin. Grind lots of pepper over the fish, inside and out, and brush the skin with oil.

Place the fish under a preheated hot grill, turning occasionally, for about 20 minutes, until the flesh is tender, depending on the size of the fish.

Meanwhile, place a rack over a flameproof tray and pile the fennel stalks underneath it. When the fish is cooked, transfer it to the rack, pour the alcohol over the fish and fennel stalks and flame. Leave to burn until the stalks have burnt away – this gives the fish the most wonderful flavour and is pretty spectacular stuff!

Serve hot with lemon halves.

me in my bass boat
at Dartmouth

Sweet and Sour Fish Kebabs

SERVES 4

2 lb (900 g) sea bass fillets, cut into slices
1½ inches (4 cm) square
8 very small tomatoes, quartered
16 small onions, halved

For the marinade:
juice of 2 lemons
1 clove of garlic, crushed
2 pinches of salt

For the basting liquid:
4 tablespoons oil
2 tablespoons dry sherry

½ teaspoon sugar
salt
freshly ground black pepper

For the sauce:
¼ pint (150 ml) natural yoghurt
4 fl oz (100 ml) double cream
juice of ½ lemon
1 tablespoon roughly chopped parsley
1 teaspoon chopped chives
salt

Mix together the ingredients for the marinade in a shallow bowl (not aluminium), put in the fish and leave to marinate for about 15 minutes or so.

Blend the ingredients for the basting liquid. Thread the fish, tomatoes and onions on to eight skewers and brush with the liquid. Cook the kebabs under a preheated moderate grill for 10 minutes, turning them and basting them regularly.

Meanwhile, mix together the ingredients for the sauce in a bowl and hand it round separately.

Serve with plain rice.

Sweet Marinated Herring

SERVES 4

4–6 salted herring fillets
milk and water, for soaking
8 oz (225 g) sugar
¼ pint (150 ml) red wine
6 tablespoons cider vinegar

6–8 white peppercorns
1 teaspoon pickling spice including a chilli
pepper
2–3 onions, sliced
few bay leaves

Soak the fillets in the milk and water. Put the sugar, wine, vinegar, peppercorns and spices in a pan and simmer for 3 minutes. Allow to cool. When the saltiness of the herrings is reduced to a palatable level, drain and arrange them in a plastic box or glass jar, interleaved with slices of onion and bay leaves. Pour over the marinade and leave for at least 5 days in the refrigerator. Discard the bay leaves.

To serve, cut into smallish pieces.

Herring Pie

This is an old recipe that will adapt well to fresh herrings or salted pilchards.

SERVES 4

1¼ lb (550 g) salted herring fillets
milk, for soaking
oil
2 onions, chopped
2½ oz (65 g) fresh white breadcrumbs soaked
  in milk and excess moisture squeezed out
1-2 eating apples, grated

freshly ground black pepper
7 fl oz (200 ml) milk
7 fl oz (200 ml) double cream
2 tablespoons butter, melted
butter
1 tablespoon toasted breadcrumbs
freshly grated nutmeg

Soak the fillets in milk to remove most of the salt. Drain, then skin and bone them. Lightly fry the onions in some oil and put them twice through a mincer together with the herring and the soaked breadcrumbs. Add the apples and mix well. Season with pepper and add the milk, cream and melted butter.

Place the mixture in a greased ovenproof dish, dot with butter and sprinkle with the toasted crumbs and a little nutmeg. Bake in a preheated oven, 350°F/180°C (gas mark 4), for 20 minutes, or until bubbling and brown.

Fish Pie with Lemon Sauce

SERVES 4

½ quantity of flaky pastry, see page 189
12 oz (350 g) sole fillets
6 large scallops, washed and cut into rounds
  ¼ inch (7 mm) thick
salt
freshly ground black pepper
beaten egg or milk, to glaze

For the stuffing:
2 oz (50 g) watercress, trimmed
1 egg
1 egg yolk
4 oz (100 g) white fish fillets
salt
freshly ground black pepper

For the sauce:
3 eggs
juice of 2 lemons
salt

Roll two-thirds of the pastry out on a lightly floured surface and use to line a 9 inch (23 cm) shallow tart dish. Reserve the rest for the lid.

Put all the ingredients for the stuffing in a food processor or blender and purée until smooth.

Season the sole and the scallops, which must be thoroughly dry, with salt and pepper and line the pastry case with half the fish. Then spread over the stuffing and cover with the remaining fish. Roll out the rest of the pastry and use to cover the tart. Brush with a little beaten egg or milk. Bake in a preheated oven, 400°F/200°C (gas mark 6), for 20–30 minutes.

Before serving, whisk the eggs and lemon juice in the top of a double boiler until you have a frothy sauce. Add a little salt to taste. Cut the tart like a cake, mask with the lemon sauce and serve a separate dish of mangetout peas or green beans.

Fish Fillets in Tomato Sauce

This recipe works well with John Dory, brill or turbot or, indeed, with any firm, white fleshed fish. I think the more delicate flat fish such as dabs, plaice and lemon sole are best grilled or fried in butter and served plain and on the bone.

SERVES 4

4 John Dory, brill or turbot fillets, weighing
    about 7 oz (200 g) each
juice of 1 lemon
1½ oz (40 g) butter
2 large onions, finely chopped
1 lb (450 g) tomatoes, skinned, seeded and
    chopped

salt
freshly ground black pepper
oil, for deep-frying
3 tablespoons flour
4 fl oz (100 ml) dry sherry
¼ pint (150 ml) double cream
finely chopped parsley, to garnish

Wash the fillets and pat dry. Pour over the lemon juice and leave to marinate for 30 minutes. Melt the butter in a pan and sauté the onions until golden. Throw in the tomatoes and season to taste with salt and pepper. Cook over a gentle heat for 15 minutes.

Heat the oil over a medium heat to 375°F/190°C. Dredge the fillets in the flour and deep-fry them for 2–3 minutes until golden. Drain on absorbent kitchen paper and set aside.

Add the sherry and cream to the tomato mixture and cook gently for a further 3 minutes. Return the fillets to the pan and cook slowly for another 2 minutes.

To serve, lift out the fillets on to a warmed serving dish, quickly purée the sauce in a food processor or blender and strain over the fish fillets. Garnish with the parsley.

Fish with Rice

SERVES 4-6

2-3 lb (900 g-1.4 kg) fish, filleted (cod,
  plaice, flounder or other white fish fillets)
4 oz (100 g) long-grain rice per person,
  cooked

For the fish paste:
1 small bunch of spring onions, trimmed and
  roughly chopped
3 onions, diced
2 fl oz (50 ml) oil
several sprigs of parsley
½ teaspoon salt
½ teaspoon freshly ground black pepper
2 red chilli peppers or 1 teaspoon cayenne
  pepper
2 tomatoes, quartered

For the vegetable stew:
4 fl oz (100 ml) white wine vinegar
8 fl oz (250 ml) water
2 large carrots, chopped
2 turnips, chopped
½ small cauliflower, chopped
2 medium tomatoes, chopped
1 teaspoon salt
1 teaspoon freshly ground black pepper
1 red chilli pepper, crushed or ½ teaspoon
  cayenne pepper
pinch of chopped thyme
2 bay leaves

Bake or boil the fish, then flake it into small pieces, removing the bones.

Using a food processor, blender or pestle and mortar, reduce the onions, oil, parsley, salt and peppers to a fine paste. Add the fish and tomatoes and grind again. Divide and shape the paste into tiny balls about the size of large pearls. Set aside.

To make the stew, mix together the vinegar and water in a heavy-based pan. Add the vegetables along with the salt, peppers and herbs. Bring to the boil, then reduce the heat and simmer for 30 minutes. Add the fish balls for the last 5 minutes to cook through.

To serve, arrange the hot rice on a platter that has raised edges. Pour on the stew and scatter the fish paste pearls evenly across the top. Remove the bay leaves before serving.

A colourful and spicy dish from sun baked Africa well worth the trouble for a genuinely original taste.

The Classic Bouillabaisse

SERVES 6-8

1 fl oz (25 ml) olive oil
2 large onions, finely chopped
white part of 1 leek, finely chopped
4 cloves of garlic, crushed
5 ripe tomatoes, chopped
1 sprig of thyme
1 sprig of fennel
1 tablespoon grated orange zest
4 pints (2.25 litres) water or fish stock, see
  page 44
5 lb (2.3 kg) mixed fish (choosing at least 4-6

different types of fish from John Dory,
gurnard, wrasse, dogfish, small, soft-shelled
crabs, saithe, weever fish, racasse, monkfish,
red mullet, for example), scaled, cleaned
and gutted
salt
freshly ground black pepper
2 sachets of saffron threads
½ pint (300 ml) rouille, see page 35
½ pint (300 ml) aïoli, see page 34

Heat the oil in a large pan and fry the onions, leek, garlic and tomatoes until golden. Throw in the thyme, fennel and orange zest, mix in thoroughly and cook for a further 5 minutes.

Bring the water or stock to the boil and pour it, boiling, into the pan. Increase the heat to high and beat vigorously for a minute or two, until the sauce thickens. (It has to boil hard to amalgamate the oil and water.) Perhaps add another dash of olive oil at this stage and keep boiling for a few minutes until the sauce is of the right consistency.

Reduce the heat and add the fish. Season to taste with salt and pepper, add the saffron and simmer for about 10-15 minutes, until cooked.

Lift each fish out carefully from the sauce as soon as it is cooked and remove the skin and bones. Arrange in a serving dish and pour over a cupful or two of strained sauce. Strain the remaining sauce into a tureen and serve as a soup with the rouille and aïoli floating on top. Eat the fish with plain boiled potatoes and more aïoli.

Garlic Fish Stew (Bourride)

The poached shellfish stew known as a bourride is thought to have been invented by the Phoenicians hundreds and hundreds of years ago. It's much older than the more common bouillabaisse and, to my mind, the better dish.

It's really quite easy to prepare, but fresh, fresh fish is essential. You can use either lobsters or crayfish and thick fillets of turbot or bass or even hake or haddock.

The best way to enjoy the dish is to take half the sauce, which should be yellow and have the consistency of a thin custard, and serve it as a soup with freshly toasted croûtons of bread lightly spread with some chilli paste and with a dollop of garlic mayonnaise (aïoli) floating in it. Then you eat the fish with the remainder of the sauce, more aïoli and some plain boiled potatoes. A strong white wine like a Sancerre should be drunk to cut through the richness of the sauce and the garlic. This is truly a feast and you shouldn't have much planned for the rest of the afternoon, because you'll feel quite bloated. But very happy.

SERVES 4

2 pints (1.2 litres) fish stock, see page 44
2 live lobsters or crayfish
4 thick, white fish fillets (see above), weighing about 8 oz (225 g) each

7 fl oz (200 ml) double cream
½ pint (300 ml) aïoli, see page 34
toasted croûtons spread with chilli paste

Put the fish stock in a large pan and drop in the lobsters or crayfish. Cover the pan tightly and slowly bring to the boil, then reduce the heat and simmer for 20 minutes.

Remove the lobsters or crayfish and keep warm while you poach the fish fillets in the same stock for about 15 minutes, depending on their thickness. Halve the lobsters or crayfish and arrange on a large serving dish with the fish fillets. Keep warm.

Boil the remaining stock briskly until it is reduced by about two-thirds. Reduce the heat to low, stir in the cream and carefully whisk in half the aïoli, stirring with a wooden spoon, until the sauce looks like a thin custard. The sauce must not boil or it will go grainy.

Pour half the sauce over the fish and serve the rest as soup as described above with the remaining aïoli and some croûtons spread with chilli paste.

Fried Eel

Central TV once invited me to cook something on an angling programme.
As I was very busy, it was agreed that they would choose the recipe and
I'd just whizz in and cook the prepared ingredients. I arrived at the studio
to find the kitchen set brilliantly ready. Only one thing was missing –
the fish.
'Where's the fish?' I said.
'In a bucket over there,' they said lightly.
To my horror, the bucket contained half-a-dozen wriggling and
very live eels.
'We thought you'd like something really fresh,' they said.
Ugh. But somehow I despatched the wretched things and, of course,
cooked them superbly well. They tasted good, too. But if I were you I'd
get someone else to do the first bit for you.

SERVES 6

3 lb (1.4 kg) eels – buy your eels alive and
    ask the fishmonger to kill, bleed, clean,
    skin, gut and cut into lengths for you on
    the spot
1 fl oz (25 ml) water
2 fl oz (50 ml) white wine vinegar
2 bay leaves
1 medium onion, diced
juice of 1 lemon

salt
freshly ground black pepper
2 oz (50 g) flour
½ oz (15 g) ground paprika
5 oz (150 g) olive oil
1 bunch of parsley heads
milk
flour, for dredging
lemon wedges, to garnish

Wipe the pieces of eel. Mix together the water, vinegar, bay leaves, onion, lemon juice, salt and pepper in a bowl (not aluminium) and place the eels in it. Leave to marinate for 2 hours. Lift out the eels and discard the marinade.

Mix the flour with the paprika and turn the eel slices in it. Heat the oil in a large pan and fry the eels over a medium heat for at least 10–15 minutes. Drain the eels on absorbent kitchen paper.

Lift the eels on to a warmed serving dish. Dip the parsley heads in a little milk, dredge in flour and deep-fry until crisp. Scatter over the eels and serve very hot with lemon wedges.

Seafood Paella

SERVES 6

1 small chicken or rabbit, jointed
salt
freshly ground black pepper
1 teaspoon hot ground paprika or cayenne
    pepper
olive oil for frying – 1 coffee cup at least
1 large onion, diced
4 cloves of garlic, chopped
1 lb (450 g) 'quick cook' rice

1 red pepper, seeded and finely diced
14 oz (400 g) can tomatoes and their juice
2 pints (1.2 litres) fish stock, see page 44, or
    water
1 tablespoon ground turmeric
24 mussels, scraped and cleaned, see page
    141
4 oz (100 g) peeled prawns
6 large prawns in their shells

Season the chicken or rabbit joints with salt, pepper and paprika or cayenne pepper.

Heat some of the olive oil in a large frying pan and gently fry the chicken or rabbit, onion and garlic until golden. Add more oil and throw in the rice, stirring until the oil is absorbed – about 5 minutes.

Tip in everything else except the mussels and prawns and cook gently until the rice is almost tender – roughly 20 minutes. Add the mussels and prawns and scatter over the giant prawns (unshelled), increase the heat and cook for a further 10 minutes, until the liquid has bubbled away.

A large cast iron frying pan with high sides and 2 handles is necessary. A lid is quite useful too – the rice will cook better – as is a lot of iced rosé.

Mussels are wonderful. They're delicious and not expensive – you can even get them for free on seaside holidays as you scramble over the rocks. One of the best ways to cook them is in white wine or dry cider, but they are also good stuffed in the half shell or grilled with garlic butter.

Stuffed Mussels

Scrape the mussels carefully with a small, sharp knife, removing any seaweed or barnacles, and pull off their 'beards' – the hairy bits that hang out of the shells. Wash the mussels thoroughly in several changes of water. Discard any with broken shells and that do not shut when tapped. If any mussel seems heavy for its size, prise it open as it may be full of sand or mud.

Put the mussels in a big pan with no liquid at all. Cover and cook them over a high heat, shaking the pan occasionally, until they open. Discard any that remain shut. Allow to cool, then strain off and reserve the juices that have come from the mussels. Remove and discard one shell of each mussel. Meanwhile, mix equal quantities of Tomato Sauce, see page 37, with fresh white breadcrumbs and fill each half mussel with a teaspoonful or so of this mixture. Dot each one with a knob of garlic butter and arrange them in a single layer in a grill pan. Pop under a preheated very hot grill until the top of the stuffing starts to crisp up. Serve liberally strewn with chopped coriander or parsley.

Grilled Mussels with Garlic Butter

Prepare and cook the mussels as described left, but instead of filling them with a tomato and breadcrumb mixture, simply fill each half shell with some garlic butter mixed with fresh white breadcrumbs and a generous amount of finely chopped herbs (parsley, chives and chervil, for example) and pop them under the grill just the same.

Mussels in White Wine or Cider

For 4–6 people, scrape and clean 6 lb (2.75 kg) mussels, as described left. Melt 2 oz (50 g) butter in a large pan and cook 2 large chopped onions and 3 chopped cloves of garlic for 2–3 minutes. Tip in ½ pint (300 ml) dry white wine or cider and bring to the boil. Add the mussels, cover and cook over a high heat, shaking the pan occasionally, until the mussels open. Discard any that remain shut.

Serve with extra knobs of butter and chopped parsley and plenty of fresh bread.

Scallops in Wine with Basil, Bacon and a Julienne of Vegetables

Robert Harrison at Congham Hall, King's Lynn

Robert, although young (compared to me, that is), has no time for jokes
and slapdash methods as I learnt to my cost when I visited him at
Congham Hall – sorry I poured in too much lime juice when we worked
together Robert!

S E R V E S 4

9 oz (250 g) unsalted butter, diced
3 oz (75 g) shallots, finely chopped
4 oz (100 g) unsmoked bacon, cut in fine
   strips
16 scallops, washed and sliced in half
salt
freshly ground black pepper

¼ pint (150 ml) Gewürztraminer wine
juice of 1 lime
julienne of vegetables (selection of peppers,
   leeks, carrots and celery, for example)
1 small bunch of basil, chopped
basil leaves, to garnish

Melt 1 oz (25 g) of the butter and sauté the shallots and bacon over a high heat, but without allowing them to brown. Season the scallops with salt and pepper and add to the pan. Cook the scallops until they have just lost their opaque look, about 2–4 minutes, lift out and keep warm.

Add the wine and lime juice to the pan and boil rapidly until reduced by two-thirds. Add the vegetable julienne and over a high heat shake in the remaining butter, piece by piece. Return the scallops to the pan to heat through and add the chopped basil at the last moment.

Arrange the scallops on plates, spoon over the sauce and garnish with some basil leaves.

Crayfish

This is a feast for the fairly self-indulgent. A crayfish – as my friend John
Noble says – is like a goose or a magnum of claret, too much for one but
not enough for two! That's gourmandising for you.

F O R E A C H S E R V I N G

1 live crayfish
2 tablespoons oil
3 oz (75 g) butter, softened
2 shallots, finely chopped

1 tablespoon finely chopped herbs (parsley,
   chervil and tarragon, for example)
salt
½ teaspoon black peppercorns, finely crushed

For the very best taste of a crayfish, or a lobster for that matter, I am afraid that you have to hold it firmly by the head and, with a very sharp, large knife, push the point of the blade into the cross on the back of the head. It will then die instantly. Cut it in half straight down its back. I appreciate that this is repugnant to many people and you may prefer to buy an already boiled fish – so be it, but the taste won't be the same.

Brush the flesh with the oil and pop under a preheated hot grill, flesh-side down, for 5 minutes. Then turn it back the other way, shell-side down, and grill for a further 20 minutes. While the crayfish is cooking, mix the butter with the shallots, herbs, salt and pepper. By now the flesh of the fish will have contracted, leaving a channel between the fish and the shell. Spoon the seasoned butter into this channel. Once the butter has melted, the crayfish is ready to eat.

Dublin Bay Prawns, Prawns (Langoustines)

These little lobster-like shellfish are caught in vast quantities around the Scottish coast and are rushed by plane to France and Spain before their little claws stop wriggling. Even so, you can still buy them and, considering their excellence, they are not desperately expensive. In fact, bearing in mind the job the fishermen have to catch them, they're cheap.

A plate piled high with boiled, cold, pink prawns accompanied by a wobbly pile of mayonnnaise and fresh bread plus a bottle of iced Chablis is an easily achievable state of heaven. You just throw as many prawns as you can into a pan of boiling salted water. As soon as a white scum appears on the surface, remove from the heat, drain and rinse them under cold running water to arrest the cooking process. Eat while they are still very slightly warm.

Or select the biggest ones you can find and cut them in half lengthways. Dab them with melted butter and whack them under a preheated hot grill for a few moments. You could add a little crushed garlic and chopped parsley to the butter but really fresh prawns like

this are so sweet that you only need a squeeze of lemon juice.

Another method is to cook them in a piquant tomato sauce. For 4 people you'll need about 48 prawns. Cook them briskly for about 3 minutes in 5 tablespoons olive oil with 1 finely chopped onion and carrot. Pour in 1 fl oz (25 ml) Cognac or *eau de vie* and flame. Tip in 4 fl oz (100 ml) dry white wine and cook for a further 2 minutes. Add ¾ pint (450 ml) Tomato Sauce, see page 93, ¾ teaspoon *harissa* or chilli sauce and 1 bouquet garni (parsley, thyme and bay leaf, for example) and simmer for 4–5 minutes more, depending on the size of the prawns – but take great care not to overcook them. Remove the bouquet garni before serving.

Lobster and Mussel Stew

This is a good way to make a very expensive lobster feed lots of people. Be sure that the mussels are fresh and serve with lots of boiled new potatoes to mash into the sauce.

S E R V E S 6

1 pint (600 ml) dry cider
1¾ pints (1 litre) dry white wine
3 lb (1.4 kg) mussels, scraped and cleaned, see page 125
5 shallots, minced
3 sprigs of parsley, chopped
2 cloves of garlic, crushed
freshly ground black pepper
1 tablespoon nut oil
2 oz (50 g) butter

2 live lobsters, weighing about 1½ lb (675 g) each, cut in half from head to tail, stomach sac from near the head and dark thread-like intestine removed, claws cracked and tail cut through the joints. (Reserve the pink matter from the head.)
1 small wineglass of Calvados
bouquet garni (thyme, parsley and bay leaf, for example)
¾ pint (450 ml) double cream

Bring half the cider and a quarter of the wine to the boil in a large pan. Toss in the mussels, shallots, parsley and garlic and plenty of pepper. Cover and cook over a high heat for 10 minutes, shaking the pan now and then.

Lift out the mussels, reserving the juice, and discard any that remain shut. Take them out of their shells, keeping back a few good-looking ones for the garnish and set aside.

Heat together the oil and butter in a large pan, add the lobsters and stir around until they turn red. Remove from the heat, pour over the Calvados and flame. Return to the heat and add the remaining cider, wine, strained mussel liquid and bouquet garni. Boil rapidly until reduced by one-third.

Add the pink matter from the head of the lobster to the cream and beat together. Add to the stew and throw in the mussels. Cook, stirring frequently, until the sauce thickens.

Discard the bouquet garni. Lift out the lobsters, arrange on a warmed serving dish and surround with the mussels. Garnish with the mussels still in their shells and pour over the sauce.

POULTRY

T hanks to modern farming techniques, all manner of poultry from guinea fowl to geese are easily available; unfortunately, no thanks to modern methods, most of them taste like compressed blotting paper that has been injected with fish-flavoured water. Not only depressing for us, but damned miserable for the birds. I once worked on a chicken farm and I was given the gruesome task of cutting their beaks so that when they fought each other – which they naturally did having been driven wild with frustration by being cooped in horrific little cages – damage to their flesh (and, of course, profitability) was minimised. Ugh. But I'm not here to campaign for animal rights, and although I abhor cruelty, unnecessary suffering or killing for pleasure, I am a fully paid-up member of the meat-eating society and am very concerned about the taste of things.

Since you must go to a lot of trouble to cook a meal you must also take trouble to find your ingredients and the dishes that follow will taste so much better if you buy free range birds. Make sure you get the giblets as well since these are essential for making gravies or soups. Or you can save the livers up in the deep freeze till you have enough to make a pâté or terrine.

If you are roasting or frying, buy small, plump young birds. Free range, maize-fed ones with a yellow skin are good. If you are casseroling or currying, ask for an older tougher creature who's been hurtling around the farmyard for some time. Best of all is a cockerel, if you can persuade a farmer to sell you one. Make friends with your butcher or poulterer and if he doesn't stock free range stuff get him to order what you want. Of course, because I live a lot of the time in the country it's easy for me to buy good farm produce. Specially my Christmas goose that I buy from my friend John Sullivan in Abergavenny. Around October time he selects one for me and ensures that it's well fed and happy and ready for the oven on Christmas Day. Incidentally, a goose benefits from being kept (plucked and drawn etc) in a cool larder for a couple of days before you cook it.

Ducks don't have as much meat on them in relation to their size as you might think. Try to choose small, heavy ones that have a comfortable feel in your hands. Avoid those with protruding chest bones and concave breasts.

On the subject of turkeys I think I shall maintain a diplomatic silence, because unless you can buy a genuine free range one of about five to six pounds, I don't think they're much cop. Except if you raise a few yourself of course.

Glazed Spring Chickens

Spring chickens are really only good if they are fresh. Although I do keep hammering the point about fresh produce in this book, it is very important, and it isn't too much of a headache to find a fresh spring chicken nowadays. Lots of supermarkets have them, chilled rather than frozen, and if you can find a free range one, better still. It will make all the difference.

SERVES 4

2 poussins, weighing about 1½-2 lb
  (675-900 g) each
salt
freshly ground black pepper
2 oz (50 g) butter

For the glaze:
5 tablespoons water

dash of lemon juice
5 tablespoons sugar
dash of apple juice
1 tablespoon grated lemon rind
salt

grated lemon zest, to garnish

Put all the glaze ingredients in a pan, heat gently until the sugar dissolves and then boil for 5 minutes. Wipe the birds and season them inside and out with salt and pepper. Truss them neatly, brush with the glaze and the butter and place on a rack or the wire shelf over a roasting tin.

Roast the birds in a preheated oven, 425°F/ 220°C (gas mark 7), for about 20-30 minutes, basting and turning the poussins frequently with the glaze. Remove the trussing strings and place the poussins on a warmed serving dish. Garnish with a little grated lemon zest to serve.

Stuffed Spring Chickens with Red Fruit Sauce

SERVES 4

4 small poussins, weighing about 1 lb
  (450 g) each
salt
freshly ground black pepper

For the stuffing:
4 oz (100 g) fresh white breadcrumbs
2 oz (50 g) wheatgerm
2 oz (50 g) celery heart, finely diced
4 fl oz (100 ml) chicken or veal stock, see
  page 43 or 41
1 tablespoon grated lemon rind

1 tablespoon chopped parsley
1 teaspoon sugar
1 clove of garlic, finely chopped
4 oz (100 g) butter, melted

For the sauce:
10 oz (275 g) redcurrant jelly
3 oz (75 g) sultanas
2 oz (50 g) butter
dash of lemon juice
large pinch of ground cinnamon

Mix together all the ingredients for the stuffing using three-quarters of the butter in a large bowl. Wipe the birds and season them inside and out with salt and pepper. Stuff them with the prepared mixture, tucking in the loose bits of skin neatly. Brush the chickens with the remaining melted butter and place them on a wire rack in a roasting tin. Roast in a preheated oven, 425°F/220°C (gas mark 7), for about 20–30 minutes, or until they're golden brown.

Meanwhile, prepare the sauce. Put all the ingredients into a pan and cook gently for about 10 minutes, stirring occasionally to mix well. When the chickens are almost cooked, brush them generously all over with the sauce. Return to the oven and continue roasting for a further 10–15 minutes.

Arrange the poussins on warmed serving plates, heat the remaining sauce, add to it any juices from the roasting tin and hand it round separately.

Chicken with Sour Cherry Sauce

Sour cherry sauce is great for pouring over chicken, pork or any white meat – and, if you are one of those good people who have made your chicken stock and stored it in the deep freeze, you can make it very quickly.

SERVES 4-6

4 lb (1.75 kg) boiling fowl
1 onion, chopped
1 carrot, chopped
bouquet garni (parsley, bay leaf and thyme, for example)
8 oz (225 g) fresh cherries, stoned

2-3 tablespoons chopped parsley
1 tablespoon chopped dill
1 wineglass of dry white wine
1 oz (25 g) flour ⎱ *mashed together*
1 oz (25 g) butter ⎰

Put the chicken in a large pan and cover with cold water. Add the onion, carrot and bouquet garni. Bring to the boil, reduce the heat and simmer for about 1½-2 hours, or until tender. Lift out the chicken, skin and joint it either on or off the bone. Set aside and keep warm. Boil the cooking liquid rapidly to produce a well-flavoured stock. Discard the bouquet garni.

In another pan, pour some of the stock over the cherries and herbs so that they are just covered and add the wine. Simmer gently for about 10–15 minutes, or until the cherries are soft. Add the knobs of flour and butter mix and thicken the sauce gradually, stirring constantly. Boil rapidly for 2 minutes, then pass the mixture through a sieve or process in a food processor or blender. Return the sauce to the pan, heat through and pour over the chicken pieces.

Serve with rice.

PS You can use gooseberries or plums instead of cherries when in season.

Gumbo

'Let the good times roll' or '*laissez les bons temps rouler*' as they put it –
that's the Cajun motto and all that Louisiana-style zest for the spice of life
is here in this great Cajun/Creole soup-cum-stew.

S E R V E S 8

3 lb (1.4 kg) chicken, jointed
8 oz (225 g) smoked, spicy sausage, chopped
1 teaspoon salt
1 lb (450 g) fresh, unpeeled prawns
4 oz (100 g) butter
2 oz (50 g) flour
2 large onions, chopped
2 cloves of garlic, crushed
2 tablespoons chopped parsley

1 teaspoon chopped thyme
2 bay leaves
¼ teaspoon cayenne pepper
freshly ground black pepper
4 oz (100 g) cooked ham, chopped
4 tomatoes, skinned and chopped
2 tablespoons file powder (ground sassafras
*   leaves), available from delicatessens*
24 fresh oysters

Put the chicken pieces in a large pan with the chopped sausage. Cover with water, add the salt and simmer for 45 minutes. Lift out the chicken and sausage and strain the stock. Remove the chicken flesh from the bones, dice it and set aside.

Wash the prawns, cover with water in a large pan, add a little salt and boil for 3 minutes. Strain, reserving the liquid. Peel off the prawn shells and heads and reserve the flesh. Return the shells and heads to the prawn broth, boil vigorously for 15 minutes, then strain the prawn liquid into the chicken stock.

To make the *roux*, melt the butter in a heavy skillet or frying pan over a low heat. Add the flour and stir until the mixture is creamy and free from lumps. Reduce the heat and continue to stir for about 10 minutes, until it is nut brown. Take care not to burn it, keep stirring and don't take your eyes off the pan. When the

roux is browned, add the onions and garlic and cook slowly until soft. Stir in the parsley, thyme, bay leaves, cayenne and pepper to taste.

Transfer to a large pan, add the sausage, chicken, chopped ham and tomatoes and cover generously with the chicken and prawn broth – make up the liquid with extra chicken stock or water if necessary. Stir in the file powder and simmer gently for 1 hour. Scrub the oysters, open carefully and add the oyster flesh and liquid to the gumbo with the reserved prawns. Cook for a further 5 minutes.

Check the seasoning. Do not be timid about adding more salt as an insipid gumbo is considered to be a disaster. Turn off the heat and leave the gumbo to stand for 5 minutes. Fish out and discard the bay leaves.

Serve the gumbo in warmed soup bowls with a little steamed or boiled rice in the bottom of each bowl.

Chicken Jambalaya

This is jazz cooking, a spicy rice dish from way down in Louisiana. Actually, it's Cajun cooking, which has its roots in France, and just like New Orleans Dixieland jazz, improvisation is the name of the game. You can vary this recipe by using rabbit instead of chicken and different kinds of seafood – do your own thing and have a bit of fun. 'Son of a gun, we'll have big fun on the bayou . . .' and all that.

SERVES 8-10

4-5 lb (1.75-2.25 kg) chicken, with giblets
bouquet garni (parsley, bay leaf and thyme,
   for example)
½ pint (300 ml) water
2 oz (50 g) oil or butter
1 large onion, chopped
2 spring onions, trimmed and sliced
   (including the green parts)
1 green pepper, seeded and cut into strips
3 sticks of celery, chopped
2 cloves of garlic, crushed
8 oz (225 g) smoked sausage, sliced
4 oz (100 g) cooked ham, diced

1 lb (450 g) can tomatoes, roughly chopped
   and their juice
1 bay leaf
1 teaspoon chopped thyme
½ teaspoon ground cumin
3 whole cloves
4 whole allspice, crushed, or ¼ teaspoon
   ground allspice
¼ teaspooon cayenne pepper
10-12 oz (275-350 g) long-grain rice
6 oz (175 g) cooked and peeled prawns
salt

Wipe the chicken and put in a heavy-based pan with the giblets, bouquet garni and water. Bring to the boil, then cover and simmer gently for 1½ hours, until the chicken is tender. Strain the stock from the pan and reserve. Allow the chicken to cool slightly, then remove the flesh from the bones and cut into strips. Dice the chicken liver, if liked. Discard the rest of the giblets, bones and skin. Clean any scum from the pan. When cold, skim off the fat from the surface of the chicken stock.

Heat the oil or butter in the pan, add the vegetables including the garlic, and sauté, stirring frequently, for 3-4 minutes. Throw in the smoked sausage and fry for a further 5 minutes. Stir in the ham, tomatoes, bay leaf, thyme,

cumin, cloves, allspice and cayenne pepper. Add ½ pint (300 ml) of the reserved chicken stock and return the sliced chicken and diced liver, if using, to the pan.

Rinse the rice under cold running water and add to the pan. Bring the contents to the boil, then cover the pan and cook for about 20 minutes, until the rice is tender and the stock has been absorbed. If the Jambalaya looks too moist, remove the lid towards the end of the cooking time to allow the remaining liquid to evaporate. Five minutes before the end of the cooking time, stir in the prawns. Before serving, fish out the bay leaf, season to taste with salt and add extra cayenne pepper if you like a spicy flavour.

Chicken Couscous

The great African dish, couscous, can vary from just a plate of couscous
with a little olive oil, a few chopped herbs and a bit of vegetable to a
grand affair with chicken, lamb and small black sausages.

Here is a quite simple but typical version. Make
vast quantities and serve with strong Moroccan
red wine.

To serve it, you must have a tube or tin of hot
spicy paste called *harissa*, which you should be
able to get from most delicatessens. Then you
either serve the strained liquid from the pot
separately as a soup, spiced up with *harissa*, or
pour just a little of it over the couscous and vegetables and spread the *harissa* on the chicken.

SERVES 4

3½ lb (1.5 kg) chicken, jointed
3 tablespoons olive oil
2 tablespoons clarified butter, see page 35
1 onion, sliced into rounds
1 large ripe tomato
1 cinnamon stick
salt, to taste
½ teaspoon freshly ground black pepper

3 tablespoons chickpeas, soaked overnight
  and drained
3 or 4 small turnips, quartered
2 courgettes, sliced
8 oz (225 g) precooked couscous
butter (optional)
few tablespoons harissa (spicy chilli paste),
  available from delicatessens

Mix together the chicken, oil, butter, onion,
tomato, cinnamon, salt and pepper in a large
heavy pan. Cook over a moderate heat, stirring
to coat and brown the chicken. After about 5
minutes, cover with 12 fl oz (350 ml) cold water
and bring to the boil. Toss in the chickpeas,
cover and simmer for 30–40 minutes, or until
the chicken is tender. Lift out the chicken
pieces and set aside.

Continue to cook the mixture in the pan
until the chickpeas are tender – perhaps
another 1½ hours, adding the turnips and
courgettes about 30 minutes before the end of
cooking. Add more water if necessary. Meanwhile, cover the couscous with water and leave
to absorb the liquid for 15 minutes. About 15
minutes before the end of the cooking time,
set the couscous to steam above the stew (it
should really be put into a muslin-lined
steamer or *couscoussier*, but a wire sieve lined
with a 'J'-cloth is fine). Cover with the pan lid
and steam for 15 minutes. Remove the couscous and keep warm. Return the chicken to the
pan to heat through and stir a little butter into
the couscous before serving, if liked.

Serve with the *harissa* as described above.

Herby-fried Chicken with Cream Sauce

SERVES 4-6

3 lb (1.4 kg) chicken, jointed or 8 chicken
  pieces
¼ pint (150 ml) buttermilk or milk and
  1 teaspoon cream of tartar
8 oz (225 g) flour
1 teaspoon salt
freshly ground black pepper
2 teaspoons chopped marjoram
2 teaspoons chopped parsley
oil for deep-frying

For the sauce:
1½ oz (40 g) bacon fat or butter
1½ oz (40 g) flour
½ pint (300 ml) chicken stock, see page 43
½ pint (300 ml) double cream
salt
freshly ground black pepper

Remove the skin from the chicken pieces. Place the chicken in a large bowl (not aluminium) with the buttermilk or milk and cream of tartar mixture and leave to marinate for 2 hours.

Sift the flour and salt into a small bowl and stir in the pepper, marjoram and parsley.

Heat the oil in a frying pan. Shake the chicken pieces gently to remove any excess buttermilk, and dip them into the herbed flour, to coat all over. Deep-fry the pieces slowly for 15–20 minutes, turning to brown on all sides and ensuring that they cook right through. Drain on absorbent kitchen paper.

To make the sauce, heat the bacon fat or butter in a medium-sized pan, add the flour and cook for 1 minute. Remove from the heat and gradually stir in the chicken stock. Return to the heat and cook, stirring constantly, until the sauce thickens. Cook for 3 minutes, then remove from the heat and stir in the cream. Season to taste with salt and pepper.

To serve, arrange the chicken pieces on a large plate and hand round a bowl of the hot cream sauce separately. If the sauce needs to be reheated, do not allow it to boil or it will separate.

NOTE
Although I don't really like the great British turkey, I'm sad to say, I must say a word in favour of the small, free range French turkey. A 5 lb (2.25 kg) one with three sliced truffles inserted under the skin, wrapped in fatty bacon and roasted breast down, served with the juices from the roasting tray deglazed with a little red wine, is a gastronomic treat of the highest excellence.

Coriander Chicken

SERVES 4-6

4 tablespoons oil
1 tablespoon butter
4 lb (1.75 kg) chicken, jointed
4 large cloves of garlic, peeled and left whole
1 teaspoon ground turmeric or saffron
1 small bunch of coriander leaves, finely
  chopped, or 2 teaspoons ground coriander

4 oz (100 g) purple olives, stoned (Greek or
  Italian rather than the ripe American type)
1 lemon, sliced
salt
freshly ground black pepper

Heat together the oil and butter in a large, heavy-based frying pan and brown the chicken pieces over a moderate heat. Add the garlic, spices and coriander. Cook for about 10 minutes, turning the chicken pieces occasionally to coat them evenly. Stir in enough water to cover, about 8 fl oz (250 ml), cover and simmer over a low heat, adding more water if necessary, for about 20-30 minutes, or until the chicken is tender. Increase the heat, add the olives and lemon and season to taste with salt and pepper. Cook for a further 8-10 minutes, or until the sauce is reduced.

Serve with rice or couscous.

Chicken Paprika with Dumplings

Like couscous, this recipe benefits from an elderly chicken, rather than a blander spring one – you can tell an old chicken by its brown legs and white breasts. Since this is a typical eastern European dish, such as you might find in Hungary, paprika snobs should use Hungarian paprika, which should tax your shopping skills to the point of frustration!

SERVES 6

4 lb (1.75 kg) chicken, with giblets
2 tablespoons vegetable oil
2 oz (50 g) butter
1 large onion, finely chopped
½ oz (15 g) ground paprika
salt

4 oz (100 g) red pepper, seeded and sliced
4 oz (100 g) fresh or canned tomatoes
3 oz (75 g) flour
¾ pint (450 ml) soured cream
3 fl oz (75 ml) double cream
Dumplings, see page 172

Joint the chicken into 8-10 pieces. Heat together the oil and butter in a pan and fry the onion until golden. Stir in the paprika and add the chicken pieces, together with the liver, heart and giblets. Season to taste with salt and cook the chicken joints, over a low heat, in their juices, stirring frequently.

After about 20 minutes, add the pepper, tomatoes, and a little water. Continue cooking with the lid on over a gentle heat, stirring occasionally, for about 30–40 minutes, until tender. Mix the flour into the soured cream and add to the chicken. Pour the double cream over the chicken and bring to the boil, stirring constantly, until the sauce thickens slightly.

Serve hot with buttered dumplings.

Breasts of Chicken Stuffed with Spinach and Mushrooms

Juan Martin at Sharrow Bay Hotel, Ullswater

S E R V E S 6 - 8

2 oz (50 g) butter
4 shallots or 1 small onion, chopped
8 oz (225 g) mushrooms, wild if possible,
* finely chopped*
8 tablespoons cooked spinach
salt
freshly ground black pepper
2 teaspoons chopped chervil
6-8 chicken breasts
butter

For the sauce:
½ oz (15 g) butter
2 shallots or 1 small onion, chopped
½ pint (300 ml) chicken stock, see page 43
¼ pint (150 ml) dry white wine
5 mushrooms, chopped
1 pint (600 ml) double cream
salt
freshly ground black pepper

Melt the butter in a pan and sauté the shallots or onion until softened. Add the mushrooms and cook for 2 minutes. Stir in the cooked spinach, season to taste with salt and pepper and add the chervil.

With a sharp knife, cut a lengthways pocket in each of the chicken breasts and fill it with the prepared stuffing. Lightly butter the breasts and wrap them in separate pieces of foil to form loose but secure parcels. Place on a baking tray and bake in a preheated oven, 425°F/220°C (gas mark 7), for 10–12 minutes.

To make the sauce, melt the butter in a pan and sauté the shallots or onion. Add the stock, wine and mushrooms and boil rapidly to reduce by three-quarters. Add the cream and cook for a minute or two longer to allow the sauce to thicken slightly. The sauce should have a thin coating consistency. Season to taste with salt and pepper.

Unwrap the foil parcels, lift the chicken breasts on to warmed plates and pour over the sauce.

Ragoût of Chicken and Mussels in a Basil and Aniseed Sauce

Paul Gayler at Inigo Jones, London

SERVES 4

butter
1 oz (25 g) shallots, roughly chopped
1 tablespoon parsley stalks
1¾ pints (1 litre) fresh mussels, scraped and cleaned, see page 125
¼ pint (150 ml) dry white wine
1 pint (600 ml) chicken stock, see page 43
olive oil
1 leek, finely diced
2 carrots, finely diced
1 stick of celery, finely diced

1 small fennel bulb, finely diced
1 clove of garlic, crushed
1 tablespoon chopped thyme
1 bay leaf
3 tomatoes, skinned, seeded and diced
salt
freshly ground black pepper
4 × 6 oz (175 g) chicken breasts
5 tablespoons Pernod or Ricard
¼ pint (150 ml) double cream
6 basil leaves, finely shredded

Lightly butter a pan, add the shallots and parsley stalks and place the mussels on top. Moisten with the white wine and half the chicken stock. Cover the pan, place it on a high heat and steam until the mussels open their shells – about 1 minute. Pour the mussels into a colander, reserving the cooking liquid, and discard any that do not open. Set aside.

In another pan heat together a little oil and butter and sweat the vegetables, including the garlic, the thyme, bay leaf and tomatoes for 2–3 minutes with the lid on. Remove the lid and place the seasoned chicken breasts on top. Moisten with the Pernod or Ricard, pour over the reserved mussel liquid and the remaining stock. Cover with buttered greaseproof paper and poach for about 10–15 minutes, or until the chicken is tender.

Remove the chicken breasts and keep warm. Fish out and discard the bay leaf. Boil the sauce rapidly to reduce, add the double cream and whisk in a few small pieces of butter to give a rich smooth sauce.

Cut the chicken into small escalopes or thin slices and arrange on a warmed serving dish. Add the mussels to the sauce and reheat them without boiling. Check the seasoning, add the basil leaves and pour the sauce over the chicken.

Serve immediately.

Chicken Suprêmes Jacqueline

Allan Holland at Mallory Court, Bishops Tachbrook

SERVES 6

8 oz (225 g) raw, skinless and boneless duck
  meat
1 egg white, stiffly beaten
8-10 fl oz (250-275 ml) chilled double
  cream, lightly whipped
salt
pinch of white pepper
6 skinned and boned chicken breasts,
  weighing about 6-7 oz (175-200 g) each
¾ pint (450 ml) chicken stock, see page 43

For the sauce:
¼ pint (150 ml) tawny port
½ pint (300 ml) double cream
lemon juice
salt
freshly ground black pepper
1 oz (25 g) butter

For the garnish:
2 oz (50 g) flaked almonds, sautéed in butter
  until golden
6 thin slices of truffle
sprigs of chervil or parsley

To make the duck mousse, chop the duck meat coarsely and purée in a food processor or blender. Alternatively, put it through a mincer and then pound the meat in a mortar. Beat in the egg white until the mixture is smooth. Pass through a sieve into a bowl and chill for 1 hour. Set the bowl into a larger bowl filled with ice and, using a wooden spoon, gradually beat in the whipped cream until the mixture looks light and mousse-like. If the mixture is too firm, add more cream. Season with salt and white pepper, cover the bowl and chill again.

Using a sharp knife, make a lengthways slit in the chicken breasts to make a pocket. Fill them with the duck mousse. Do not overfill as the mousse expands during cooking. Place the stuffed chicken breasts in a single layer in a lightly buttered frying pan and pour in the chicken stock. Cover, bring slowly to simmering point and poach the breasts very gently for 8-10 minutes, or until they are just cooked. Remove the breasts to a dish, reserving the stock, cover and keep warm while making the sauce.

Pour the port into a pan with the reserved stock and boil rapidly until they are well reduced and syrupy. Add the cream and continue to simmer, over a gentle heat, until the sauce has a coating consistency. Remove from the heat, and season to taste with lemon juice, salt and pepper. Whisk in the butter. Pass the sauce through a very fine sieve.

Arrange the breasts on individual warmed plates and coat with the sauce. Sprinkle with the almonds and garnish with truffle slices. Surround with sprigs of chervil or parsley.

Roast Duck with Cranberry Glaze

SERVES 4

4-5 lb (1.75-2.25 kg) free-range duck, with
   giblets
6 fl oz (175 ml) chicken stock, see page 43
salt
flour
4 tablespoons red wine

2 tablespoons cornflour
2 tablespoons lemon juice
14 oz (400 g) jar whole berry cranberry
   sauce
watercress sprigs, trimmed, to garnish

Put the duck giblets and chicken stock in a pan, bring up to the boil and simmer for 1 hour.

Wipe the bird and rub the skin well with salt. Prick all over with a fork. Place on a rack in a roasting tin and roast in a preheated oven, 400°F/200°C (gas mark 6), for 20 minutes per 1 lb (450 g), basting occasionally. About 15 minutes before the end of the cooking time, baste the duck, sprinkle with flour and add the wine to the roasting tin. Increase the oven temperature to 425°F/220°C (gas mark 7) and finish cooking. Strain the juices into a bowl and skim off the fat from the surface.

Meanwhile, mix together the cornflour and lemon juice in a pan and stir in the strained giblet stock, skimmed cooking juices and cranberry sauce. Bring to the boil, stirring, then simmer for 3-4 minutes. Strain about one-third of the sauce and use it to brush over the duck to glaze it for about 5 minutes or so in the oven. Pour the remaining sauce into a sauceboat and keep warm. Carve the duck, garnish with some watercress sprigs and serve with the hot sauce.

Breast of Duck with Ginger, Mango and Spring Onions

Stephen Ross at Homewood Park, Hinton Charterhouse

SERVES 6

6 duck breasts
½ pint (300 ml) game or chicken stock, see
   page 43
1 large piece of fresh root ginger, grated

2 fl oz (50 ml) Malibu liqueur
4 ripe mangoes
¼ pint (150 ml) double cream
4 spring onions, trimmed and finely chopped

Either buy six duck breasts or remove the breasts from three ducks, using the legs for another dish and the carcasses for stock.

Grill the breasts until the skin is really brown and crisp and then cook them in a preheated oven, 450°F/230°C (gas mark 8), for 5-10 minutes, until just cooked – the flesh must be still pink. Pour off and reserve any juices.

To make the sauce, put the stock, ginger and Malibu liqueur in a pan and boil rapidly until they are reduced by half. Peel two of the mangoes and cut the flesh from the stones. Purée in a food processor or blender and beat into the sauce. Add the cream and cook for 1–2 minutes to thicken slightly. Just before serving, stir in the spring onions.

Peel the remaining mangoes and slice them lengthways into thin slices. Slice the cooked duck breasts lengthways and interleave the duck with the mango. Return to the oven to keep warm. Pour the sauce on to individual serving plates and arrange the duck breasts and mangoes on top.

Roast Goose with Celery and Almond Stuffing

The goose is the queen of poultry, and rather like a magnum of good claret, it is a little too much for one, and not quite enough for two. I think it is the ultimate in self-indulgence and luxury to tuck into a goose, crisply roasted one day, and then to tuck into the cold meat, with some Pickled Damsons, see page 39, the next.

SERVES 8-10

13 lb (6 kg) prepared goose
salt

For the stuffing:
1 tablespoon oil
1 large onion, finely chopped
2 sticks of celery, finely chopped
1 apple, peeled, cored and finely chopped

8 oz (225 g) pork sausagemeat
4 oz (100 g) fresh white breadcrumbs
2 oz (50 g) flaked almonds, chopped
goose liver, finely chopped
½ teaspoon ground nutmeg
freshly ground black pepper

Wash and dry the goose, prick the skin and rub with salt. Place on a wire rack in a roasting tin.

To make the stuffing, heat the oil in a pan and sauté the onion, celery and apple until softened. Remove from the heat and mix with the sausagemeat, breadcrumbs, almonds, goose liver, nutmeg and salt and pepper to taste. Form into small balls and place in a greased ovenproof dish, then cover with foil.

Roast the goose in a preheated oven, 425°F/220°C (gas mark 7), for 20 minutes. Reduce the oven temperature to 325°F/160°C (gas mark 3), turn the goose breast side down and strain

off excess fat. Cover the goose with foil and roast for a further 2 hours.

Add the stuffing balls to the oven, remove the foil, turn the goose breast side up, and cook for a further 50–55 minutes to allow the skin to crisp.

To serve, place the goose on a warmed serving dish with the cooked stuffing balls. Skim any fat from the roasting juices, reduce rapidly to make a slightly thickened gravy and serve with the goose.

PS Save the goose fat for cooking sautéed spuds – etc, etc.

Although guinea fowl can be treated in much the same way as pheasant, I think it should be included in this poultry section since anything you can do to a chicken you can do to a guinea fowl.

Guinea Fowl with Peaches

I've cooked this one more times than I care to remember but on my first ever television performance I had to use a frozen bird and forgot to remove the plastic bag of giblets before roasting it. I flamboyantly cut it in half in front of millions of people and whoops there was the plastic sack. The television company did not think it very funny!

SERVES 4

1 large guinea fowl, weighing about 2 lb (900 g)
salt
freshly ground black pepper
chopped thyme
chopped basil
juice of 1 lemon

3 oz (75 g) butter
4 ripe peaches, halved
1 wineglass of dry white wine
1 measure of brandy or peach liqueur
about 4 tablespoons chicken stock or jelly, see page 43

Wipe the bird and season it inside and out with salt, pepper, thyme and basil. Rub with lemon juice and butter and place in a roasting tin, breast side down. Roast in a preheated oven, 425°F/220°C (gas mark 7), for 15 minutes.

Add the peaches and wine and cook for a further 15 minutes, breast side up, basting frequently. When the skin is brown and the flesh moist (it must not be overcooked), remove the bird and joint it. Place with the peaches on a warmed serving dish, pour over the brandy or peach liqueur and flame.

Meanwhile, bubble the juices in the roasting tin over a high direct heat until they are reduced by half. Then add the stock or jelly plus the juices that have oozed out from the flamed bird on the serving dish. There is not much sauce but it is delicious so don't cook it away. Strain over the guinea fowl and serve immediately.

Grilled Breast of Guinea Fowl with Lentils and Foie Gras

Shaun Hill at Gidleigh Park, Chagford

Shaun told me that if he hadn't become a cook he'd like to have been a gardener – I'm sure he would have grown brilliant vegetables, but I'm glad he chose the kitchen.

SERVES 4

4 guinea fowl breasts
4 oz (100 g) brown lentils
4 oz (100 g) foie gras
oil
1 onion, chopped
1 carrot, chopped
2 rashers of streaky bacon, chopped

1 clove of garlic, chopped
1 pint (600 ml) chicken stock, see page 43
salt
freshly ground black pepper
melted butter
2 tablespoons veal glaze, see page 42

Lightly beat the breasts to an even thickness between sheets of greaseproof paper, but don't allow them to become very thin.

Wash and sort through the lentils, removing any small stones or pieces of grit. Cook them in a pan of boiling salted water for about 35 minutes, or until tender. Drain and set aside.

Pick any thin stringy nerves or skin from the foie gras, then cut into four small slices. Heat some oil in a pan and fry the onion, carrot, bacon and garlic until golden brown. Add the lentils with a few tablespoons of the stock.

Season the guinea fowl with salt and pepper and brush with melted butter. Cook the breasts under a preheated grill for 3 minutes or so. Remove and keep warm. Boil the remaining chicken stock rapidly in a pan to reduce by half. Add the veal glaze and cooked lentil mixture.

Heat a frying pan until red hot – no oil or butter – and quickly fry the foie gras. Strain the cooking juices into the lentil sauce.

Spoon the sauce on to warmed plates and place the guinea fowl and foie gras on top.

GAME

T he game-loving gourmet does not need to spend time in the quiet, sombre shop of a gunsmith in St James's any more than he or she needs to spend time cutting out coupons from the Sunday supplements to buy a special overwaxed coat. The only equipment we need – and after all the game's the thing – is a superb kitchen and a brilliant wine cellar, which probably cost about the same as a good gun anywhere these days and which I think are a more useful investment.

Because game (and I include the humble rabbit in this category) lives in the wild and feeds off the nuts, berries, grains and grasses that are available, it has a highly individual flavour and in most cases its meat or flesh will be tougher than that of domestic fowl and this brings us on to the question of hanging.

To hang or not to hang is a question that should occupy gourmets much more than it does politicians. I have had more disgusting meals in my life with the red-faced, hearty traditionalist who has insisted on hanging the game until it is virtually putrid than I care to remember. A happy balance must be struck between the degree of tenderising that the hanging process gives and what is acceptable to our palates. Here, then, are the Floyd guidelines on this subject.

Pheasant, grouse and partridge should be hung in a cool airy place for two to three days, and then plucked. If you are going to freeze your birds for future use you must hang and pluck them first and don't forget to mark carefully which are old birds and which are young birds. Obviously, young for roasting and old for casseroling. Small birds like snipe or woodcock need one or two days' hanging. Wild ducks need no hanging at all. Pigeons are unquestionably best when young and need no hanging either and neither do rabbits.

Venison and hare both need hanging. So far as venison is concerned, it is probably best to arrange with your butcher to keep it for you for a week to ten days before you decide to use it. A hare should be hung for two to three days before being skinned and paunched. Both hare and venison are quite dry meats and benefit enormously from marinating after they have been hanging, and in the case of a whole hare or venison, it is a good idea either to lard the thighs with bacon fat or to wrap them well in fatty bacon.

As a general rule with small game birds, it is best to wrap them in the fatty tissue known as caul which you will probably have to order from your butcher, and also to roast them breast-down since this allows the juices to flow through the drier breast meat thus making it more succulent.

The old game die-hards are full of quaint expressions and rules of thumb such as 'a properly cooked snipe merely flies through a hot oven', implying that the birds should be served practically raw but I think if you like a well-cooked snipe you should cook it that way. It is all too like the wine thing where everybody says you must have white wine with fish and red wine with meat. That is stuff and non-sense; the best way to enjoy wine as to enjoy game is to have what you like, how you like and when you like. Having said all that, with some game birds by the time the breast is nicely cooked, the legs can still be raw so it is not a bad idea to serve the breast first and then pop the legs under the grill for a moment or two and serve them a little later on in the meal.

Roast Pheasant

Pheasants are no longer the preserve of the landed gentry or the wealthy (some supermarkets sell them these days) and since they are plump and meaty they are good value for a dinner party. I don't agree that they should be 'hung' for days before cooking – rotted flesh of any sort is unpalatable.

SERVES 4

1 brace of pheasants, and their giblets
6 rashers of streaky bacon
3 oz (75 g) butter
2 tablespoons flour
4 oz (100 g) fresh white breadcrumbs

½ pint (300 ml) game stock, see page 43
salt
freshly ground black pepper
butter, to finish

Truss the birds and wrap them with bacon. Place them, breast down, side by side in a roasting tin on a trivet with the giblets underneath. Soften 2 oz (50 g) of the butter and spread over the legs and wings. Roast in a preheated oven, 450°F/230°C (gas mark 8), for 10 minutes, then reduce the temperature to 400°F/200°C (gas mark 6), and continue to cook for 15–20 minutes, basting frequently with the butter in the tin.

Remove the bacon rashers, turn the birds breast side up and sprinkle the breasts with the flour. Baste the birds again and cook for a further 15 minutes.

Melt the remaining butter in a pan and fry the breadcrumbs until they are golden brown, turning them occasionally to ensure even browning. Lift the pheasants on to a heated serving dish and remove the trussing strings. Spoon the fried breadcrumbs round the birds and keep hot.

Skim the fat from the cooking juices. Place the tin over a direct heat, add the stock and scrape up any sediment stuck to the bottom. Boil for 2–3 minutes and season to taste with salt and pepper. Then strain the sauce into a pan and, over a low heat, whisk in a knob of butter until the sauce is smooth.

Pheasant Cooked in Red Wine with Pig's Trotters

Joyce Molyneux at The Carved Angel, Dartmouth

Joyce has to be the mother superior of British cooks. This is one of her
personal favourites.

S E R V E S   3 - 4

1 oz (25 g) butter
12 small onions, peeled
4 oz (100 g) pickled belly of pork or streaky
   bacon, cut in strips
1 pheasant, trussed
salt
freshly ground black pepper

brandy
2 cooked pig's trotters with about ½ pint
   (300 ml) reserved pig's trotter stock
12 button mushrooms
bouquet garni (thyme, bay leaf and parsley,
   for example)
½ pint (300 ml) red wine

Melt the butter in a heavy flameproof casserole
and brown the onions and belly of pork or
bacon. Remove with a slotted spoon.

Season the pheasant with salt and pepper
and add it to the pan. Brown it on all sides.
Return the onions and belly of pork or bacon to
the casserole. Pour over a little brandy and
flame.

Split the trotters in half or four and tuck
round the pheasant. Add the mushrooms and
bouquet garni. Pour over the stock and red wine.
Bring to the boil and check the seasoning.

Cover and cook in a preheated oven, 350°F/
180°C (gas mark 4), for 30 minutes, or until the
pheasant is tender. Check the seasoning again
and remove the bouquet garni and trussing
strings.

Carve the pheasant and serve.

Pheasant – an Alsace Way

A super dish for an old pheasant or couple of partridges too tough to roast. Slow cooking is the secret here.

S E R V E S   3 - 4

1 firm cabbage
1 pheasant, jointed
salt
freshly ground black pepper
1½ oz (40 g) butter
1 onion, finely chopped
9 oz (250 g) smoked bacon, diced
1 carrot, finely chopped

1 × 6 oz (175 g) pepperone sausage, sliced
few sprigs of thyme
1 bay leaf
2 cloves of garlic, crushed
4 juniper berries, crushed
1 bottle of dry white wine or cider
large knob of butter

Core the cabbage and blanch in boiling water. Rinse under cold running water and drain thoroughly, then separate the cabbage into leaves.

Season the pheasant with salt and pepper and brown in the first lot of butter. Lift out the joints and set aside. Add the onion, bacon and carrot to the pan and fry until golden. Remove and place in the base of a casserole.

Wrap each piece of pheasant in two or three cabbage leaves and add them to the casserole along with the sausage, herbs, garlic, juniper berries and wine or cider.

Bake in a preheated oven, 350°F/180°C (gas mark 4), for at least 1½ hours; add a little more wine as necessary. Remove the pheasant parcels to a heated serving dish and keep warm. Add the knob of butter to the sauce and whisk over a high direct heat for 2–3 minutes. Check the seasoning and pour over the pheasant. Remove the bay leaf before serving.

Stuffed Roast Partridges

SERVES 4

4 young partridges

For the stuffing:
4 oz (100 g) fresh white breadcrumbs
grated rind of 1 large lemon
2 tablespoons chopped parsley
1 tablespoon minced onion

few crushed juniper berries or 1 oz (25 g)
   seedless raisins
salt
freshly ground black pepper
beaten egg, to bind
8 fat rashers of bacon
2 oz (50 g) butter, melted

Wash and dry the partridges. To make the stuffing, mix the breadcrumbs with the lemon rind, parsley, onion, juniper berries or raisins and salt and pepper to taste. Bind with beaten egg and use to stuff the birds. Truss, wrap in the fat bacon rashers and place in a roasting tin. Brush generously with some of the melted butter.

Roast in a preheated oven, 350°F/180°C (gas mark 4), for 1 hour, basting occasionally with the juices and melted butter. Remove the trussing strings and serve immediately.

Braised Partridge with Cabbage

This is a brilliant winter dish with some Châteauneuf-du-Pape or Barolo.

SERVES 4

2 oz (50 g) butter or bacon fat
1 brace of partridges, trussed, and their giblets
1 firm cabbage
6 oz (175 g) streaky bacon
salt
freshly ground black pepper

1 carrot, roughly chopped
1 onion, stuck with 2-3 whole cloves
bouquet garni (parsley, bay leaf and thyme,
   for example)
about 1 pint (600 ml) veal, chicken or game
   stock, see pages 41-3

Melt the fat in a frying pan and brown the partridges well on all sides. Trim, quarter and wash the cabbage. Cook in boiling salted water for 5 minutes, then drain well. Line a flameproof casserole with the bacon and lay half the cabbage over it. Season to taste with salt and pepper.

Place the partridges on top with the remaining cabbage, the carrot, onion, bouquet garni and giblets. Bring the stock to the boil and pour enough into the casserole to cover the birds. Cover and simmer for about 1¼ hours.

Remove the trussing strings, halve the partridges and chop the cabbage. Arrange the cabbage on a heated serving dish, place the partridges on top and surround with the bacon.

Roast Grouse

On the odd occasion in my life when I feel like celebrating but have to do so on my own I cook grouse. A terrific, tangy, dark meat bird with a wonderful breast and chewy legs, which, by the way, you can detach from the bird when cooked, if you like, and leave in the oven till you've finished eating the breast.

FOR EACH SERVING

1 young grouse, trussed, liver reserved
1 croûton, trimmed to fit each bird
butter

salt
freshly ground black pepper
pinch of chopped thyme

Remove the liver from the bird. Place the liver on the croûton with a knob of butter.

Season the grouse with salt, pepper and thyme. Melt some butter until foaming in a frying pan and seal the bird rapidly on all sides. Place the bird on the croûton and put into a roasting tin. Pop into a preheated oven, 425°F/ 220°C (gas mark 7), for 20–30 minutes, depending upon size, basting frequently with lots of butter.

Remove the trussing strings, whack the grouse on to a hot plate and strain all the butter from the roasting tin over it.

Serve with watercress and fried potatoes.

Roast Snipe

SERVES 4

4 snipe, prepared, trussed and barded
2 oz (50 g) butter, melted
salt

1 tablespoon brandy
freshly ground black pepper
large fried bread slices, to serve

Brush the snipe thoroughly with the butter and place in a roasting tin. Roast in a preheated oven, 425°F/220°C (gas mark 7), for 9–11 minutes. Remove any trussing strings from the snipe, salt the birds, draw them and cut into halves. Place on a dish and keep warm.

Pour any cooking juices from the roasting tin into a small pan with the brandy. Add any juices from the birds and mix well. Mash the innards with a fork and add to the mixture with salt and pepper to taste. Heat gently but do not boil.

To serve, place the fried bread on a serving dish, spoon over the sauce and top with the cooked snipe. Serve immediately.

Grilled Quail

Make sure the poulterer gives you their hearts and livers, which you can then chop up and spread on to the croûtons as well – it's the little extra effort that makes a simple dish taste really special.

FOR EACH SERVING

2 quail
sprigs of rosemary and thyme
salt
freshly ground black pepper
2 rashers of bacon

2 croûtons, trimmed to fit each bird
2-4 anchovy fillets
8 cloves of garlic, unpeeled and par-boiled
olive oil
1 measure of brandy, eau de vie or Armagnac

Stuff each quail with a sprig of rosemary and thyme. Truss the birds, season with salt and pepper and wrap each in a rasher of bacon. Chop up the hearts and livers and spread on each croûton, cover with 1 or 2 anchovy fillets and place the quail on top.

Place the quail in a lightly oiled grilling pan and surround with the garlic, still in its skin.

Sprinkle the lot with olive oil and place under a preheated very hot grill for about 15 minutes, turning the birds from time to time to ensure that they cook evenly.

When the birds are cooked, pour over the warmed brandy or alcohol and flame the lot. Remove the trussing strings and serve immediately with a salad of dandelion leaves.

If you burn the edges of the croûtons just trim them.

Rabbit Cooked in Ale and Mustard

Clive Imber at Michael's Brasserie, Newcastle upon Tyne

I love this dish, which I discovered at Michael's Brasserie in Newcastle,
because it demonstrates the wonderful way in which the best young
cooks – particularly in Britain – are combining local ingredients and
cooking them in a thoroughly modern way to create something that
tastes both traditional and delicious.

S E R V E S 4

1 large or 2 small rabbits, jointed
1 tablespoon flour
1 tablespoon dry English mustard
4 tablespoons oil
1 oz (25 g) butter
1 onion, diced
½ pint (300 ml) chicken stock, see page 43
¼ pint (150 ml) light ale
salt
freshly ground black pepper

1 tablespoon white wine vinegar
2 tablespoons brown sugar
2 teaspoons made English mustard

For the topping:
2 tablespoons oil
2 oz (50 g) butter
2 oz (50 g) fresh white breadcrumbs
1 tablespoon chopped tarragon
1 tablespoon chopped chives

Dip the rabbit joints in the flour and dry mustard. Reserve any flour and mustard that is left over. Heat the oil in a heavy frying pan and fry the joints until golden brown on all sides. Lift out the joints and place them in a casserole.

Add the butter to the pan and sweat the onion until soft. Stir in any remaining flour and mustard and cook for 1 minute. Add the stock and ale and bring to the boil. Season to taste with salt and pepper and add the vinegar, sugar and the made mustard. Pour over the rabbit and cook in a preheated oven, 325°F/160°C (gas mark 3), for 1 hour.

Meanwhile, heat together the oil and butter and fry the breadcrumbs until brown. Stir in the tarragon and chives.

To serve, arrange the rabbit on four heated plates and sprinkle with the herbed crumbs.

Rabbit Casserole

If you are lucky enough to live in the country you might be able to find a few wild mushrooms to pop into this dish – but do read your 'Mushroom Guide' first!

S E R V E S 4 - 6

knob of butter
1 large or 2 small rabbits, jointed, liver etc
  reserved
2 tablespoons tomato purée
8 juniper berries
1 clove of garlic, crushed
¼ pint (150 ml) red wine
½ pint (300 ml) well-flavoured game or
  chicken stock, see page 43

1 teaspoon chopped mixed herbs
2 bay leaves
1 teaspoon salt
freshly ground black pepper
8 oz (225 g) back bacon, rind removed
4 slices of white bread
lard or butter for frying

Melt the butter in a large flameproof casserole and brown the rabbit joints on all sides. Add the tomato purée and cook for 1–2 minutes, stirring constantly. Next, add the juniper berries with the garlic and wine. Boil for 2 minutes until the wine has reduced.

Pour the stock over the rabbit and add the chopped liver, mixed herbs, bay leaves and salt and pepper to taste. Cover and cook in a preheated oven, 325°F/160°C (gas mark 3), for about 2 hours.

Meanwhile, halve the bacon rashers and roll up. Thread on to skewers and grill until crisp. Remove from the skewers. Add the bacon rolls to the casserole and cook for a further 30 minutes.

Trim the crusts from the bread, then cut into triangles and fry until crisp in a little lard or butter.

To serve, pile the rabbit into a heated serving dish and remove the bay leaves. Arrange the croûtons around the dish.

Claud Arnaud's Stuffed Rabbit

Claud's restaurant in St Saturnin-d'Apt is my favourite in France. It's not the grandest place but his dishes, which reflect the very essence of Provence – both its physical and gastronomic characteristics – are so tasty that a 500-mile journey to get there is no hardship at all.

S E R V E S 4

2 rabbit saddles, weighing about 12 oz
* (350 g) each, livers and kidneys reserved*
3 fl oz (75 ml) nut oil
5 tablespoons dry white wine
½ pint (300 ml) water
salt
freshly ground black pepper

1 sprig of thyme
1 sprig of rosemary
some pig's caul
butter
1 lb (450 g) cooked broccoli, puréed, to
* garnish*

Carefully bone the saddles. First, using a small sharp knife, remove the back ribs by making a slit along either side of each rib to separate it from its surrounding flesh. Pull each rib up and twist sharply to break it away from the backbone. Loosen the backbone by cutting into the flesh covering the backbone inside the carcass – this exposes the bone. Cut away the flesh on either side of the backbone and slit round the bones that protrude from the vertebrae. Pull up the backbone, starting at the rib end, and snap it off at the pelvic bone. Cut the pelvic bone free from its surrounding flesh and remove.

Heat the oil in a pan and sauté the livers and kidneys for a few minutes, then set aside. Place the bones in the same pan and fry until browned. Pour in the wine and water. Cook gently for 30 minutes. Strain the stock through a fine sieve, discarding the bones, and reserve.

Season the saddles with salt and pepper and the herbs. Put the livers and kidneys inside and roll both saddles into cylinders. Cover each one with a piece of caul. Place in a roasting tin and roast in a preheated oven, 450°F/230°C (gas mark 8), for about 15 minutes, then remove and keep warm. Pour off the fat from the roasting tin, taking care to keep the little bits of juice from the rabbit, which you now reduce over a brisk direct heat.

Add the stock which you made earlier, whisking all the while. Bubble away until it is reduced by about one-third. To enrich it, beat in a knob of butter, so the sauce is smooth and shiny, and strain through a fine sieve.

Put a little of the sauce on each plate. Slice the rabbit and add to the plates. Garnish with the puréed broccoli.

Rabbit with Prunes

It is important to buy a wild rabbit from a good butcher's. Reared, frozen
rabbit pieces will not give the right flavour.

S E R V E S 4

1 large rabbit, jointed
salt
freshly ground black pepper
2 oz (50 g) butter
20 very small onions, peeled
4 oz (100 g) smoked bacon, diced

1 heaped teaspoon strong made mustard
2–3 sprigs of thyme
½ pint (300 ml) dry white wine
6 prunes, stoned and soaked in Armagnac
 or water
1 measure of brandy

Season the rabbit joints with salt and pepper. Melt the butter in a large pan and brown the rabbit pieces on all sides. Remove with a slotted spoon and set aside. Place the onions and bacon in the same pan and brown, then remove and put to one side.

Spread the mustard over the rabbit joints and put in a casserole. Add the onions, bacon and thyme and cover with the wine. Cook in a preheated oven, 350°F/180°C (gas mark 4), for about 1 hour.

Add the soaked prunes and brandy and cook for a further 30 minutes or so. Then strain off the juices and boil rapidly to reduce by one-third – pour back over the rabbit and onions etc.

Serve with baby turnips.

In the middle ages
rabbits were the exclusive
preserve of the nobility
and cost over £20 each
by modern standards.
Amazing ain't it?

Raised Winter Pie

The real luxury of good home-made food is having the time to prepare it
– but I reckon this pie is worth taking the day off work to cook.

S E R V E S 8

4 oz (100 g) cooked ham, diced
6 oz (175 g) rump or sirloin steak, diced
leftover cold meat from 1 cooked pheasant or
  2 pigeons or hare or whatever, boned and
  cut into small pieces
12 oz (350 g) minced pork
salt
freshly ground black pepper
¼–½ pint (150–300 ml) dry Madeira-
  flavoured game, chicken or veal glaze, see
  pages 41–3 (this is stock which has been
  reduced by three-quarters in a pan so that
  when cold it will set like a jelly)

For the hot water crust pastry:
1½ lb (675 g) plain flour
3 teaspoons salt
6 oz (175 g) lard (best quality)
½ pint (300 ml) milk or milk and water
beaten egg, to glaze

To make the pastry, sift the flour and salt into a large bowl and make a well in the flour. Melt the lard in the milk or milk and water, bring to the boil and pour into the dry ingredients. Working quickly, beat to form a soft dough. Lightly pinch together with one hand. Knead until smooth. Cover with clingfilm and leave to rest for 20–30 minutes, or until cool enough to handle. Cut off three-quarters of the pastry and roll it out on a lightly floured surface to an oval about ¼ inch (7 mm) in thickness. Keep the remaining pastry covered to prevent it drying out.

Place a 7 inch (18 cm) hinged pie mould on a baking sheet and lift the pastry into it. Press it carefully into the mould and trim to stand ¼ inch (7 mm) above the rim.

Mix together the ham, steak, game and minced pork. Season lightly to taste with salt and pepper. Spoon the mixture into the pie mould.

Roll out the remaining pastry and use it to cover the pie. Cut a hole in the centre of the pastry lid and brush the lid with a little of the beaten egg. Bake in a preheated oven, 425°F/220°C (gas mark 7), for 15–20 minutes, then reduce the temperature to 350°F/180°C (gas mark 4) and bake for a further 1 hour, or until tender when tested through the hole with a skewer. Remove the sides of the tin and brush the pie with the beaten egg.

Bake the pie for about another 30 minutes so that the sides cook to a golden colour, then cool. Pour the warm stock through the hole in the pastry lid. Allow to cool completely. Top up with extra stock, if necessary, to fill the pastry shell and leave overnight so the jelly is properly set and has absorbed all the flavours of the meat filling.

You can also make a similar pie using all uncooked meats, but it will take longer in the oven and should be cooked at a slightly lower temperature so the top crust doesn't burn before the filling is ready.

Hare in Soured Cream

I don't know how often the average Russian gets to eat a hare but when
he does this is probably how he'd cook it!

SERVES A GOOD 4

1 hare, skinned and jointed
small pieces of fat bacon (optional)
salt
2 carrots
1 turnip
1 parsnip
1 large onion
1 stick of celery
3 tablespoons oil or bacon fat
2 tablespoons butter
1-2 tablespoons flour
⅓ pint (200 ml) game stock, see page 43, or
    water
2-3 small ¼ pint (150 ml) cartons soured
    cream
freshly ground black pepper

For the marinade:
1 small carrot, finely chopped
1 celery root, finely chopped
½ small parsnip or 1 Hamburg parsley root,
    finely chopped
1 onion, finely chopped
6 bay leaves
12 whole allspice
6 whole cloves
seeds from 3 whole cardamom pods, crushed
⅓ pint (200 ml) cider vinegar
⅔ pint (400 ml) water
½ head of garlic, finely chopped

To make the marinade, mix together all the ingredients, except the garlic, in a pan and bring to the boil. Add the garlic. Allow to cool.

Pour the marinade over the hare. Cover and leave to marinate for 3-4 hours or overnight. Ideally, the meat should be larded by making small incisions and filling them with the fat bacon.

Lift the hare out of the marinade and pat dry. Salt the hare and put in a roasting tin with a macédoine (very finely chopped mixture) of carrot, turnip, parsnip, onion and celery and a little oil or bacon fat, and brown in a preheated oven, 425°F/220°C (gas mark 7), for about 20 minutes. Alternatively, put the hare and vegetables in a frying pan and cook on top of the

stove. Baste occasionally with the pan juices.

Melt the butter in a pan and stir in the flour. Cook the roux for a minute or two without allowing it to colour. Add the stock or water gradually, stirring constantly, and cook for 3-4 minutes. Tip in the soured cream and the juices from the roasting tin and season to taste with salt and pepper. Transfer the hare to a baking dish, pour over the soured cream mixture and cover. Reduce the oven temperature to 350°F/180°C (gas mark 4) and bake for a further 30-40 minutes at least.

Serve with boiled potatoes.

NB Hares can vary in toughness – always allow a little more cooking time if you are unsure.

Jugged Hare – a French Way

Do you ever get one of those days when disaster stalks you at every turn?
I recall coming home one New Year's Eve after being pulled up for
speeding *and* then getting a puncture and thinking well, never mind, at
least I've got a hare marinating and ready to cook for supper. I arrived
only to find that the bloody dog had eaten the raw hare, the marinade,
the lot. I had nothing else and, being New Year's Eve, all the restaurants
were booked so we just ate *foie gras*, cheese, Champagne and Burgundy,
and went hungry. And I'm afraid to admit I clouted the dog as well.
So, if you are going to prepare this elaborate and delicious recipe, lock
the dog out first.

SERVES 4

*1 hare, skinned and jointed, blood and liver
  reserved*
1 teaspoon vinegar
10 small onions, peeled
2-3 whole cloves
3 cloves of garlic, peeled and left whole
5 oz (150 g) lean smoked bacon, diced
*bouquet garni (1 sprig of thyme, 1 sprig of
  rosemary and 2 bay leaves, for example)*
2 tablespoons chopped parsley
salt
freshly ground black pepper
*2 fl oz (50 ml) plum brandy or any fruit
  alcohol*
2 bottles of strong red wine

4 fl oz (100 ml) olive oil
10 oz (275 g) butter
3 large carrots, chopped
*7 oz (200 g) field mushrooms or chanterelles,
  blanched*
knob of butter
1 tablespoon tomato purée (optional)

For the dumplings:
1 lb (450 g) plain flour
4 eggs, beaten
½ oz (15 g) salt
¼ pint (150 ml) water
butter for cooking

Wash and wipe dry the pieces of hare. Put the
hare, blood, liver and vinegar into a large bowl
(not aluminium) and toss in the onions, cloves,
garlic, bacon, bouquet garni, parsley and salt
and pepper. Add the brandy or alcohol and the
wine. Finally, pour in the oil. Cover and leave to
marinate in the refrigerator for 2 days.

Melt the first lot of butter in a large
flameproof casserole, lift out the onions from
the marinade and fry until golden. Add the
hare, bacon and carrots and fry until sealed,
then add the strained marinade and bouquet
garni. Pop in a preheated oven, 350°F/180°C

(gas mark 4), for at least 1 hour. After 45 minutes, add the mushrooms.

Meanwhile, make the dumplings. Sift the
flour into a large bowl. Make a well in the
centre and pour in the eggs and salt. Slowly add
the water and mix from the centre, gradually
drawing in the flour, to make a smooth batter.

Bring 5 pints (2.8 litres) salted water to the
boil. Pour some of the dough on to a plate and
plunge the plate into the water for a few seconds. Remove and cut the dough into very
small pieces. Return the dumplings to the
water. They will be cooked when they float to

the surface. Use up the remaining dough in the same way.

Just before serving the hare, warm the dumplings by tossing them in butter in a large pan.

When the hare is tender, strain the sauce into a pan and bring to the boil. Reduce it a little, add pepper and the knob of butter and, if it's too winey, the tomato purée. Whisk together, strain the sauce back over the hare, onions, bacon, carrots and mushrooms and serve.

Roast Saddle of Hare

I spend a lot of time in Devon and a friendly farmer often gives me a hare – just about my favourite 'game'. Not only that but in a stream at the bottom of my garden is a wild watercress bed! So I cook this recipe quite often.

SERVES 2

1 oz (25 g) butter
1 saddle of hare
about 8 fl oz (250 ml) rich game stock, see
  page 43
1 teaspoon tomato purée

2 tablespoons double cream
walnut-sized knob of butter
salt
freshly ground black pepper

Melt the first lot of butter in a large pan and brown the hare on all sides. Place it, breast side down, in a roasting tin with a bit of butter and pop it into a preheated oven, 425°F/ 220°C (gas mark 7), for about 10 minutes. Turn it breast side up, add the stock and cook for a further 10 minutes or so. Remove the tin from the oven and put the hare to one side in a warm place (it should be pink inside and this 'resting period' will allow the cooking process to finish).

Meanwhile, over a low heat, bubble up the juices in the roasting tin and thoroughly stir in the tomato purée and cream, then whisk in the knob of butter. Season to taste with salt and pepper. By this time some of the juices may have run from the saddle, so tip those into the sauce. Carve the hare lengthways in thin slices and strain the sauce over them.

Serve with some crisp, winter vegetable and small roast or fried potatoes. Or, simply, some fresh, plain pasta and a salad of watercress.

You can prepare small birds like teal in the same way. And if you find the cream too rich, simply leave it out and you will be left with a brown, gamey sauce, which is just as delicious. Quite rightly, many object to the killing of wildlife as gluttony – but as the man said, '*Chacun à son goût.*'

Venison with Cherry Liqueur

This is truly a gastronomic dish but very simple to prepare as long as
you have some good stock to hand.

SERVES 4

*1¾ lb (800 g) venison fillet, trimmed of all
tough membrane, fat and sinew and cut
into eight ½ inch (1 cm) slices – ask the
butcher to do this for you
freshly ground black pepper
little butter for frying
good drop of morello cherry liqueur*

*¾ pint (450 ml) rich game stock, see page 43
1 tablespoon tomato purée
walnut-sized knob of butter
salt
sprigs of watercress, trimmed, to garnish*

Pat the meat dry, then season well with lots of
black pepper. Melt the butter until foaming in
a heavy-based frying pan and cook the meat
for a minute or two on each side so that it
sears and chars well – just like a regular steak.
Reduce the heat and cook for a minute or two
on each side, then tip in the cherry liqueur
and flame it. As the liquid all but disappears,
tip in the stock, remove the meat with a
slotted spoon and set aside in a warm place
(let it rest and add any juices that seep out to
the finished sauce at the last minute).

Increase the heat, add the tomato purée
and bubble the sauce until it begins to
thicken and go a dark vermilion shiny colour.
Reduce the heat and whisk in the knob of butter. Check the seasoning and add a lot more
black pepper. Pour the sauce on to a heated
serving dish, place the cooked venison fillet
on top and garnish with sprigs of crunchy
watercress.

Serve with plain noodles, or fried potatoes
and a fresh green vegetable.

Medallions of Venison with Shallots in Marsala Sauce

Kate Smith at Royal Oak Hotel, Sevenoaks

This is pure hedonism: a rich dish of wild mushrooms, offal and game. Nature and gastronomy in perfect harmony.

SERVES 6

2 oz (50 g) calves' or lambs' sweetbreads
1 saddle of venison, preferably roebuck that has been well hung for two to three weeks (of course, the butcher does that)
¾ pint (450 ml) veal stock, see page 41
clarified butter, see page 35

6 oz (175 g) shallots, chopped
2 tablespoons Marsala
salt
freshly ground black pepper
6 oz (175 g) girolles, chopped, but leave some whole
chopped parsley, to garnish (optional)

Soak the sweetbreads in cold water for several hours to remove any blood. Drain and blanch them in a pan of boiling salted water. Drain and allow to cool. Press them between two boards or plates with a weight on top for 1–2 hours. Pick over the sweetbreads, removing all skin and membrane, slice them evenly and set aside.

Remove the meat from the bones and trim off any tough sinew or fat. Cut the meat into medallions, about ½ inch (1 cm) thick. Put the stock in a pan and boil briskly until it is reduced by about ¼ pint (150 ml) and is of a slightly syrupy consistency.

Melt a little clarified butter in a pan and sauté the shallots until softened. Deglaze the pan with Marsala and add the reduced stock. Cook for perhaps 20 minutes, until the stock is reduced by one-third. Season the medallions with salt and pepper and either grill under a fierce heat or sauté them in a little clarified butter for 3–5 minutes, leaving them very pink. Set aside and keep warm while you gently sauté the girolles and sweetbreads in some more clarified butter for 6–8 minutes, until lightly cooked. Stir in the cooked shallots and sauce.

Arrange the medallions on a warmed serving dish, pile the sauce around them and sprinkle with a little chopped parsley, if liked. Serve with whole baby carrots.

EAT MORE MEAT

CHAPTER 8

The Brown Rice Conspiracy

T he greatest novel of the future ever written. The chilling story of a government plot code-named 'Green for Lettuce' and one man's deadly mission to thwart it.

'It's all too likely to come true.' – *The Independent*
'Unnerving.' – *Farmer's Weekly*
'A masterpiece.' – *Green Cuisine*

'After a bloodless coup a dictator crazed by spinach juice brutally imposes his masterplan on an unsuspecting nation. Squads of armed vegetarians ransack restaurants, execute butchers, burn cookery books and destroy farms as a helpless population watches. Terrified.

'Not since Herod has the world witnessed mass slaughter on such a scale. Every ox, cow, lamb, goat, sheep and pig is allowed to run amok. Meat-eating citizens caught by the dreaded Secret Meat Police are force-fed lentils and water.

'Publishers, journalists, TV producers and food guide editors squeal like castrated lambs as restaurant, after wine bar, after pub is razed to the ground. The pavements of London are awash with claret and Burgundy. Weeping editors desperately licking the bloody torrent are dragged screaming from the gutters and interned on forced labour mushroom farms.

'And every word is hammered on the anvil of truth.'

Of course, dear gastronauts, such a book does not exist. It's just my little joke and I think a rather neat way to introduce the next set of recipes. Meat. I can't imagine a world without meat, can you? *Bon appetit.*

Roast Beef

There are two things to say about roast beef. One, even if you can afford it only once a year, you must buy the best joint, marbled with fat, and not one of those blood red slabs you find in certain shops, which has a piece of fat from some other animal wrapped around it encased in a plastic net. Forget it.

Two, you must roast the beef slowly on a rack in the oven, allowing the dripping to dribble on to the potatoes and/or Yorkshire pudding beneath – delicious!

Make sure the meat is at room temperature before cooking. Mix 2 tablespoons flour, 1 tablespoon dry mustard and some freshly ground black pepper – quite a lot – then coat the fat of the beef with the mixture.

Seal the juices by frying the meat quickly on all sides in a little beef dripping. Place the joint on a rack in a roasting tin, fat-side up, and roast in a preheated oven, 400°F/200°C (gas mark 6), for 20 minutes. Reduce the temperature to 325°F/160°C (gas mark 3) and continue cooking, basting regularly, for 15–20 minutes per 1 lb (450 g), or longer, if you like well done meat. Test with a skewer to see if it is cooked enough – the juices run clear when it's done.

Allow the meat to rest in a warm place before serving, so that it carves easily and is succulent and tender.

Steak

Grilled

An elaborate fillet steak stuffed with morels à la Roux Brothers is a very fine feast – but I'd like to say a word or two in praise of the humble, unadorned steak.

As a confirmed carnivore, I happen to think that a well grilled steak is pretty unbeatable, but it is a dish frequently ruined by people who think that, thanks to some special magic, it will taste delicious without them having to pay any attention to it whatsoever.

Well, that isn't the case. Here are the golden rules:

■ You must buy meat of the finest quality you can afford: bright red, firm, finely grained and not moist.

■ The steak must be at room temperature before you start cooking.

■ The grill must be absolutely hot before you put the steak anywhere near it, so that the juices are sealed in immediately, keeping the meat tender and moist.

The same principle applies to the barbecue. Cooking over an open fire is almost as old as man, yet we still have trouble getting it right. The rule is:

■ You must not start cooking on your charcoal grill until the flames have died away and the ashes are covered in a fine white dust.

Fried/Sautéed

My favourite way of cooking steaks is in a cast iron griddle pan, which allows the fat to drain away. You use it on top of the stove, but again, it's the same maxim: you must get it blasting hot before you put the steak in.

■ The second thing you must do, if you are using a griddle pan, is to hold the steak, which must be very lightly brushed with oil, vertically against the griddle, on its fatty edge, so that the fat sizzles and crisps up and the excess runs away. Then, if you like your steak rare, the fat won't be uncooked and disgusting.

■ You must not salt the meat too early, or it will draw the blood and leave the steak soggy. Wait until the meat is sealed all round. Pepper turns bitter during cooking and is best put on the table.
■ After going through the trauma of grilling or frying, the meat must be allowed to 'rest' before you eat it. It is behaving just as you would if you put your hand on to a red hot grill: tensing up with shock. So we have to keep it warm and let it relax for a few minutes so that it will be tender.

Simply grilled steaks are terrific with the kind of sauce you can prepare separately and then pour over the top.
The more sophisticated way of cooking steak with a sauce, Roux Brothers' style, involves sautéing the meat in unsalted butter, removing it, and then making the sauce in the same pan, scraping up all those brilliant meaty bits, which cling to the bottom of the pan, to enrich the sauce.
Most of the recipes that follow can be prepared in either way.

Red Wine Sauce with Beef Marrow

SERVES 4

½ oz (15 g) unsalted butter
½ teaspoon chopped shallot
½ wineglass red Bordeaux wine
pinch of crushed peppercorns

small piece of bay leaf
1 sprig of thyme
¼ pint (150 ml) veal glaze, see page 42
1 oz (25 g) beef marrow, very fresh

Melt half of the butter in a pan until very hot, add the shallot and brown lightly. Add the wine and seasonings, bring the sauce to the boil and reduce rapidly until 2 tablespoons remain. Tip in the veal glaze and boil for 15 minutes. Strain the sauce through a very fine sieve, return to the pan and bring to the boil again. Check the seasoning and set aside until ready to serve.

Poach the marrow in a bowl of lightly salted hot water for 3–5 minutes. Drain and put to one side. Just before serving, warm the sauce slightly. Remove from the heat and, stirring constantly with a wooden spoon, add the remaining butter. Remove the bay leaf and pour the sauce over the steaks. Pop the marrow on top.

Blue Cheese Sauce

For best results, use this sauce with a thick-cut steak. Grill the steak to
your liking, remove and slice. Spread with an ample quantity of the sauce
and return to the grill to melt the cheese until it bubbles –
about 1 minute. Then serve immediately.

SERVES 6

1 clove of garlic
2 tablespoons brandy
4 oz (100 g) blue cheese, rinded

3 tablespoons olive oil
freshly ground black pepper

Pound the garlic to a paste and mix with the
brandy. Gradually beat in the blue cheese, oil
and pepper to taste.

(Maybe add a tiny drop of cream too.)

Chasseur Sauce

SERVES 4

1 tablespoon oil
1 oz (25 g) unsalted butter
2 oz (50 g) mushrooms, white and firm,
  washed, drained and finely chopped or
  sliced
½ teaspoon chopped shallots

1-2 ripe tomatoes, skinned, seeded, juice
  removed and coarsely chopped
½ wineglass of dry white wine
¼ pint (150 ml) veal glaze, see page 42
chopped chervil and tarragon

Heat together the oil and a little of the butter in
a sauté pan and brown the mushrooms over a
high heat. At that point add the shallots and
heat for a few seconds. Stir in the tomatoes,
wine and veal glaze.

Just before serving, remove from the heat
and finish the sauce by adding the remaining
butter and a good sprinkling of the chervil and
tarragon.

NOTE
Don't forget that while the steak is resting it will release some juices – always pour this
juice back into the finished sauce.

Mushroom Sauce

S E R V E S   4

1 oz (25 g) unsalted butter
3 shallots, chopped
4 oz (100 g) mushrooms (of course, you
can use wild mushrooms, chanterelles or
morels etc)

½ wineglass of dry white wine
½ pint (300 ml) veal glaze, see page 42
1 sprig of parsley, chopped
dash of lemon juice

Melt a little of the butter in a sauté pan until light brown and slowly cook the shallots. Then add the mushrooms, washed, drained and finely chopped at the last moment to keep them from turning brown. Cook the mushrooms over a very high heat and, stirring constantly, let the juices reduce. Pour in the wine and reduce it almost completely. Add the veal glaze. Simmer the sauce over a low heat for 10 minutes. Finish the sauce by removing from the heat, adding the remaining butter and, at the last minute, the parsley and lemon juice.

N O T E
If any of the sauce recipes using veal glaze need a little more liquid you can always add one of your cubes of veal stock. (Remember the stock section at the beginning of the book! – see pages 41–4.)

Fillet Steaks Béarnaise

A simple but delicious dish. Do not swamp it with soggy vegetables as they tend to in restaurants. All this needs is a few matchstick chips or sauté potatoes and a sprig of watercress.

S E R V E S   4

freshly ground black pepper
4 fillet steaks, cut 1 inch (2.5 cm) thick
oil
½ oz (15 g) butter
6 tablespoons strong beef stock, see page 42

For the béarnaise:
3 tablespoons red wine vinegar
2 shallots, finely chopped

5 teaspoons chopped tarragon
1 teaspoon white peppercorns, coarsely
*   crushed*
1 bay leaf
4 egg yolks
8 oz (225 g) butter, at room temperature
3 teaspoons chopped chervil
salt

Put a good few twists of pepper on each side of the steaks, brush with a little oil and leave to marinate for at least 1 hour at room temperature.

To make the sauce, pour the vinegar into a pan with the shallots, tarragon, peppercorns and bay leaf. Simmer until the mixture is reduced by half. Remove from the heat, discard the bay leaf and allow to cool. Place the egg yolks in a bowl with a knob of the butter and pour on the vinegar mixture. Set the bowl over a pan half-filled with very hot water. Whisk well for several minutes, until the mixture is very creamy. Add the butter a knob at a time, whisking constantly, but do not overheat.

When all the butter has been added and the sauce has the consistency of whipped cream, remove from the heat. Stir in the chervil and a little salt to taste. Keep warm by setting the bowl over another bowl filled with warm water.

Set a heavy frying pan or steak griddle over a very high heat for 15 seconds, drop in the butter and immediately put in the steaks. Turn over, reduce the heat slightly, cook for 3 minutes, turn again and cook for a further 3 minutes. Lift on to a warmed serving dish. Deglaze the pan with the stock, reduce a little, check the seasoning and pour round the steaks.

To serve, put a teaspoonful of béarnaise on the top of each steak.

Roast Sirloin Steak with Mustard

SERVES 4

1 tablespoon made mustard
4 tablespoons oil
salt
freshly ground black pepper

1 × 2 lb (900 g) sirloin steak
4 rashers of smoked bacon, rind removed
4 tomatoes

Whisk together the mustard, oil, salt and pepper in a bowl (not aluminium), add the steak and leave to marinate for at least 30 minutes. Lift out the steak and place it on a griddle over a roasting tin to collect the juices. Cook in a preheated oven, 425°F/220°C (gas mark 7), for 30 minutes, turning frequently. Apply the remaining marinade as it cooks. Just before the steak is ready, grill the bacon and tomatoes.

Carve the steak into thin slices along the grain, pour over any juices from the roasting tin and serve with the crisply grilled bacon and tomatoes.

Grilled Sirloin Steak with Wine Butter

SERVES 4

4 × 8 oz (225 g) sirloin steaks
1 tablespoon walnut oil
salt

freshly ground black pepper
3 oz (75 g) wine butter, see page 35

Rub each steak well with the oil. Cook the steaks under a preheated grill for 3–4 minutes on each side. Place them on a warmed serving dish, add salt and pepper to taste and a slice of wine butter to each steak.

Serve with sprigs of watercress and matchstick chips.

Steak Tartare

This is a simply delicious dish – but it is also the bane of the restaurateur's life, because he suffers from ill-educated customers who don't really know what it is supposed to taste like. Equally, it is the bane of the true gastronaut's life, because he is frequently confronted with ignorant restaurateurs who don't know how to make this brilliant dish truly edible.

So, this is the way to do it. Just make sure all your ingredients are cool, prepare it seconds before you want to eat it, and have on hand plenty of iced vodka, or the beer that made Milwaukee famous: iced Schlitz.

SERVES 2

8 oz (225 g) good quality steak (fillet, rump or sirloin, for example)
2 egg yolks

To serve:
2 oz (50 g) can anchovy fillets, drained and chopped

2 tablespoons chopped parsley
2 tablespoons capers, chopped
2 tablespoons finely chopped red or white onion
salt
freshly ground black pepper

Chop by hand or mince the steak until very fine in texture – chopping by hand helps to keep in the juices. Divide into two equal portions and shape each into a small mound. Place in the centre of two individual serving plates and make a small hollow in the centre of each. Carefully place the egg yolks in the hollows.

Either surround the beef mounds with equal quantities of the anchovy fillets, parsley, capers, onion and salt and pepper or place them on small separate saucers for selection.

To eat, the beef is mixed with the accompaniments according to taste. Serve with buttered rye bread.

Paupiettes of Beef with Lemon Stuffing

Colin White at Whites, Cricklade

S E R V E S   6 - 8

about 12-16 thin slices of topside or silverside
of beef
1 tablespoon vegetable oil
1 oz (25 g) butter
piece of pork skin

For the stuffing:
6 oz (175 g) butter
12 oz (350 g) bacon, chopped
12 onions, chopped
12 oz (350 g) mushrooms, sliced
4-6 cloves of garlic, chopped
6 tablespoons fresh white breadcrumbs

chopped parsley and lemon balm
grated zest of 6 lemons
4 eggs
salt
freshly ground black pepper

For the sauce:
4 onions, finely chopped
1 bottle of dry white wine
grated zest of 1 lemon
chopped parsley and thyme
enough beef stock, see page 42, to almost
cover the meat

To make the stuffing, melt the butter in a pan and cook the bacon and onions. Add the mushrooms and cook rapidly over a high heat to reduce. Add the remaining stuffing ingredients and mix well. Season to taste with salt and pepper.

Spread about 1 tablespoon of the stuffing on each steak. Roll the steaks up and tie with thin string at each end and at the centre. Heat together the oil and butter in a pan and fry the paupiettes quickly to seal. Lift out and place in a flameproof casserole.

To make the sauce, fry the onions in the pan the meat was cooked in and then deglaze the pan with the wine. Transfer to the casserole, add the remaining sauce ingredients and cover with the pork skin and a tightly-fitting lid. Cook gently for about 1½ hours, or until the meat is tender.

Lift out the paupiettes carefully, remove the string and place on a warmed serving dish. Cover with the sauce.

Winter Beef Stew with Dumplings

This is a classic example of wonderful, simple English food, born out of expediency. The dumplings were put in to stretch the meat, and the juices from the beef seeped into them, so you could almost convince yourself that you were eating a bit more meat.

SERVES 4-6

1½ oz (40 g) dripping
1½ lb (675 g) lean stewing or braising steak, gristle and fat removed and cubed
1 lb (450 g) small onions, sliced
1 tablespoon flour
1½ pints (900 ml) beef stock, see page 42
1 tablespoon tomato purée
salt
freshly ground black pepper
1 lb (450 g) carrots, cut across into chunks (if you like, you could use peeled and cubed swedes, turnips and parsnips instead)
1 bay leaf

For the dumplings:
6 oz (175 g) self-raising flour
3 oz (75 g) shredded suet
1 tablespoon chopped parsley
salt
freshly ground black pepper
water to mix

Melt the dripping in a large, heavy-based pan and fry the meat and onions until well browned on all sides. Sprinkle in the flour and mix well. Gradually add the stock and tomato purée, stirring constantly. Bring up to the boil and season generously with salt and pepper. Reduce the heat, cover and simmer for 1 hour. Add the carrots (or other vegetables, if using) and the bay leaf to the stew and simmer for a further hour.

Meanwhile, make the dumplings. Sift the flour into a bowl. Add the suet, parsley, and salt and pepper to taste. Gradually add sufficient water and mix to form a soft but manageable dough. Divide and shape the dough into eight small balls, using floured hands. Add the dumplings to the stew, cover and cook for a further 15–20 minutes, or until the dumplings are swollen, light and fluffy. Remove the bay leaf and serve immediately.

Poached Fillet Steak with Roast Shallots and Red Wine Sauce

Shaun Hill at Gidleigh Park, Chagford

SERVES 4

12 shallots
1 pint (600 ml) beef stock, see page 42
1 pint (600 ml) red wine

1¼ lb (550 g) beef fillet
1 teaspoon arrowroot

Roast the whole shallots in a small roasting tin or tray. Mix the stock and wine in a pan and bring to the boil. Add the beef fillet and poach for about 20–30 minutes, until rare – or how you like it. Lift out the meat and allow it to rest for a few minutes. Reduce the stock over a brisk heat and then whisk in the arrowroot dissolved in a little cold water. The sauce should not be too thick.

Slice the fillet and place on warmed plates with the shallots. Strain the sauce through a fine sieve over the meat.

Beef Stewed in Red Burgundy

This wonderful dish is served in different ways throughout France – but I reckon this is the classic way to prepare it. Do cook it slowly and, if possible, allow it to cool overnight once cooked. Skim off any fat from the surface, reheat gently and serve.

SERVES 6

3 lb (1.4 kg) well hung beef (shin, shoulder or
    neck)
5 onions, roughly chopped
5 carrots, roughly chopped
5 shallots, roughly chopped
3 cloves of garlic, chopped
2 sprigs of thyme
2 bay leaves
1 bunch of parsley, roughly chopped
2 bottles of red Burgundy
6 thick rashers of streaky bacon, diced

1 large wineglass of brandy
¼ pint (150 ml) Madeira or very dry sherry
1 small calf's foot or even 1 chopped pig's
    trotter (optional, but it enriches the sauce
    beautifully)
butter
9 oz (250 g) mushrooms
7 oz (200 g) baby onions
salt
freshly ground black pepper

Trim off excess fat from the beef and cut it into small cubes. Put it in a large bowl (not aluminium) with the onions, carrots, shallots, garlic and herbs and pour over the wine. Leave

174

EAT MORE MEAT

to marinate overnight. Lift out the meat and strain and reserve the liquid.

Fry the bacon, without additional fat, in a large, heavy-based pan. Add the meat and brown it on all sides. Pour over the brandy and flame. Add the Madeira or sherry and barely cover with the reserved marinade. Stir in the calf's foot or pig's trotter, if using. Cover and simmer on a low heat for 3 hours. Add more marinade if the stew seems to be drying out.

Melt a little butter in a pan and fry the mushrooms. Add to the meat and throw in the baby onions. Cook the stew for a further 10–15 minutes, until the onions are tender. Season to taste with salt and pepper and remove the calf's foot or pig's trotter before serving.

Serve very hot just with boiled potatoes or plain pasta.

PS This is also a useful dish to make in large quantities and then freeze half for another time.

Meat Fritters

This is a good way to use the remains of roast chicken, beef, lamb or pork, or any meat you fancy or happen to have in the larder.

SERVES 4

You prepare the choux pastry first by sifting 9 oz (250 g) plain flour on to a sheet of paper. Then boil ½ pint (300 ml) water with ½ pint (300 ml) dry white wine, 2 oz (50 g) butter and a pinch of salt. Reduce the heat, 'shoot' in the flour and stir like crazy until it forms a smooth ball. Pull the pan off the heat altogether and beat in 6 eggs, one at a time, mixing thoroughly between each addition. Leave to rest for about 20 minutes.

Meanwhile, chop 14 oz (400 g) meat very finely. Season to taste with salt and pepper. Heat some cooking oil in a pan. Mix together the meat and pastry. Roll into bite-sized balls and deep-fry until they swell up and turn golden. Drain them on absorbent kitchen paper.

Serve with some tartar sauce, which is simply mayonnaise, see page 34, with chopped capers, gherkins and parsley added to it.

Now all you need to do is prepare a simple salad of good crisp lettuce and open the wine.

Meat balls.

There was a terrific sequence in "the Godfather" about cooking meat balls. Anyway although fresh meat is best you can use left over cooked meats equally well. If you use a food processor don't over mince the meat or you will get a paste which will result in meat bullets. Which as the film points out are for killing people not feeding them!!

A meat bullet

A meat ball

Spaghetti with Meatballs

SERVES 4

1 lb (450 g) minced beef
1 teaspoon chopped basil, oregano or mixed herbs
salt
freshly ground black pepper
1 tablespoon olive oil
1 onion, chopped
1-2 cloves of garlic, finely chopped or crushed
1 lb (450 g) tomatoes, skinned and chopped
2 tablespoons tomato purée
1 bay leaf
8 oz (225 g) dried spaghetti or rather more if fresh
grated Parmesan cheese

Mix the minced beef in a bowl with some of the chopped herbs and salt and pepper to taste. Divide and shape the mixture into small, round balls. Heat the oil in a pan and sauté the onion and garlic for 4-5 minutes. Add the meatballs and brown on all sides, turning frequently.

Add the tomatoes, tomato purée, remaining herbs, bay leaf and check the seasoning. Cover the pan and simmer gently for 30 minutes.

Meanwhile, cook the spaghetti in a large pan of boiling salted water for about 10-12 minutes (but cook fresh for 2-3 minutes), until it is just tender but still firm, *al dente*. Drain well, then lay the spaghetti on a large, warmed serving dish and spoon the meatballs and their sauce into the centre. Fish out the bay leaf and sprinkle with a little grated Parmesan cheese to serve.

Bulgarian Meatballs

SERVES 6

2 lb (900 g) minced beef
10 oz (275 g) minced lamb
2 oz (50 g) onion, finely chopped
4 oz (100 g) cooking fat
3 cloves of garlic, crushed
½ oz (15 g) freshly ground black pepper
salt

Mince the meats together in a mincer or food processor. Mix together all the ingredients in a large bowl. Divide and shape the mixture into walnut-sized balls. Chill until the mixture becomes firm. Place under a preheated hot grill for about 10 minutes, until cooked, turning frequently.

Serve hot with potatoes and pickles.

Russian Meatballs

SERVES 4

2 oz (50 g) butter
1 tablespoon flour
¼ pint (150 ml) milk
1 lb (450 g) minced beef
2 tablespoons chopped coriander leaves
3 tablespoons chopped parsley
¾ teaspoon salt
½ teaspoon freshly ground black pepper
2 onions, chopped
2 tablespoons vodka
1 egg
veal or chicken stock for cooking the meatballs, see page 41 or 43

Melt the butter in a pan and stir in the flour. Cook the *roux* for a couple of minutes over a gentle heat, stirring constantly, then slowly add the milk until you have a thick smooth sauce. Remove from the heat and, when the sauce has cooled slightly, add to the meat with the herbs, salt and pepper, onions, vodka and egg. Tip the whole mixture into a food processor or blender and whizz for a minute, adding a couple of tablespoons of water if the mixture is too thick.

Bring the stock to a simmer in a pan and drop in the meat mixture, a heaped teaspoonful at a time, and cook gently. The meatballs are ready when they rise to the surface. Drain with a slotted spoon and place on a warmed serving dish.

Serve with potatoes or pasta.

I have a dream! I want to cook for Gorbachev. That's why I've put all these Russian recipes in the book in the hope that he might invite me to pop over and conjure up some dramatic dishes in the manner of the old Tsars. And, anyway, it's a good excuse to drink some vodka.

Russian Burgers

SERVES 4

1 lb (450 g) minced beef
2 red peppers, cored, seeded, blanched and
    finely chopped
1½ teaspoons caraway seeds
½ teaspoon cayenne pepper

1 head of garlic, finely minced
½ tablespoon chopped mint
beaten egg white and fresh white
    breadcrumbs for coating
oil for frying

Mix the beef with all the remaining ingredients except the egg white, breadcrumbs and oil and put the whole mixture through a mincer again or pound in a food processor. With floured hands shape into flattish rounds, coat in the egg white and breadcrumbs and fry for about 8 minutes on each side, depending on size.

Serve with Tomato Sauce, see page 37, or cooked tomatoes.

Beef Steak, Russian Style

SERVES 6

2 lb (900 g) minced beef steak
4 oz (100 g) butter, melted
salt
freshly ground black pepper
3 fl oz (75 ml) milk

cooking fat
2 oz (50 g) flour
1 pint (600 ml) soured cream
1½ lb (675 g) potatoes, diced
chopped sprigs of parsley, to garnish

Place the minced beef in a bowl and add some of the melted butter, salt, pepper and the milk. With floured hands divide and shape into walnut-sized balls, then fry them in a little hot cooking fat. Lift them out and keep warm. Mix the remaining butter with the flour in a pan and cook for a minute or two. Tip in the soured cream. Add salt to taste and bring to the boil. Fry the potatoes in cooking fat, then place in a serving dish. Pile on the fried meatballs and pour over the soured cream sauce. Sprinkle with the parsley.

Oxtail Stew

The British Government ought to make Oxtail Stew compulsory in places like Heathrow Airport, and ports of entry, so people can have at least one decent British meal when they arrive!

Oxtails make the most delicious stews, and they aren't expensive. But as they are fatty, you should cook the stew the day before you want to eat it, then strain off the fat before you reheat it.

SERVES 4

2 lb (900 kg) oxtail
2 tablespoons olive oil
2 oz (50 g) fat bacon, rind removed and
  chopped
1 onion, chopped
1 clove of garlic, finely chopped
8 fl oz (250 ml) dry white wine
salt

freshly ground black pepper
about ½ pint (300 ml) hot meat stock, see
  pages 41–2
2 sticks of celery, cut into 1½ inch (4 cm)
  lengths
4 tomatoes, skinned and quartered
chopped parsley, to garnish

Cut the oxtail into 2 inch (5 cm) pieces, wash and dry well. Heat the oil in a flameproof casserole and sauté the fat bacon, onion and garlic until the onion is transparent. Add the oxtail and cook on all sides until brown.

Add the wine and season with a little salt and pepper. Cover and braise over a gentle heat for about 2 hours, shaking the pan occasionally and adding a little stock from time to time to keep the oxtail moist.

About 30 minutes before the end of the cooking time, add the celery and about 10 minutes before the end of cooking, throw in the tomatoes, mixing well. Taste and adjust the seasoning before serving sprinkled with chopped parsley.

Oxtail with Grapes

Again, this dish should be cooked the day before.

SERVES 6

3 lb (1.4 kg) jointed oxtail
1 tablespoon vegetable oil
1 oz (25 g) butter
1 large onion, diced
2 large carrots, finely diced
1 clove of garlic, chopped
1 large wineglass of dry sherry

1 tablespoon tomato purée
1 bay leaf
1 teaspoon chopped thyme
1 tablespoon chopped parsley
salt
freshly ground black pepper
1 lb (450 g) seedless grapes

Trim off excess fat from the oxtail, wash and dry well. Heat together the oil and butter in a heavy-based pan and brown the meat with the onion, carrots and garlic. Strain off surplus fat, pour over the sherry and flame.

Stir in the tomato purée and add the herbs. Season to taste with salt and pepper and pour in enough cold water to cover. Bring up to the boil, then cover with a lid and cook very slowly for at least 2 hours.

When the oxtail is tender, remove the pan from the heat and allow to cool. Skim off the fat from the surface and discard the bay leaf.

To serve, add the grapes and reheat gently until the fruit is soft, about 10–15 minutes.

Saltimbocca

Elizabeth David's recipe for Saltimbocca has never been bettered by any Italian restaurant I have visited in twenty years. I include it here as a token of respect to the single most influential cookery writer this country has ever produced. This recipe is taken from *Italian Food* (Penguin Books, 1954).

VARY THE QUANTITIES DEPENDING ON THE NUMBER YOU ARE SERVING

2 or 3 slices of veal per person
2 or 3 slices of raw or cooked ham, the same
   size as the slices of veal
sage leaves
salt

freshly ground black pepper
butter
1 wineglass of Marsala or dry white wine
croûtons, to garnish

Flatten out the slices of veal between sheets of greaseproof paper with a rolling pin or meat mallet until they are as thin as possible. On each one lay a slice of ham and a leaf of sage. Season to taste with salt and pepper. Make each one into a little roll and secure with a toothpick. Melt some butter in a pan and cook the rolls gently until they are well browned all over, then pour over the Marsala or white wine. Let it bubble for a minute, cover the pan and simmer for about 10-15 minutes, until the meat is tender.

Serve with croûtons.

Blanquette of Veal

This is one of those dishes you get offered all the time in France when you visit friends for lunch. It's simple and traditional – peasant food really – and I like it very much.

S E R V E S 4 - 6

1 stick of celery, chopped
1 carrot, chopped
2 whole cloves
1 bay leaf
1½ lb (675 g) lean boneless pie veal, trimmed
    and cut into 1½ inch (4 cm) chunks
about 1 pint (600 ml) veal or chicken stock,
    see page 41 or 43

4 fl oz (100 ml) dry Martini or white wine
12 button onions, peeled and blanched in
    boiling water for 2-3 minutes
12 oz (350 g) button mushrooms
2 egg yolks
4 tablespoons double or whipping cream
chopped dill, to garnish

Put the celery, carrot, cloves and bay leaf on a square of muslin and tie into a bag with string to make a bouquet garni. Put the bouquet garni, veal and stock into a pan and bring to the boil. Skim off any scum from the surface. Reduce the heat, add the Martini or wine, cover and simmer for about 1 hour.

Add the onions and mushrooms, bring back to the boil, then cover again and simmer for a further 30 minutes, or until the veal is tender.

Fish out and discard the bouquet garni.

Whisk together the egg yolks and cream, then whisk in a little of the hot cooking juices. Slowly pour the mixture into the pan, stirring rapidly to prevent lumps forming. Reduce the heat to very low. Cook gently, stirring constantly, until the sauce has thickened, without allowing it to boil.

Serve with hot noodles or rice and garnish with the dill.

Wiener Schnitzel

These are great. Just beat them out thinly and fry them quickly in butter and fresh crumbs.

SERVES 6

6 veal escalopes, cut about ¼ inch
   (7 mm) thick
2 eggs
salt
½ teaspoon freshly ground black pepper
5 tablespoons flour
6 oz (175 g) fresh white breadcrumbs
2-4 oz (50-100 g) butter

For the garnish:
lemon wedges
chopped parsley
anchovy fillets
capers

Put the escalopes between two sheets of greaseproof paper and pound them with a meat mallet or rolling pin until they are about ⅛ inch (3 mm) thick.

Beat together the eggs, salt and pepper in a bowl. Spread the flour on a sheet of greaseproof paper and the breadcrumbs on another. Roll the escalopes in the flour, shake, then dip them in the egg and coat well, pressing in the breadcrumbs. Melt 2 oz (50 g) of the butter in a large frying pan. Fry the escalopes, two at a time, for 3-4 minutes on each side, until well browned. Add more butter to the pan if necessary.

Transfer to a warmed serving dish and serve garnished with lemon wedges and parsley, anchovies and capers. Serve immediately.

Veal Paprika

SERVES 6

1½ oz (40 g) butter
2 lb (900 g) leg of veal, diced
2 large onions
1 tablespoon ground paprika
1½ teaspoons salt

veal or beef stock, see page 41 or 42
4 fl oz (100 ml) soured cream
2 egg yolks, beaten
chopped coriander, to garnish

Melt the butter in a flameproof casserole and brown the veal, a few pieces at a time, adding more fat to the pan if necessary. Lift out the pieces as they brown and set aside.

Reduce the heat, add the onions and paprika and cook, stirring occasionally, for about 10 minutes, or until the onions are tender. Return the veal to the casserole, add the salt and enough stock to cover. Bring to the boil, then reduce the heat, cover and simmer for 1¼ hours, or until the meat is tender and the sauce quite reduced.

Remove the casserole from the heat and strain the sauce into a smaller pan. Over a low heat stir in the soured cream mixed with the egg yolks until the sauce thickens. Pour immediately back over the meat in the casserole.

Sprinkle with the coriander and serve with boiled noodles.

I adore roast lamb so I have included several subtly different ways of preparing it. Its natural brilliance depends on buying the best quality English or Welsh meat with plenty of fat. Legs should be slightly undercooked and breast and shoulder slightly overcooked.

Simple Roast Lamb

Much as I admire the rugby teams of the southern hemisphere, when it comes to a leg of lamb, Welsh or English is best!

SERVES 4-6

2 tablespoons salt
1 teaspoon freshly ground black pepper
1 tablespoon chopped fresh rosemary or
1 teaspoon crushed dried rosemary

2 oz (50 g) butter, melted
4½ lb (2 kg) leg of young lamb

Mix the salt, pepper and rosemary with the butter and use this to coat the meat as evenly as possible all over. Place the lamb in a shallow roasting tin and sear in a preheated oven, 450°F/230°C (gas mark 8), for 20 minutes. Reduce the temperature to 350°F/180°C (gas mark 4) and roast for a further 40–60 minutes, or until the lamb is cooked to your taste.

Roast Lamb and Potatoes

SERVES 6-8

2 tablespoons cold water
4½ lb (2 kg) leg of lamb
salt
2 oz (50 g) butter, melted
2-2½ lb (900 g-1.25 kg) potatoes, very thinly
    sliced and rinsed free of starch

1 onion, thinly sliced
1 clove of garlic, crushed
1 bay leaf
2 sprigs of thyme
freshly ground black pepper

Place the cold water in a shallow earthenware dish and put in the lamb. Salt it and paint it with half of the melted butter. Roast in a preheated oven, 425°F/220°C (gas mark 7), for 40 minutes, basting from time to time. Meanwhile, mix together the potatoes, onion, garlic, bay leaf and thyme and season to taste with salt and pepper.

After 40 minutes, transfer the lamb to a plate and keep it warm. Spread the potato mixture in the baking dish, pour in enough boiling salted water to come just to the height of the potatoes and place over a direct medium heat. When the water comes to the boil, put the lamb into the dish on top of the potatoes and paint with the remaining melted butter. Return the dish to the oven and roast for at least a further 20 minutes, turning the leg of lamb twice. The potatoes will be tender in 20 minutes, but continue to cook until the lamb is done - that is, still pink inside.

Roast Lamb with Garlic Sauce

SERVES 6-8

4½ lb (2 kg) leg of lamb
2½ oz (65 g) butter
salt
freshly ground black pepper

10 cloves of garlic, unpeeled
½ pint (300 ml) lamb or veal stock, see page
    42 or 41
2 tablespoons puréed tomato

Spread the leg of lamb with the butter and put it into a roasting tin. Roast in a preheated oven, 400°F/200°C (gas mark 6), for 15 minutes per 1 lb (450 g) of meat. Season with salt and pepper halfway through the cooking time.

While the lamb is cooking, prepare the garlic sauce. Bring a pan of water to the boil, add the garlic cloves and par-boil them for about 3-4 minutes. Drain and then peel them.

Purée the garlic in a food processor or blender. Tip the purée into a pan and add the stock, roasting juices from the lamb and the puréed tomato. Season to taste with salt and pepper and cook over a high heat for 5 minutes to reduce the sauce. Hand the sauce round separately.

Roast Breast of Lamb with Potatoes

SERVES 4

1¾ lb (800 g) potatoes, cut into regular-sized
    chips
salt
freshly ground black pepper
1 breast of lamb, neatly trimmed and cut
    into 4 pieces

4 juniper berries, crushed
few rosemary leaves
3 cloves of garlic, crushed
4 tablespoons olive oil
6 fl oz (175 ml) water

Place the potatoes in the bottom of a deep baking dish and season to taste with salt and pepper. Place the pieces of lamb on top and sprinkle with the juniper berries, rosemary and garlic. Season again with salt and pepper and pour over the oil and water. Cover with a closely-fitting lid or with foil and cook in a preheated oven, 375°F/190°C (gas mark 5), for 45 minutes. Remove the lid or foil and increase the temperature to 425°F/220°C (gas mark 7). Cook for a further 20 minutes, or until the meat has turned a deep golden brown. Turn it over gently and allow the other side to brown, about 10–15 minutes.

Serve immediately – straight from the baking dish.

Shoulder of Lamb with Beans

SERVES 6-8

2 lb (900 g) white haricot beans, soaked for
    12 hours and drained
bouquet garni (parsley, thyme and bay leaf,
    for example)
1 whole shallot
2 large onions
1 large ripe tomato, skinned
3 cloves of garlic

freshly ground black pepper
4 lb (1.75 kg) fatty shoulder of lamb
8 potatoes, par-boiled
3½ oz (90 g) butter
thyme leaves
salt
1 chopped shallot
2 tablespoons chopped parsley

Put the beans in a large pan with plenty of cold salted water and the bouquet garni. Bring to the boil and simmer for about 2 hours, adding more water if necessary. Then add the whole shallot, onions, tomato, two of the garlic cloves and season with pepper. Simmer for a further 15 minutes or so.

While the beans are cooking, cut the other clove of garlic into four and push the pieces into the lamb with the point of a sharp knife. Put the lamb and potatoes in a roasting tin, melt ½ oz (15 g) of the butter and pour over. Sprinkle the lamb with thyme, salt and pepper. Pop the joint into a preheated oven, 350°F/

180°C (gas mark 4), and roast for about 1¾ hours, turning occasionally.

Meanwhile, drain the beans and keep warm. Melt the remaining butter in a small pan and fry the chopped shallot. Add the cooked shallot, onions and tomato from the beans. Discard the bouquet garni. With a fork crush everything in the pan until you have a coarse tomato sauce and stir this into the beans. Arrange the lamb on a serving plate and surround with the beans and potatoes. Scatter with the parsley. Don't overgild the lily by serving other vegetables. This dish is a complete meal.

Lamb Noisettes with Tarragon

SERVES 4

2 tablespoons sunflower or groundnut oil
2 oz (50 g) butter
8 lean noisettes of lamb, cut about 1 inch
    (2.5 cm) thick
salt

freshly ground black pepper
4 tablespoons brandy
2 tablespoons chopped tarragon
3 tablespoons double cream

Heat the oil with half of the butter in a heavy-based frying pan. When sizzling add the noisettes and cook until well-browned but still pink inside – about 2½–3 minutes on each side. Remove from the pan with a slotted spoon, season the noisettes on both sides with salt and pepper and keep warm.

Melt the remaining butter in the same pan and add the brandy, tarragon and cream, mixing well. Bring to the boil and reduce slightly and allow the sauce to thicken.

To serve, spoon the sauce over the noisettes. Serve immediately with creamed carrots and green beans.

Noisettes must be well trimmed of their fat and the outside skin so they can be neatly rolled.

Lamb Chops with Rosemary

S E R V E S 4

4 fl oz (100 ml) cider vinegar
4 fl oz (100 ml) water
1 tablespoon brown sugar
1 tablespoon black peppercorns, finely
  crushed

1 small bunch of rosemary, finely chopped
8 lamb chops (or 4 thick slices of leg of lamb)
1 tablespoon oil
salt

Bring the vinegar and water to the boil. Add the sugar, peppercorns and rosemary. Boil for a further 3 minutes, or until the liquid is well reduced.

Brush the chops with oil, sprinkle with a little salt and seal them quickly under a preheated very hot grill. Then, using the trusty basting brush, paint on the rosemary sauce. Reduce the heat to moderate and grill for a further 6–8 minutes, depending on your taste, turning occasionally and adding more of the rosemary sauce. Serve the remaining sauce with the chops.

Irish Stew

If the French had invented Irish Stew, it would have been fêted and copied the world over. Unfortunately, it was invented in Ireland and we think it's nothing to write home about. Well, it should be!

S E R V E S 4

8 middle neck chops
2 lb (900 g) potatoes, sliced
2 large onions, sliced

salt
freshly ground black pepper
chopped parsley, to garnish

Trim some of the fat from the chops. Place alternate layers of meat and vegetables in a heavy-based pan, seasoning with salt and pepper as you go and finishing with a layer of potatoes. Pour in enough cold water to half cover the stew.

Cover and simmer very slowly for 3 hours. Serve sprinkled with the parsley.

N O T E
All meat stews and casseroles that are normally cooked by just adding water to the ingredients will be dramatically improved if you substitute stock, see pages 41 to 43.

Boiled Lamb with Cream and Caper Sauce

SERVES 6-8

3 lb (1.4 kg) leg of lamb
3½ pints (2 litres) lamb or veal stock, see
*   page 42 or 41*

For the sauce:
1 oz (25 g) butter
1 oz (25 g) flour
2 egg yolks
3½ fl oz (90 ml) double cream
2 tablespoons capers, chopped

Wipe the meat, bring the stock to the boil in a large pan and add the lamb. Simmer for 25 minutes per 1 lb (450 g) of meat. When the lamb is cooked, remove it, reserving the stock, and keep warm.

To make the sauce, melt the butter in a small pan, stir in the flour and cook lightly, without allowing it to brown. Stir in about 16 fl oz (475 ml) of the reserved stock and simmer, stirring constantly, until the sauce is smooth and slightly thickened.

Remove the sauce from the heat, mix the egg yolks with the cream and stir them into the sauce. Return the sauce to the heat for a minute or two to thicken it, but without boiling. Stir in the capers and serve the sauce with the lamb.

Lamb Stew with Aubergines

If you have time, salt the aubergine slices, let them sweat for half an hour or so in a colander and then dry them off with kitchen paper.

SERVES 4

1 lb (450 g) stewing lamb
1 lb (450 g) onions
1 lb (450 g) potatoes
1 lb (450 g) aubergines
1 lb (450 g) fresh or canned tomatoes
2 tablespoons butter or olive oil

1 tablespoon chopped basil
2 tablespoons chopped coriander
freshly ground black pepper
½ teaspoon ground paprika
7 fl oz (200 ml) tomato juice
salt

Trim off excess fat from the meat and cut it into cubes. Slice the onions and potatoes finely and cut the aubergines and tomatoes into largish pieces. Place the meat in a buttered casserole and cover with the vegetables, the butter or oil and the herbs, pepper and paprika. Pour over the tomato juice and season lightly with salt. Cover and bake in a preheated oven, 350°F/ 180°C (gas mark 4), for 1½–2 hours. Add some water if the dish becomes dry during cooking.

EAT MORE MEAT

Moussaka

This brings back memories of my first ever restaurant where I used to cook moussaka (without ever having been to Greece, of course). I would make it up in huge trays of about twenty-four portions, cook it (absolutely magnificently) and let it get cold. Then I'd heat it up in the microwave next day. And, today, I still do the same thing, because I reckon freshly cooked moussaka is greasy and oily and the flavours haven't quite amalgamated. It's up to you but my tip is to cook it today and reheat it in the oven or microwave tomorrow.

S E R V E S 4

oil for frying
1 large aubergine, sliced into thin discs
1 large onion, finely chopped
1 lb (450 g) cooked lamb, minced - from
   Sunday's joint, say
4 cloves of garlic, chopped
1 tablespoon chopped parsley
1 teaspoon chopped thyme or rosemary
1 bay leaf
14 oz (400 g) can tomatoes, drained
salt
freshly ground black pepper
4 oz (100 g) cheese, grated

For the béchamel sauce:
½ pint (300 ml) milk
salt
freshly ground black pepper
1 onion ring
sliver of carrot
1 bay leaf
parsley stalk
2 oz (50 g) butter
2 tablespoons plain flour

To make the sauce, heat the milk gently with the salt and pepper, vegetables and herbs. Leave to infuse for 15 minutes. In another pan melt the butter and stir in the flour. Allow to cook for a minute or so without browning. Strain the milk and, stirring all the while, pour on to the *roux*. Cook over a low heat for 10 minutes, stirring constantly, until thick. Set the sauce aside.

Heat some oil in a sauté pan, enough to come about ¾ inch (1.5 cm) up the side of the pan and fry the aubergine discs until cooked, about 10 minutes. Lift out the aubergine and drain on absorbent kitchen paper. Fry the

onion in the same oil until golden. Add the meat, garlic, herbs and tomatoes. Season to taste with salt and pepper and cook for 10 minutes over a high heat until there is not much liquid left. Remove the bay leaf.

Tip the mixture into a shallow ovenproof dish and cover with the aubergine. Pour over the béchamel sauce, sprinkle with the cheese and bake in a preheated oven, 400°F/200°C (gas mark 6), for 20–30 minutes.

Serve with boiled rice or pasta.

PS Before frying, you should really salt the aubergine discs, let them sweat for 30 minutes and then dry them off with kitchen paper.

Lamb Kebabs

S E R V E S   4

1 lb (450 g) leg of lamb or boned lean
   shoulder

For the marinade:
juice of 1 lime
1 clove of garlic, crushed

2 shallots or 1 small onion, finely grated
½ teaspoon dried rosemary
2 tablespoons olive oil
salt
freshly ground black pepper

Trim off the fat from the meat and cut it into 1 inch (2.5 cm) cubes. Put them into a bowl (not aluminium). Mix together the ingredients for the marinade and pour over the meat, coating it well. Leave to marinate for at least 1 hour.

Lift out the lamb cubes and thread them on to skewers. They will taste best cooked over a charcoal grill but if you can't do that, the second best thing is to heat a flat steel frying pan –

no oil or grease – until it is very, very hot and sear the kebabs on all sides before you pop them under a preheated hot grill. Cook for 7-10 minutes (more if you like them well done). Turn the skewers regularly, basting with the marinade.

Serve with some Pickled Lemons or Limes, see page 39, a salad, warm pitta bread and rice, if liked.

Mutton Pasties

S E R V E S   8

2 breasts of lamb
1 lb (450 g) onions
1 lb (450 g) potatoes
salt
freshly ground black pepper

For the flaky pastry:
1 lb (450 g) plain flour
pinch of salt
12 oz (350 g) butter, which has been in the
   freezing compartment of the refrigerator
   for 3 hours
milk, to glaze

Cook the breasts of lamb in boiling salted water for about 1½ hours, until tender. Lift out from the pan and cook the whole onions and potatoes in the same liquid until tender.

Trim away the fat from the breasts and flake the lean meat. Strain the onions and potatoes, add the flaked lean meat and season to taste

with salt and pepper. Mix well together, mashing the potatoes as you go.

To make the flaky pastry, sift the flour and salt into a large bowl. Holding the frozen butter in foil, grate it into the flour. Keep dipping the butter in the flour to make it easier to grate. Using your hands to press the mixture together, add enough cold water to form a dough that leaves the sides of the bowl clean. Put the dough into a polythene bag and chill for 30 minutes.

Roll the pastry out on a lightly floured surface and cut into eight 4–5 inch (10–13 cm) rounds. Divide the meat mixture equally and place it in the centre of each round. Dampen the edges of the pastry and draw the edges together to form a seam at the top. Flute the edges with your fingers. Brush with a little milk and bake in a preheated oven, 425°F/220°C (gas mark 7), for about 20–25 minutes.

Roast Loin of Pork

SERVES 6-8

5-6 lb (2.25-2.75 kg) loin of pork, on the
   bone and chined with the skin well scored
2 tablespoons vegetable oil
2 teaspoons salt
¼ teaspoon freshly ground black pepper
½ pint (300 ml) veal stock, see page 41
butter
tarragon leaves, to garnish (optional)

Place the pork in a roasting tin, fat side up, rub the rind with the oil and sprinkle with the salt and pepper. Roast in a preheated oven, 425°F/220°C (gas mark 7), for 2½–2¾ hours.

Lift the pork on to a heated serving dish and keep warm. Pour the juices into a sauce separating jug and leave to stand until the fat separates. Add the stock to the roasting tin and stir well over a direct heat to loosen any sediment from the bottom of the pan. Strain off the fat from the jug and add the roasting juices to the pan. Bring to the boil, add a little butter and cook, stirring constantly, until thickened. Season to taste with salt and pepper.

To carve the meat, stand the joint upright and remove the chine bone. Cut between the ribs to make chops.

Serve with the gravy, unpeeled dessert apples, which have been cored and quartered, and roast baby onions. Garnish with tarragon leaves, if liked.

Ensure that either the butcher or you removes the outside skin to leave the loin evenly coated with fat.

Prune Stuffed Pork

SERVES 6-8

6 oz (175 g) stoned prunes
4½–5 lb (2–2.25 kg) loin of pork, boned but
   not rolled, but with the rind removed
salt
freshly ground black pepper
ground ginger

3 tablespoons flour
1 pint (600 ml) meat stock, see pages 41–2
4 fl oz (100 ml) single cream, or half cream
   and half milk
1 teaspoon redcurrant jelly

Put the prunes in a bowl, cover with boiling water and leave to soak for 30 minutes, then drain and dry thoroughly.

Sprinkle the pork with salt, pepper and 1 teaspoon ground ginger and rub them into the fat. Lay the prunes in the centre of the meat, roll up and tie with string. Place the joint, fat side up, in a roasting tin and roast in a preheated oven, 375°F/190°C (gas mark 5), for 30–35 minutes per 1 lb (450 g).

When the meat is cooked, lift on to a heated serving dish and keep warm. Pour the juices from the tin into a sauce separating jug and leave to stand until the fat separates. Then add the flour to the pan, stir and cook gently over a direct heat until browned. Strain off the fat from the jug, pour the juices and stock into the roasting tin and bring to the boil. Simmer until the gravy is reduced by one-third, then whisk in the cream, jelly and a little more ginger until the sauce is smooth and thick. Strain over the pork and serve.

Suckling Pig Stuffed with Sage and Onion

This is a terrific summer feast that, if you organise carefully, won't end in tears of frustration and blackened faces, burnt hands and meat. Alternatively, cook in the oven instead of on the spit.

SERVES 12

1 suckling pig, about 12 lb (5.5 kg), ordered
   from your butcher well in advance
salt
freshly ground black pepper

For the stuffing:
8 oz (225 g) bread, crusts removed
¼ pint (150 ml) milk
2 lb (900 g) onions, chopped
large bunch of sage, finely chopped
2–3 eggs, beaten

½ teaspoon ground nutmeg
salt
freshly ground black pepper

oil and salt for basting in the oven

For the spit roasting basting mixture (optional):
4 fl oz (100 ml) olive oil
4 fl oz (100 ml) dry white wine
3 cloves of garlic, finely chopped
1 teaspoon salt

Season the inside of the pig with salt and pepper. To make the stuffing, soak the bread in the milk, then squeeze out as much liquid as possible. Mix the soaked bread with the onions, sage and sufficient beaten egg to bind. Season with nutmeg and salt and pepper to taste. Stuff the pig and sew up the opening securely with string. For extra security (especially for spit roasting), you can wrap it in fine-gauged chicken mesh after trussing into a neat shape.

To cook in the oven, place on its belly in a large roasting tin or on a roasting rack with a dish underneath. Smear with a little oil and rub with a handful of salt. Cover the ears and tail with foil to prevent burning. Roast in a preheated oven, 350°F/180°C (gas mark 4), for 3–3½ hours, basting regularly to make the skin golden and crunchy. Remove the foil before serving.

To spit roast, remember that this little pig is going to take about 3–4 hours to cook, so don't place it too close to the fire to start with. Position over the fire on the spit and cook for 30 minutes. At this point mix together all the ingredients for the basting mixture, if using, and start to baste the piglet with it. Purists would use sprigs of rosemary as their basting brush. Turn and baste regularly during the cooking time until the flesh and stuffing are cooked and the skin is golden and crunchy.

Pork with Apple and Calvados

I never eat this dish without thinking of the great Kenneth Bell in the days when he started the Thornbury Castle Restaurant. Come back from Andorra, Kenneth, Britain needs you!

SERVES 4

4 best end chops, well trimmed with no rind and a little fat
pinch of dried sage
pinch of freshly grated nutmeg
1 oz (25 g) butter
1 measure of Calvados
4 oz (100 g) apple purée

¼ pint (150 ml) double cream
1 tablespoon meat jelly, which you have saved from your roasts
salt
freshly ground black pepper
sage leaves, to garnish (optional)

Season the chops with the sage and nutmeg. Heat a frying pan until hot, melt the butter and cook the chops gently for about 5 minutes on each side (cook for longer, of course, if the chops are a foot thick).

There should be some juice in the pan by now, so warm the Calvados, then pour over and flame it. Remove the meat and keep warm.

Add the apple purée and cream to the pan and bubble until thick. Then add your meat jelly to thin the sauce a little, season to taste with salt and pepper and pour over the chops.

Serve with fried apple rings and broad beans. Garnish with sage leaves, if liked. Eat immediately.

Russian Stuffed Cabbage

Stuffed cabbages are great things, very popular in Russia and eastern
Europe, and since we seem to grow acres of them in British gardens, why
not start serving them in the same way, as a main meal? Here's a good
recipe to start. You can change it around a bit another time and use, say,
bacon, or minced liver, or rice. And instead of the Soured Cream Sauce,
you could serve it with Tomato Sauce, see page 37 or 93.

SERVES 4

1 large Savoy cabbage
Mushroom and Soured Cream Sauce, see
* below*

For the stuffing:
1 lb (450 g) pork, minced
3 oz (75 g) cooked pearl barley
1 onion, finely chopped

5 oz (150 g) boiled mushrooms, drained and
* chopped*
1 teaspoon dried marjoram
1-2 tablespoons chopped herbs – parsley and
* chervil, for example*
1 egg, beaten

Blanch the cabbage in boiling salted water for 5 minutes. Drain, rinse under cold running water and allow to cool. Separate the leaves and cut out any thick stalks.

Mix together all the stuffing ingredients in a large bowl. Roll up small parcels of cabbage filled with the stuffing and place them, seam side down, in a shallow ovenproof dish, packing closely together. Cover with the Mushroom and Soured Cream Sauce, and bake in a preheated oven, 350°F/180°C (gas mark 4), for 30–40 minutes.

Mushroom and Soured Cream Sauce

Melt a knob of butter in a pan and add a few finely sliced mushrooms & cook until soft. Then add some sour cream & cook gently till it's reduced a bit then stir in a little grated Shanst & season with pepper, paprika & salt.

Cassoulet

The French invented this dish to use up all those odds and ends that country people used to keep in their larders. Nowadays, the ingredients take a little seeking out, but if you have the time and patience to shop and prepare, this is terrific party food with buckets of red wine – double up the quantities of this recipe.

SERVES 4-6

1 tablespoon oil or goose fat
1 onion, thinly sliced
2 cloves of garlic, chopped
4 oz (100 g) salt pork or bacon in one piece
8 oz (225 g) shoulder of pork, boned
½ small shoulder of lamb, boned
1 piece of preserved goose – buy a tin of it
 from a posh shop (optional)
8 oz (225 g) well-flavoured coarse-grain pork
 and garlic sausage

2 tablespoons tomato purée
1½ pints (900 ml) water
1 lb (450 g) dried white haricot beans, soaked
 overnight and drained
salt
freshly ground black pepper
1 bouquet garni (bay leaf, thyme and parsley,
 for example)
4-5 tablespoons fresh white breadcrumbs

Heat the oil or goose fat in a large pan and fry the onion and garlic until softened. Remove the rind from the salt pork or bacon and shoulder of pork and cut it into cubes. Add to the onion mixture, increase the heat to high and brown the cubes on all sides. Remove the onion and rind mixture and set aside.

Dice the flesh of the salt pork or bacon, shoulder of pork, lamb, and goose, if using, and chop the sausage, add to the pan and again cook until browned on all sides. Remove the meat pieces and place in a flameproof casserole with the onion mixture. Add the tomato

purée and half of the water to the cooking pan and stir around to loosen any sediment, then transfer to the meat mixture.

Add the soaked beans and remaining water to the meat mixture with salt and pepper to taste and the bouquet garni, mixing well. Slowly bring to the boil, stirring occasionally.

Sprinkle with the breadcrumbs and bake in a preheated oven, 300°F/150°C (gas mark 2), for 2½-3 hours, pressing the crust down several times during cooking.

Remove the bouquet garni before serving and serve hot straight from the dish.

Boiled Ham and Vegetables

When I'm asked what is my favourite meal, I nearly always lie. I mention my latest fad. In fact, outside of cheese on toast, which has consistently been my favourite meal since I was twelve, and faggots and peas, high, high on my list of favourites is Boiled Ham and Vegetables. I eat it even in summer. For me, it's one of the greatest dishes of all time.

If you want to be modern and trendy, you can purée the vegetables and serve thin delicate slices of ham, but I like great chunks of it, with masses of carrots, turnips, butter beans, potatoes and parsley sauce. Amazing how I keep so trim really!

SERVES 6-8

3 lb (1.4 kg) ham shoulder
4 lb (1.75 kg) ham hock
6 carrots
1 cabbage, tough leaves and core removed,
    cut in 4
thyme, bay leaves and parsley

1 onion, stuck with 2 whole cloves
2 lb (900 g) potatoes, peeled
salt
freshly ground black pepper
butter

Cover the hams with cold water and leave to soak for at least 6 hours, depending on how salty they are.

Drain and put the hams in a large pan. Cover with fresh cold water and bring to the boil. Skim off any scum that rises to the surface. Simmer for 1½ hours, then add the carrots, cabbage, herbs and onion. After 30 minutes, add the potatoes. When the potatoes are cooked, lift out the meat and slice it. Place the meat on a heated serving dish and surround it with the drained vegetables. (Save the stock if it's not too salty and use it as a base for a green pea soup.) Remove the bay leaves, season to taste with salt and pepper, if necessary, and pop lots of butter on the vegetables.

Serve with some fresh English mustard. Wonderful.

Boiled Bacon with Pease Pudding

If you don't have time to make a pease pudding, you can boil the bacon with cabbage instead. Just before the bacon is cooked, you chuck in a load of shredded cabbage and then serve it alongside the bacon with lots of salt and freshly milled black pepper, melted butter and masses of lovely mustard.

SERVES 4-6

For the pease pudding:
8 oz (225 g) split peas
salt
1 oz (25 g) butter
1 egg
freshly ground black pepper
pinch of sugar

For the bacon:
3 lb (1.4 kg) bacon joint, forehock or collar
1 bay leaf
few whole cloves
1 onion, sliced

Wash the peas and soak overnight in cold water. Drain and tie loosely in a cloth. Place in a pan with a pinch of salt and cover with boiling water. Boil for 2–3 hours until soft.

Meanwhile, put the bacon in a pan with the bay leaf, cloves and onion. Cover with water and boil for 25 minutes per 1 lb (450 g), plus 25 minutes.

Rub the peas through a sieve or purée them in a food processor or blender. Add the butter, egg and season to taste with salt and pepper and the sugar. Beat until lightly mixed. Tie up tightly with a floured cloth and boil for a further 30 minutes.

Serve the pudding with the strained hot bacon and carrots or swede and parsley sauce.

OFFAL IS GREAT

M ention offal to the Anglo-Saxon in general and the English-man in particular and he will clasp his stomach and groan. Distant memories of tough pig's liver served with burnt onions and lumpy gravy that 'they' forced him to eat at school or in the army will come flooding back leaving a nasty taste in his mouth.

Start talking offal to a Frenchman and his eyes will light up and he will spread his arms heavenwards in a gesture of praise and antici-pation. Not for him horrid memories, just thoughts of charcoal-grilled ox heart brochettes or light fluffy brains served in foaming butter with capers. He will tuck into a plate of tripe like a man possessed.

I am passionately fond of offal whether it is a pickled ox tongue at Christmas or a body-building plate of faggots and peas on a cold winter's day and in summer what could be better than a thin sliver of calves' liver lightly grilled so that it is still pink inside and served with a couple of fine bacon rashers?

Those too prejudiced by unhappy youthful experiences and who are not open-minded (I would rather say open-hearted but I think the pun is too obvious) are missing a great deal of pleasure.

On a holiday in France I once made a 300-kilometre detour to eat at a restaurant where the speciality was a whole chicken poached inside a sheep's stomach. The journey to Lambesc to eat was not wasted. The only trouble was that the chef so jealously guarded his recipe that he wouldn't give it to me.

Anyway, since you have bought this book, I know that you are going to start eating more offal but, before you cook the recipes, perhaps I should give you a few tips.

Tripe This is sold by butchers already cleaned and blanched, which is called dressed, and except for a quick rinse in cold water needs no further preparation before cooking.

Kidneys It is best to buy all kidneys encased in the creamy white fat that you can peel off yourself rather than the butcher and render down and use for frying. All kidneys are surrounded by the ubiquitous membrane, which must be removed before cooking. When cut through the middle they reveal a grizzly hard core, which must also be removed. Calves' and lambs' kidneys are the most delicate and are best for dishes like the Fluffy Omelette with Kidneys on page 201 or for simple grilling. Ox and pigs' kidneys are best in casseroles and stews, pies and puddings.

Liver This should be smooth and shining, heavy and firm to the touch. Buy it cut in thin slices and remember to remove any pipes and the fine membrane, which is like very thin clingfilm, from the edges before you cook it. Calves' liver is the best and, of course, the most expensive. Lamb's liver comes next, then pig's then ox. Ox and pig's to my mind are best either braised or used in composite dishes like faggots or pâtés.

Sweetbreads Soak them in water for several hours to remove any blood. Drain and blanch them in a pan of boiling salted water. Then drain again, allow to cool and put them between two flat boards or plates with a weight on top to press them for an hour or two before cooking. Peel away the outer membrane and skin and now they are ready to cook.

Tongues These are covered in a thickish skin. If this skin is rough then the tongue comes from an old animal and should be rejected. If you buy a fresh tongue it is a good idea to pickle it for a few hours before cooking. If your tongue has already been pickled or salted, then soak it for a few hours in cold water before cooking. I suppose Ox Tongue (see page 211) is the classic one served and cooked in very different styles but equally delicious and quite different is a warming dish of Braised Lambs' Tongues (see page 210).

Brains Like all offal these must be very fresh and consumed within, at most, twenty-four hours of buying them. The first thing with brains is to soak them in cold water for 30 minutes or so and rinse off any blood. Trim away as much membrane and tissue that surrounds them as possible. Then it is best to pop them into boiling salted water for 2–3 minutes to blanch them. Lift them out carefully, because they are fragile. Now they are ready to cook in whichever way you choose.

Tripe and Onions

Ten reasons for eating tripe:

1. It tastes very good.
2. It's very good for you.
3. It's not expensive.
4. I like it very much.
5. Prove to your friends that you're not a food snob.
6. You can choose the other four reasons.

S E R V E S 4

1 lb (450 g) dressed tripe, cut into slices
10 oz (275 g) onions, sliced
1 pint (600 ml) milk
salt
freshly ground black pepper

1 oz (25 g) butter
1 oz (25 g) flour
freshly grated nutmeg
chopped parsley
dollop of double cream

Put the tripe, onions, milk and salt and pepper in a pan, cover and simmer for 2 hours, or until tender. Strain off the liquid, reserving 1 pint (600 ml). Cut the tripe into bite-sized pieces.

Melt the butter in a pan, stir in the flour and cook for 2 minutes or so. Remove the pan from the heat and gradually stir in the reserved liquid. Return to the heat, bring slowly up to the boil and continue to stir until the sauce has thickened. Add the tripe and onions and reheat. Check the seasoning, add the nutmeg and grind even more black pepper over it. Sprinkle with the parsley. Finally, stir the cream into the sauce.

Serve with toast or plain, boiled potatoes.

My Favourite Meal of All

This is Mum's recipe (see page 10).

SERVES 4

caul
1 set of pig's lights and heart*
2 lb (900 g) pig's liver*
3 large onions, cut in half
1 bay leaf
2 teaspoons salt
1 tablespoon dried sage
2 sage leaves or 1 teaspoon dried sage
1 tablespoon chopped parsley

1 teaspoon dried thyme
salt
freshly ground black pepper
6 oz (175 g) fresh white breadcrumbs
2 Oxo cubes – yes Oxo cubes!
cornflour
1 packet of marrowfat dried peas cooked
    according to the recipe on the box, but add
    1 tablespoon sugar

*known as a pig's pluck in the Black Country!

When you ask the butcher for pig's lights, he will give you an unspeakable mess of intestines – make sure he gives you lots of caul, a sort of fat netting without which a faggot is not a faggot!

Put the lights, heart, liver and onions in a pan and cover with cold water. Pop in the bay leaf, salt and the first lot of sage. Bring to the boil and simmer for about 1 hour until the onions et al. are cooked.

Strain off the stock into another pan. Put on to a low heat to reduce by about one-third.

Remove and discard the bay leaf. Put the offal and onions through the coarse blade of a mincer or a food processor. Mix in the sage, parsley, thyme, salt and pepper and breadcrumbs.

Form the mixture into balls a bit smaller than tennis balls and wrap each one with a generous section of caul. Place in a roasting dish and moisten liberally with some of the stock. Bake in a preheated oven, 400°F/200°C (gas mark 6), for about 10 minutes until the caul is cooked.

Meanwhile, add the Oxo cubes to the rest of the stock and thicken with just a little cornflour.

Serve the faggots with the gravy and marrowfat dried peas that you have cooked until mushy.

I really love food like this – any invitations gratefully accepted!

Once a regular feature in a working home in Britain, you are now more likely to find this in simple restaurants in France as *Fromage de Tête* or just offered without name as a starter on a set menu. It is very simple to make.

SERVES 4-6

1 pig's head
1 onion, chopped
1 good sprig of parsley

salt
freshly ground black pepper
plenty of freshly grated nutmeg

Wash the head and put into a large pan with the onion and parsley. Cover with cold water, bring to the boil and simmer very gently for some hours, until the meat is dropping off the bones. When the meat is cooked, leave it in the liquid for an hour or so to cool, but before it gets cold, remove the meat on to a large dish or tin and start to cut it up. Use every scrap of meat and put it into a big bowl. While you are doing this, keep the liquid on the heat simmering gently, meanwhile throwing in every bone that comes from the meat.

Finally, when all the meat is finely chopped, season to taste with salt and pepper and nutmeg.

Put the meat into small basins. Boil rapidly to reduce the liquid in the pan to half and strain a small amount into each basin of meat. Leave to set.

Eat with toast and mustard, with cold beetroot or a caper and vinaigrette dressing. Any liquid left can be used as stock for soup – specially for dried peas or lentils, which are ideal pulses for pork stocks.

Fluffy Omelette with Kidneys

I always cook this for breakfast when friends are staying. It's an excellent excuse for drinking red wine in the early morning!

SERVES 2

3 eggs, separated
1 tablespoon cream or milk
1 tablespoon freshly grated Parmesan cheese
salt
freshly ground black pepper
½ oz (15 g) butter

For the filling:
4 lambs' kidneys
1½ oz (40 g) butter
2 shallots, finely chopped
2 teaspoons flour
1 teaspoon tomato purée
2 tablespoons dry sherry
¼ pint (150 ml) good stock, see pages 41-3

Prepare the filling first. Skin, core and halve the kidneys and cut them into large pieces. Melt the butter in a small sauté pan and fry the kidneys and shallots briskly until brown. Dust with the flour, then stir in the tomato purée, sherry and stock. Bring to the boil and simmer for about 8 minutes.

To make the omelette, beat the egg yolks with the cream or milk, half of the cheese and the salt and pepper. Whisk the egg whites until they hold stiff peaks and fold carefully into the yolk mixture. Melt the butter in a heavy flameproof dish. Turn the egg mixture into this, shape into an oval, and make a hollow down the middle. Scatter over the remaining cheese and place in a preheated oven, 400°F/ 200°C (gas mark 6), for 8–10 minutes. Reheat the kidney mixture if necessary and, when the omelette is ready, spoon it down the centre. Serve immediately.

Grilled Kidneys with their Fat

I served this dish in my restaurant to please a particular customer, Cyril Woodgate, who hated 'messed-up food' but loved fine wine, Champagne, Cognac and port. 'Stuff the sautéed larks' tongues and caviar – give me a grilled kidney any day.' So I did. This recipe is dedicated to his late daughter and him with love.

SERVES 4

8 lambs' kidneys with the fat around them
2 tablespoons Madeira
2 cloves of garlic, crushed
3 oz (75 g) butter, softened
1 small onion, finely chopped
3 tablespoons chopped parsley

1 teaspoon Worcestershire sauce
½ level teaspoon dry mustard
salt
freshly ground black pepper
4 slices of bread

Lift the kidneys from their fat, then skin and core them, keeping each in one piece. Open them out flat and put them back on to the fat. Place, cut side up, on a greased rack in the grill pan. Sprinkle with the Madeira.

Mix the garlic with the butter, onion, parsley, Worcestershire sauce, mustard and salt and pepper and spoon the mixture over the kidneys.

Grill the kidneys for 6–10 minutes, until the fat is crispy. Toast the bread and cut each slice in half to form eight triangles. Place a kidney on each piece of toast and spoon over some of the pan drippings.

Lambs' Kidneys in Cognac and Cream Sauce

A delicious 'plat' this one – specially if you cook the kidneys a little pink.

S E R V E S   4

about 1½ lb (675 g) lambs' kidneys	4 tablespoons double cream
3 tablespoons oil	salt
1 onion, chopped	freshly ground black pepper
1 clove of garlic, crushed	1 oz (25 g) butter
1 tablespoon seasoned flour	pinch of sugar
3 tablespoons Cognac	2 teaspoons made mustard

Skin, core and halve the kidneys and slice thinly or leave in halves as liked.

Heat the oil in a pan and sauté the onion and garlic until transparent. Dip the kidneys lightly in the seasoned flour and add to the pan. Cook until tender, stirring or turning over frequently. Pour over the Cognac, flame and leave until the flames have died away.

Meanwhile, season the cream with salt and pepper. Stir into the kidneys, mixing well. Add the butter, sugar and mustard, stirring thoroughly and heat gently until lightly thickened but do not allow to boil.

Serve hot with rice and a crisp salad.

Chicken Livers

S E R V E S   4

1½ lb (675 g) chicken livers	2 fl oz (50 ml) dry sherry
3 oz (75 g) butter	salt
1 onion, very finely diced	freshly ground black pepper
1 oz (25 g) flour	buttered toast triangles, to serve
¾ pint (450 ml) chicken stock, see page 43	chopped parsley or watercress, to garnish

Wash the chicken livers, removing any strings or bitter green bits, and dry well on absorbent kitchen paper. Melt 2 oz (50 g) of the butter in a pan and sauté the chicken livers and onion for about 10 minutes, stirring all the time.

Lift out the chicken livers and onion from the pan, leaving the cooking juices behind. Add the flour and bubble for a moment or two, then add the stock and sherry and boil until the sauce is reduced slightly. Whisk in the remaining butter and cook until the sauce has thickened. Return the livers and onion to the pan and season with salt and pepper to taste.

Serve with buttered toast triangles and garnish with parsley or watercress.

Calves' Liver with Honey Glazed Parsnips

Clive Imber at Michael's Brasserie, Newcastle upon Tyne

SERVES 4

2 tablespoons vegetable oil
2 oz (50 g) butter
4 × 6-8 oz (175-225 g) slices of calves' liver,
    trimmed of all pipes and skin
6 fl oz (175 ml) port
¼ pint (150 ml) beef or veal stock, see page
    42 or 41
1 oz (25 g) butter, chilled and diced
salt
freshly ground black pepper

For the parsnips:
1½ lb (675 g) parsnips, peeled and cut into
    thin batons
2 oz (50 g) butter
1 large tablespoon heather honey (the runny
    variety)

Place the parsnips in a pan of boiling salted water and blanch for 2 minutes. Refresh in iced water and drain. Melt the butter in a frying pan and sauté the parsnips until they are golden brown. Add the honey and toss gently to cover and glaze the parsnips. Remove and keep warm.

Heat together the oil and butter in a large, heavy frying pan and sauté the liver gently over a moderate heat for about 1 minute on each side. Lift out the liver and keep warm. Pour off any excess fat from the pan. Add the port, scraping up all the brown bits, and boil briskly to reduce by half. Add the stock and boil until the sauce is of a syrupy consistency. Whisk in the chilled butter, bit by bit, and stir until well mixed. Season to taste with salt and pepper.

To serve, arrange the liver on four warm plates, top with the honey glazed parsnips and pour the sauce around.

This expensive and delicious liver must be finely + evenly sliced — nt hacked into slabs.

Calves' Liver with Potatoes and Red Wine Sauce

SERVES 4

2 large potatoes
oil for frying
salt
freshly ground black pepper
4 × 6 oz (175 g) slices of calves' liver,
* trimmed of all pipes and skin*

For the sauce:
about 1½ oz (40 g) frozen unsalted butter
2 shallots, roughly chopped
¼ pint (150 ml) red wine
¼ pint (150 ml) veal stock, see page 41,
* reduced by half to double strength*

2 spring onions, finely chopped or chopped
* chives, to garnish*

To make the sauce, melt about one-third of the butter in a pan and brown the shallots slowly (this brings out the natural sugar). Add the red wine and boil rapidly to reduce by half. Add the reduced veal stock and simmer for 2–3 minutes. Pass the sauce through a sieve. Whisk in the remaining butter to enrich and give the sauce a shine. Season to taste with salt and pepper and keep warm.

Wash and peel the potatoes. Grate on a normal cheese grater, then dry in a clean tea towel. Heat a little oil in a heavy-based frying pan, sprinkle in the potatoes and spread evenly over the pan to give a 4 inch (10 cm) diameter. Season to taste with salt and pepper. Cook over a moderate heat for 5 minutes, keeping the potato crisp and golden. Turn over and repeat four times. Keep warm.

For the liver, heat a little oil in a heavy-based pan. Season the liver and fry for 2 minutes or so on each side, keeping the meat a little pink inside.

To serve, put the potato in the centre of a serving dish, place the liver on top and pour the sauce around. Sprinkle with the spring onions or chives.

Liver Stroganoff

When I first started cooking for a living, Beef Stroganoff was all the rage – now it has become a non-dish. So try this version and don't forget to sear the liver well but leave it pink in the middle.

SERVES 4

1 lb (450 g) calves' or lambs' liver, trimmed
    of all pipes and skin
¼ pint (150 ml) milk (optional)
1½ oz (40 g) butter
1 onion, cut into rings
1 tablespoon flour

3 fl oz (75 ml) soured cream
1 tablespoon tomato purée or 2 tablespoons
    tomato juice or 1 teaspoon made French
    mustard
salt
freshly ground black pepper

Soak the liver in the milk for a few hours or use straightaway, depending on how mild a flavour you require. Drain and cut the liver into strips. Melt the butter in a pan and cook the liver together with the onion rings over a high heat for no more than 5 minutes. Add the flour, cook for a couple of minutes, then stir in the soured cream and tomato purée or juice or mustard. Season to taste with salt and pepper and serve with plain rice.

Cold Liver Soufflé

SERVES 4 AS A LIGHT LUNCH OR
6 AS A COLD STARTER

1 lb (450 g) lambs' liver, trimmed of all pipes
    and skin
4 fl oz (100 ml) milk
1 onion, finely chopped

½ head of garlic, very finely chopped
salt
freshly ground black pepper
2 eggs, separated

Soak the liver in the milk. Drain, reserving the milk. Put the liver into a pan of boiling water and simmer until just cooked. Drain, chop finely and pound to a smooth paste with the onion, garlic and a little salt and pepper to taste. Beat the egg yolks into the reserved milk and stir into the liver paste. Whisk the egg whites until they hold stiff peaks and gently fold them into the liver mixture.

Pour into a buttered soufflé dish or six individual ones and place in a shallow baking dish half-filled with water. Bake, uncovered, in a preheated oven, 350°F/180°C (gas mark 4), for 1–2 hours or until set.

Leave to cool, then tip out and serve with a fresh Tomato Sauce, see page 37, and a salad.

Calves' Sweetbreads in Brioche with Grapes Marinated in Fino Sherry

Stephen Ross at Homewood Park, Hinton Charterhouse

For those who don't know, Stephen was a disciple of the great Kenneth Bell. Ergo the recipe needs no explanation.

SERVES 6

1 lb (450 g) calves' sweetbreads
1 lb (450 g) white grapes, peeled, seeded and
 soaked in Fino sherry for 24 hours

For the brioche:
½ oz (15 g) fresh yeast
8 oz (225 g) strong plain flour
½ teaspoon salt
½ oz (15 g) caster sugar

2 eggs, beaten
2 oz (50 g) butter, softened

For the filling:
½ pint (300 ml) chicken stock, see page 43,
 reduced by half to double strength
¼ pint (150 ml) dry white wine
2 oz (50 g) butter, diced

About 24 hours before you intend to eat the sweetbreads, soak them in cold water for several hours to remove any blood. Drain and blanch them in a pan of boiling salted water. Drain and allow to cool. Press them between two boards or plates with a weight on top for 1–2 hours. Pick over the sweetbreads, removing all skin and membrane and slice them evenly.

To make the brioche, blend the yeast with 2 teaspoons warm water and set aside until the yeast has dissolved and frothed up. Sift the flour with the salt and sugar into a bowl. Make a well in the centre and add the yeast liquid, eggs and butter. Mix together, using your hands, to form a soft dough, then knead on a lightly floured surface until smooth and elastic. Cover with a damp cloth and leave in a warm place to rise for 1 hour. Knead the dough again on a

lightly floured surface. Divide and place a ball of dough in six buttered fluted brioche tins and leave to rise until doubled in size. Bake in a preheated oven, 375°F/190°C (gas mark 5), for 20–30 minutes, until golden brown and hollow sounding when tapped on the base. Cool on a wire rack.

To make the filling, boil the chicken stock and wine rapidly until reduced by half. Reduce the heat, add the sweetbreads and cook for 2 minutes, then remove and keep warm. Add the grapes and sherry to the sauce and stir in the butter until the sauce is smooth.

To serve, remove the brioche tops and hollow out. Add the sweetbreads with some of the sauce. Pour the remainder of the sauce on each plate around the brioches and replace the tops. Serve with sautéed chanterelles.

Sweetbreads Meunière

This is a simple way of preparing sweetbreads, but if you want a real treat ring my pal Shaun Hill at Gidleigh Park – he is probably the best offal cook in the Kingdom.

SERVES 3-4

1 lb (450 g) sweetbreads – calves' are best, or
2nd best, lambs'
salt
lemon juice
white wine vinegar or dry sherry

4 oz (100 g) butter
pinch at least of ground ginger
1 oz (25 g) fresh white breadcrumbs
chopped parsley, to garnish

Soak the sweetbreads in cold water for several hours to remove any blood. Drain, put them in a pan and cover with hot water. Add salt and a dash of lemon juice and vinegar or sherry. Bring to the boil and simmer for about 15 minutes, then drain the sweetbreads and cool them with cold water. Next, press them between two boards or plates with weights on top for at least 1 hour so they flatten out. Pick over the sweetbreads, removing all skin and

membrane and cut them into equal-sized pieces.

Melt some of the butter in a pan and fry the sweetbreads for a moment or two. Sprinkle them with the ginger. Remove the sweetbreads from the pan and roll them in the breadcrumbs. Melt the remaining butter in a clean pan and fry the sweetbreads until golden. Garnish with the parsley to serve.

Calves' Sweetbreads

SERVES 4

1½ lb (675 g) calves' sweetbreads
salt
freshly ground black pepper
flour for dusting
4 oz (100 g) butter

1 tablespoon capers
1 tablespoon finely chopped parsley
pinch of freshly grated nutmeg
4 lemon halves

Some time before you intend to eat the sweetbreads, soak them in cold water for several hours to remove any blood. Drain and blanch them in a pan of boiling salted water for 2-3 minutes. Drain and allow to cool. Press them between two boards or plates with

weights on top for an hour or so. Pick over the sweetbreads, removing the fine outer skin and any membrane. If they are large, slice them into scallops 2 inches (5 cm) in diameter.

Dry them carefully, season with salt and pepper and sprinkle with flour. Melt half of the butter in a pan and fry the sweetbreads gently until they become absolutely golden. The pan will now be thick with little bits of burnt butter and flour so take out the sweetbreads, get a new pan and gently melt the remaining butter until it foams and turns brown.

Pop the sweetbreads back in with the capers, parsley and nutmeg and swish them quickly around the pan. Serve immediately on hot plates with your lemon halves and another bottle of rosé from the case which you bought for your kidneys.

Goulash of Lambs' Sweetbreads

From Hungary – with love! A delicious creamy sauce to complement the delicate taste of the sweetbreads. Serve with a few sauté potatoes.

SERVES 4

1½ lb (675 g) lambs' sweetbreads
1 lemon slice
salt
3 oz (75 g) butter
1½ lb (675 g) Spanish onions, finely sliced
2 teaspoons ground paprika, preferably Hungarian – the best kind

½ oz (15 g) flour
½ pint (300 ml) good veal or chicken stock, see page 41 or 43
freshly ground black pepper
2½ fl oz (65 ml) double cream
1 red pepper, skinned, seeded and shredded

Soak the sweetbreads in cold salted water for several hours to remove any blood. Drain, place them in a pan of cold water and add a slice of lemon and salt. Bring slowly to the boil and simmer for 1–2 minutes, drain and rinse well. Press them between two boards or plates with weights on top for about 1 hour. Remove all the fine outer skin and any membrane from the sweetbreads.

Melt 2 oz (50 g) of the butter in a sauté pan and allow the onions to soften, uncovered, for about 20 minutes. Remove the onions from the pan. Add the remaining butter and quickly brown the well drained sweetbreads, then remove from the pan. Reduce the heat, add the paprika, cook for 1–2 minutes and then mix in the flour and stock. Season lightly to taste with salt and pepper and return the sweetbreads to the pan. Cover and simmer very gently for 20–30 minutes until tender.

Just before serving, add the cream and red pepper.

Braised Lambs' Tongues

SERVES 6

6 lambs' tongues
4 rashers of streaky bacon, rinds removed
2 onions, sliced
3 carrots, sliced
1 stick of celery, sliced
bouquet garni (1 bay leaf and sprig of parsley, thyme and rosemary, for example)
8 black peppercorns
½ pint (300 ml) meat glaze, see page 42

For the sauce:
1 oz (25 g) butter
1 small onion, finely grated
1 tablespoon flour
¾ pint (450 ml) jellied veal or lamb stock, see page 41 or 42
1 dessertspoon tomato purée
1 wineglass of dry sherry
salt
freshly ground black pepper

Soak, blanch and refresh the tongues as described in the note on opposite page, then simmer gently in the fresh water for about 1½ hours until tender. Drain and plunge into a bowl of cold water. When cool enough to handle, remove the skin and trim away the roots and any bones.

Lay the bacon on the bottom of a flameproof casserole and add the onions, carrots and celery. Cover the casserole and place over a gentle heat for about 10 minutes until the onion starts to brown.

Place the tongues on top of the vegetables together with the bouquet garni, peppercorns and glaze. Cover the tongues with a double thickness of greaseproof paper and the lid. Braise in a preheated oven, 350°F/180°C (gas mark 4), for 45 minutes.

To make the sauce, melt the butter in a pan and cook the onion slowly for 2 minutes. Stir in the flour and continue cooking until nut brown. Remove from the heat, add ½ pint (300 ml) of the stock, the tomato purée and sherry and mix well. Return to the heat and bring up to the boil, stirring constantly. Reduce the heat and simmer gently with the lid half off the pan. Pour in the remaining stock, skim the surface and bring up to the boil again. Simmer for 5 minutes, then set aside.

Strain the braising liquid from the tongues into another pan and boil rapidly until it has reduced by half. Strain the sauce into this liquid and boil up together. Season to taste with salt and pepper.

To serve, slice the tongues in half and pour over a little of the sauce. Hand round the remainder separately. This dish is lovely served with a potato purée.

This recipe will give lambs' tongues a lovely flavour but make sure they are stewed until tender in the first stage.

Boiled Ox Tongue

211

OFFAL IS GREAT

The cold ox tongue is at its happiest on a sideboard or buffet table on
Christmas Eve or Boxing Day along with pickles, crisp celery
and chutneys.

SERVES 8-10

For the pickle:
1½ lb (675 g) coarse or kitchen salt
¼ oz (7 g) saltpetre
3 oz (75 g) brown sugar
4 pints (2.25 litres) water

Tongue:
1 ox tongue, weighing about 3½ lb (1.5 kg)
6 black peppercorns
large bouquet garni (1 bay leaf and sprigs of
*   parsley and thyme, for example)*
2 carrots
1 celery stalk
1 onion

If the butcher has not already salted the tongue for you, then it is essential to place it in a pickle and leave it to soak for 5-10 days, according to size.

Put all the pickle ingredients in a large pan, bring up to the boil, skim to remove any scum and cook for about 30 minutes, or until no more scum rises. Allow to cool.

Meanwhile, rub the ox tongue with salt and leave to stand for about 1 hour. Rinse well, then immerse it in the prepared brine and leave for 5-10 days.

To cook, remove the ox tongue from the pickle and wash thoroughly. Tie the tongue securely into a neat shape, then place it in a large pan of cold water so that the water comes about 3 inches (7.5 cm) above it. Add the peppercorns, bouquet garni, carrots, celery and onion. Bring slowly to the boil, skimming if necessary. Cover the pan tightly and simmer gently for 3½-4 hours, or until tender when a sharp knife is inserted into the tip of the tongue. Quickly plunge the tongue into cold water and remove the skin. Remove any root and throat bones with a sharp knife. Curl and shape it so that it will fit tightly into a 6 inch (15 cm) deep round tin or baking dish. Cover with a plate and weight heavily overnight.

Serve cold with mustard and pickles. To serve hot do not curl and weight, but simply slice thinly and serve sprinkled with sea salt and accompanied by root vegetables and a parsley sauce.

NOTE

All tongues are improved by soaking in cold water, fresh tongues for 3 hours and salted tongues for a little longer. Then rinse them well by placing in a roomy pan with fresh cold water, bringing to the boil, draining and returning to the pan with fresh cold water.

Brains in Black Butter Sauce with Capers

Despite other exotic ways of preparing brains with cream or truffles, I reckon this is the classic way to eat brains. Yum Yum!

SERVES 4

4 pairs of lambs' brains
2 tablespoons white wine vinegar
salt
4 oz (100 g) butter

1 tablespoon capers
freshly ground black pepper
chopped parsley, to garnish

Wash the brains and leave to soak in cold water for 30 minutes.

Trim away as much membrane and tissue as possible and place in a pan with just enough water to cover. Add 1 tablespoon of the vinegar and ½ teaspoon salt. Bring to the boil and simmer gently for 15 minutes. Drain and place in cold water then dry on absorbent kitchen paper.

Melt half of the butter in a frying pan. Add the brains and brown on all sides. Remove and place in a hot serving dish. Keep warm.

Add the remaining butter to the pan and heat until dark brown, without burning. Stir in the remaining vinegar, capers and salt and pepper to taste. Spoon over the brains and sprinkle with some chopped parsley. Serve immediately.

FAR FLUNG FEASTS

T he cooking of India, China and Japan lends itself to parties, feasts and fun and, with a little careful shopping, a dollop of patience, a dash of ingenuity, you can travel to the East and savour the exotic flavours and aromas of Oriental cooking without leaving the comfort of your own home. I once made a highly successful armchair tour of the Scottish whisky distilleries with the aid of a map and several dozen miniature bottles containing the fine amber liquid of that fair country and, although I wasn't wearing a kilt, I gave (I think) a fine rendering of *Loch Lomond* before retiring unsteadily to bed.

Because you eat the food in the following recipes with chopsticks, your fingers or with pieces of Indian bread, and because there is an endless array of little dishes exquisitely arranged on black square plates or served in delicate porcelain bowls you can transport yourself and friends on a gastronomic magic carpet journey leaving mundanity and mediocrity far below you.

The drinks you can serve make a refreshing change from the average dinner party's routine of gin and tonic followed by the latest and cheapest Spanish or New World wine. Kingfisher lager, iced salted Lassi, tepid sake or rice wine. Mint tea and Turkish coffee served with crystallised fruits and Turkish delight will take you to the max as a change from getting the Max and After Eights.

The variety of spices, herbs, textures, colours and flavours and the dazzling way you can decorate the plates give you a wonderful sense of culinary and artistic achievement. With a dozen well-chosen friends you can make one hell of a meal of it all. And without getting boozed out of your brains, your senses and your spirit will lift skywards like the haunting notes of a snake charmer's flute.

But for this unbridled hedonism there is a price to pay: you must have the right equipment. So see page 31 for what you have to have before you begin.

Middle Eastern Mint Tea

SERVES 4
(MAKES ABOUT 1¾ PINTS [1 litre])

1½ tablespoons green tea leaves
1¾–2¼ pints (1–1.25 litres) boiling water

about 2 oz (50 g) mint leaves
5–6 oz (150–175 g) sugar

Heat the teapot. Add the tea leaves and about ¼ pint (150 ml) of the boiling water. Swirl around, then quickly pour out the water, retaining the tea leaves. Add the mint and sugar and the remaining boiling water. Cover and leave to infuse for about 5–8 minutes.

Skim off the mint that has risen to the surface. Serve in small glasses, adding a little more sugar if necessary.

Lassi

SERVES 2–3
(MAKES ABOUT ¾ PINT [450 ml])

12 fl oz (350 ml) rich, creamy (and slightly
  sour) yoghurt
3 tablespoons double cream
1 tablespoon rose water

3 oz (75 g) sugar – you may like it salted
  instead of sweet – so omit sugar and add
  salt to taste
about 9 ice cubes

Place the yoghurt, cream, rose water and sugar or salt in a blender and process for about 30 seconds, until the sugar or salt has fully dissolved.

Add the ice cubes and blend for a further 30 seconds until the mixture is thick and frothy but still has ice crystals.

To serve, pour into chilled glasses.

To make ahead, mix the yoghurt with the cream, rose water and sugar or salt and blend as above. Chill in the refrigerator for up to three days. Blend again before adding the ice cubes to serve.

Turkish Coffee

S E R V E S 3 - 4
(M A K E S A B O U T 6 F L O Z [175 ml])

6 fl oz (175 ml) water
3 teaspoons sugar

3 teaspoons pulverised coffee

Boil the water with the sugar in a small pan (or special long-handled copper or brass Turkish coffee pot). Add the coffee, stir well and heat until the froth reaches the rim of the pan. Remove from the heat and allow the grounds to settle. Repeat this heating and settling process twice.

Serve hot in small coffee cups as soon as the grounds have settled for the final time.

You'll be surprised how much your enjoyment can be enhanced if you serve these authentic drinks with a meal instead of booze — for a change.

SERVING INDIAN FOOD

Although wine and Indian food can be a tricky combination, I reckon a slightly sweet wine from Bergerac or Monbazillac, served nicely chilled, goes jolly well with hot curries.

If you can't be bothered to make one of those strange sweets that look like fudge, but are really made of things like semolina, you are better off serving fresh exotic fruits like mangoes, with a dish of Turkish Delight and perhaps some crystallised fruit.

But who says that you have to serve a meal that is ethnically correct all the way through? After a dish of curry there is absolutely nothing wrong with a plate of raspberries and cream. You don't have to be a slave to style – or to silly cookery writers!

Lobster or Prawn Curry

In this section I've included my very favourite curries, with some emphasis on fish, because it seems to me that we don't appreciate that all kinds of fish and shellfish can be curried as happily as meat. We tend to think that the delicate flavours will be drowned but, in fact, these recipes are aromatic and spicy and complement the fish delightfully.

SERVES 4

*1 cooked lobster or 2 lb (900 g) large prawns,
  peeled
2 oz (50 g) ghee, see page 217, or fat
1 large onion, chopped
4 cloves of garlic, sliced
½ teaspoon ground turmeric*

*6 thin slices of fresh root or pickled ginger
½ pint (300 ml) coconut milk
3 fresh or dried chilli peppers, cut lengthways,
  then in halves
1 teaspoon salt*

Lay the cooked lobster, if using, on its back, detach the legs, then insert the pointed end of a sharp knife between the body and the tail. Cut down the length of the lobster to the tail

end, cutting completely in half. Remove the thread of dark gut that runs down the length of the lobster to the tail with the gravel sac at the top of the head. Remove and mash the creamy liver and coral. Crack the claws with a small mallet and remove the flesh. Break the legs apart at the central joint, then remove the flesh with a thin skewer. Remove the tail flesh and cut into bite-sized pieces. Remove the body meat and add the flesh attached to the shell. You should now have tail flesh, body meat, leg flesh, claw meat and mashed liver and coral to use in the curry.

Melt the ghee or fat in a pan and fry the onion and garlic to a golden brown. Add the turmeric, ginger, coconut milk and chillies. Simmer for 10 minutes and add the salt. Then mix in as many prawns or as much lobster as will be covered by the amount of curried sauce, cover and cook gently for 10 minutes more.

Serve immediately with plain poppadoms, fresh peas – and plain boiled rice.

Bombay Fish Curry

I like to serve this with finely chopped onion and cucumber, with a little mint stirred into it – it makes a nice crunchy contrast to the soft texture of the fish and curry.

S E R V E S 4

2 oz (50 g) ghee, see below, or fat
1 onion, finely chopped
2 cloves of garlic, sliced
2 dried chilli peppers, seeded and finely chopped
½ teaspoon ground chilli powder
1 teaspoon ground coriander
½ teaspoon ground turmeric

½ teaspoon ground mustard seeds
½ pint (300 ml) coconut milk
1 teaspoon rice flour – this is a gluten-free flour, but use plain flour if you can't get it
juice of 1 lemon
salt
2 lb (900 g) any kind of fish fillets, skin removed

Melt the ghee or fat in a large pan and brown the onion lightly. Add the garlic, chillies and ground spices. Mix the coconut milk with the rice flour and pour in. Squeeze in the juice of a lemon and add salt to taste. Cook over a low heat until the mixture thickens, then slide in the fish and coat it with the curry sauce.

Cover and cook over a gentle heat until the fish is tender, about 10–15 minutes.

N O T E
Ghee is clarified butter and is available, ready-made, from supermarkets and Asian grocers. It really is the best frying ingredient for Indian recipes and should be used at all times instead of lard or oil. If you want to make it yourself, see the recipe for clarified butter on page 35.

Indian Deep-fried Fish Fillets

SERVES 4

1 lb (450 g) fish fillets, skin and bones
  removed
2 cloves of garlic, crushed
½ inch (1 cm) fresh root ginger, grated
1 teaspoon poppy seeds, roasted and ground
½ teaspoon garam masala
1 teaspoon dry mustard

½ teaspoon chilli powder
2 oz (50 g) flour
2 oz (50 g) gram flour or finely ground
  yellow split peas
8 fl oz (250 ml) natural yoghurt
1 teaspoon salt
oil for deep-frying

Cut the fish into 2 inch (5 cm) wide pieces. Wash and pat dry. Mix the garlic, ginger, poppy seeds, garam masala, mustard and chilli powder thoroughly.

Make a smooth thick batter with the flour, gram flour and yoghurt. Add the spices and the salt. Add the pieces of fish and coat well with the batter. Set aside for 3–4 hours.

Heat the oil over a medium heat to 375°F/ 190°C, add the fish in batches and fry for about 8 minutes, until golden. Drain on absorbent kitchen paper.

A really crisp onion salad, plus various chutneys such as mango and lime, and some Baked Bread (Naan), see page 229, are excellent accompaniments to this dish.

Fish Curry

All you need with this are poppadoms, Naan Bread (see page 229) and loads of iced Kingfisher lager.

SERVES 6-8

8-10 thick-fleshed white fish fillets (hake, cod
  or monkfish, for example)
1¼ teaspoons ground turmeric
1½ teaspoons salt
½ teaspoon chilli powder
1 teaspoon ground cumin
3 tablespoons hot water

6 tablespoons vegetable oil
½ teaspoon onion seeds
2-3 green chilli peppers, cut in half and
  seeded
12 fl oz (350 ml) water
1 large potato, peeled and cut into thin slices
1 tablespoon chopped coriander leaves

Wash the fish and pat dry. Cut into equal-sized serving pieces. Sprinkle ½ teaspoon each of turmeric and salt on the fish and rub into the pieces.

In a small bowl mix together the remaining turmeric, salt, chilli powder and cumin with the hot water and set aside. Heat the oil in a pan, add the pieces of fish, a few at a time, and fry until light brown in colour. Drain on absorbent kitchen paper.

Add the onion seeds and chilli peppers to the oil and let them sizzle for 3–4 seconds. Add the spices and stir-fry for 1–2 minutes. Pour in the water and bring to the boil. Gently stir in the potato. Lastly, add the fish fillets. Cover, reduce the heat and cook for about 15 minutes until the fish is cooked and the potato tender. Sprinkle with chopped coriander leaves.

Tandoori Chicken

S E R V E S 4

2½ lb (1.25 kg) chicken
1 teaspoon whole coriander seeds
1 teaspoon whole cumin seeds
1 knob of fresh root ginger, finely grated
4 cloves of garlic, crushed
1½ teaspoons salt

1 teaspoon chilli powder
8 fl oz (250 ml) natural yoghurt
ghee, see page 217, or fat, for basting
juice of ½ lemon
lemon wedges, to garnish (optional)
sprigs of coriander, to garnish (optional)

Skin the chicken and joint into eight pieces. With a sharp knife make two or three slits in each piece of chicken. In a heavy frying pan dry roast the coriander and cumin seeds, stirring constantly, until they turn a few shades darker. Grind to a fine powder.

Mix together the coriander and cumin powder with the ginger, garlic, salt, chilli powder and yoghurt. Place the chicken pieces in a large bowl (not aluminium) and pour the yoghurt mixture on top, coating the chicken pieces thoroughly. Cover and leave to marinate overnight.

Place the chicken pieces and marinade on a baking tray and cook in a preheated oven, 375°F/190°C (gas mark 5), for about 1 hour, basting with the ghee or fat and marinade occasionally, and turning the pieces so that they become evenly browned.

Place the chicken pieces without the juices under a preheated very hot grill for 5–7 minutes each side so that they become dry. Pour the lemon juice over the pieces before serving. They won't be as red as in some Indian restaurants because we are not adding artificial colouring! You can, but you shouldn't.

Garnish with the lemon wedges and coriander, if you like, and serve with some Baked Bread (Naan), see page 229.

Chicken Curry

A really good chicken curry that uses all the spices. This is medium hot,
but you can always increase the strength by adding more spice paste.
Make this curry twenty-four hours in advance and reheat.

SERVES 4

2 oz (50 g) ghee, see page 217, or butter
2 onions, finely sliced
3 lb (1.4 kg) chicken, jointed
2½ fl oz (65 ml) water
1 dessertspoon coconut cream softened in 2
*   tablespoons hot water*
2 tomatoes, skinned and chopped
1 teaspoon salt
5 tablespoons infusion of tamarind (this is
*   the dried, sticky pod – simply infuse it in*
*   water) or 1 tablespoon redcurrant jelly*
*   mixed with the juice of ½ lemon in 2½*
*   fl oz (65 ml) water*
1 tablespoon ground almonds

For the spice paste:
1 tablespoon ground coriander
1 teaspoon whole cumin seeds, freshly ground
½ teaspoon ground fenugreek
½ teaspoon ground turmeric
1 teaspoon chilli powder
1 clove of garlic, crushed with salt
½ teaspoon ground ginger
½ teaspoon garam masala

Mix all the spices to a paste with a little water.
Melt the ghee or butter in a large pan and fry
the onions until brown. Stir in the spice paste
and fry very gently for 2 minutes. Add the
chicken pieces and cook for 3–4 minutes, turning them over once during this time. Pour in
the water and coconut mixture and add the
tomatoes and salt. Cover and cook gently until
the chicken is tender, about 30–40 minutes.

Add the infusion of tamarind or the redcurrant jelly, juice and water, if using. Mix the
ground almonds with a little water to moisten
and stir them into the curry. Remove the lid to
reduce the liquid if necessary and check the
seasoning.

Serve with Fried Rice (see page 228).

NOTE

I find the best kind of coconut for Indian recipes is the sort sold in tins in supermarkets
for making cocktails like Pina Colada, as long as it is unsweetened. Failing that, go for
coconut in block form – but not desiccated.

And if you can't find any of those, use tinned evaporated milk. Don't sneer at it,
because in hot countries like India, where fresh milk is hard to come by, they use it frequently. So it will give an authentic flavour to the food. You can also use it in stews and
casseroles whenever the recipe calls for cream.

Chicken Korma

You can make this dish even more exotic by stirring in a little double cream before you serve it and, if you have a specialist Indian shop near you, buy some of that brilliant, edible silver paper and just float it on top before serving – it will look superb.

SERVES 6

5 oz (150 g) ghee, see page 217, or butter
12 large onions, sliced
1 teaspoon ground chillies
4 teaspoons ground onion powder
1 teaspoon coriander seeds
2 tablespoons ground cinnamon
½ teaspoon ground ginger
10 black peppercorns
5 whole cloves
6 whole cardamom pods, ground

2 cloves of garlic, crushed
3 lb (1.4 kg) chicken, jointed
1 teaspoon salt
½ pint (300 ml) natural yoghurt
3 bay leaves
3 blades of lemon grass, bashed with a knife
* handle to release the flavours*
½ pint (300 ml) chicken stock, see page 43, or
* water*
juice of 1 lemon

Melt the ghee or butter in a large pan and fry the onions to a golden brown. Remove them with a slotted spoon and set aside. Then fry all the spices and garlic and, when brown, throw in the pieces of chicken and salt and cook until brown. Add the yoghurt, bay leaves, lemon grass, chicken stock or water and return the fried onions to the pan. Bring to the boil,

reduce the heat, cover with a tight-fitting lid and simmer for 1½–2 hours, until the chicken is tender.

Remove the pan from the heat, pour in the lemon juice and mix well. Remove the lemon grass and bay leaves and serve with plain boiled rice or Wholemeal Flat Bread – Chapatis (see page 228).

The important thing with curries is to do your shopping carefully and well in advance of the cooking session. And always buy small quantities of the freshest of spices so that you don't end up with a store cupboard of stale aromas.

Lamb Korma

Since this is a mild dish, it's a good idea to have a side dish of spicy potatoes or fried precooked spinach, or perhaps freshly cooked broad beans fried with some hot curry spices and a little onion and tomato.

S E R V E S 4

1 lb (450 g) lean mutton
1 pint (600 ml) water
Indian bouquet garni (pinch of fennel seeds,
*   pinch of green ginger, 4 cloves of garlic,*
*   pinch of coriander seeds and 1 small*
*   onion in a muslin twist)*
1 oz (25 g) ghee, see page 217, or butter
1 large onion, cut in thick slices
pinch of ground coriander

pinch of grated fresh root ginger
1 cinnamon stick
2 whole cloves
2 whole cardamom pods
½ teaspoon cumin seeds
4 cloves of garlic
¼ pint (150 ml) natural yoghurt
½ teaspoon ground saffron
2 teaspoons salt

Cut the meat into cubes and place in a pan with the water and the bouquet garni. Bring to the boil and simmer the meat and spices until the mutton is well cooked and tender and the water has reduced by half to about ½ pint (300 ml), about 1¼ hours.

Melt the ghee or butter in a pan and fry the onion until brown. Add the spices, garlic and yoghurt and fry for 10 minutes. Then add the meat and stock. Mix the saffron into a thin paste with a little boiling water and pour over. Add salt to taste and remove the muslin twist.

N O T E

Before you use dried spices, like peppercorns or coriander, always warm them for a few moments in a dry frying pan, to bring out more flavour. Then proceed with the recipe.

Lamb or Chicken Biriyani

This is probably my favourite Indian meal – I love the taste of the slowly
cooked lamb and the saucy little vegetable stew.

SERVES 4

½ teaspoon ground cloves
½ teaspoon ground cardamom
¼ teaspoon chilli powder
1 teaspoon ground cumin
½ teaspoon freshly ground black pepper
1 teaspoon ground coriander
6–10 cloves of garlic, chopped
1 teaspoon finely chopped fresh root ginger
½ pint (300 ml) natural yoghurt
juice of 2 large lemons
salt
3 lb (1.4 kg) boned lean lamb (leg or
    shoulder), cut into cubes, or 3 lb (1.4 kg)
    chicken, jointed
8 oz (225 g) ghee, see page 217, or butter
6 large onions, finely sliced

For the rice:
10 whole cloves
10 black peppercorns
10 whole cardamom pods
6 cinnamon sticks
1 lb (450 g) Patna rice, washed and soaked
    in water for 2 hours
½ teaspoon saffron
2 teaspoons hot milk

For the garnish:
sliced hard-boiled eggs
chopped almonds or cashews or sultanas
chopped coriander leaves (optional)

Mix together the ground spices, garlic, ginger, yoghurt, lemon juice and salt to taste in a large bowl (not aluminium) and stir in the lamb or chicken. Leave to marinate for an hour or so. Melt the ghee or butter and fry the onions until crisp and brown. Divide the onions into two portions. Finely mince one portion and mix with the meat and spices. Set aside the remainder for the rice.

Then on to the complicated bit, which is to prepare the rice. Fill a large pan three-parts full with water and put in the spices with 1 dessertspoon salt. The salt will eventually be drained away. Bring the water to the boil and pour in the Patna rice. When par-boiled and the grains still hard, after about 5 minutes, remove from the heat and drain through a fine sieve. Do not remove the spices from the rice.

When completely drained, place the rice on a tray to cool and divide in half.

Mix the saffron with the hot milk. Put one portion of the rice into a large pan that has a tightly-fitting lid. Empty the meat and spices over the rice together with the remainder of the onions, saffron and milk. Cover the pan and bring to the boil. Immediately it boils, turn down the heat as low as possible and simmer for about 1½ hours, when the meat should be tender.

Cook the remainder of the rice until each grain is tender and separate, then drain. When the rice is dry spread it out on a flat dish. Ladle over the meat and rice mixture and decorate with hard-boiled eggs, or almonds, cashews or sultanas – or some of each. Garnish, if you like, with fresh chopped coriander.

Lamb Rogan Josh

SERVES 4-6

6 tablespoons vegetable oil
good pinch of ground asafetida
1 cinnamon stick
1¾ teaspoons fennel seeds, ground to a
    powder
4 whole cardamom pods
4 whole cloves

2 lb (900 g) boned shoulder of lamb, cut into
    1 inch (2.5 cm) cubes
2 teaspoons ground paprika
2 teaspoons chilli powder
1½ teaspoons ground ginger
1 teaspoon salt
18 fl oz (550 ml) natural yoghurt, lightly
    beaten

Heat the oil in a large pan over a high heat. Add the asafetida and after 2 seconds add the cinnamon, ground fennel, cardamom and cloves and let them sizzle for 4–5 seconds. Throw in the lamb and fry, stirring constantly, for about 5–7 minutes. Whack in the paprika, chilli, ginger and salt and fry for another 2–3 minutes.

Add the yoghurt, mix with the lamb, and cook for 10 minutes. Cover the pan, reduce the heat and cook for about 1 hour, stirring occasionally, until the meat is tender and the gravy thickened.

Serve with rice.

Vindaloo

SERVES 6-8

2 lb (900 g) lean boneless pork, beef or
    chicken
4 oz (100 g) malt vinegar
1 tablespoon ground ginger
1 teaspoon ground chilli, use fresh chilli
    peppers if possible
1 teaspoon ground coriander
½ teaspoon ground cumin
5 whole cardamom pods, ground

1 tablespoon ground cinnamon
6 whole cloves, ground
2 cloves of garlic, crushed
½ teaspoon salt
6 oz (175 g) ghee, see page 217, or lard or
    dripping
12 black peppercorns
2-3 bay leaves

Cut the meat into large cubes. Mix together the vinegar, ground spices, garlic and the salt thoroughly in a large bowl (not aluminium) and stir in the meat. Leave to marinate for at least 12 hours. (This impregnates the flesh, which can then be kept for two or three days without the slightest danger of it going off.)

Melt the ghee or fat in a heavy-based pan, toss in the meat and marinade and add the peppercorns and bay leaves. Simmer gently over a low heat for 2 hours until tender.

Remove the bay leaves and serve hot with rice, raita (see page 229) and sweet pickles.

My Favourite Meal of All – Faggots (page 200)

Calves' Liver with Honey Glazed Parsnips (page 204)

Tandoori Chicken (page 219)

Clockwise from top: *Potatoes with Fenugreek Leaves (page 226); Lamb Biriyani (page 223); Raita (page 229); Dhall (page 226); Poppadoms; Wholemeal Flat Bread – Chapati (page 228)*

Roast Duck Peking Style with Mandarin Pancakes (pages 232–3)

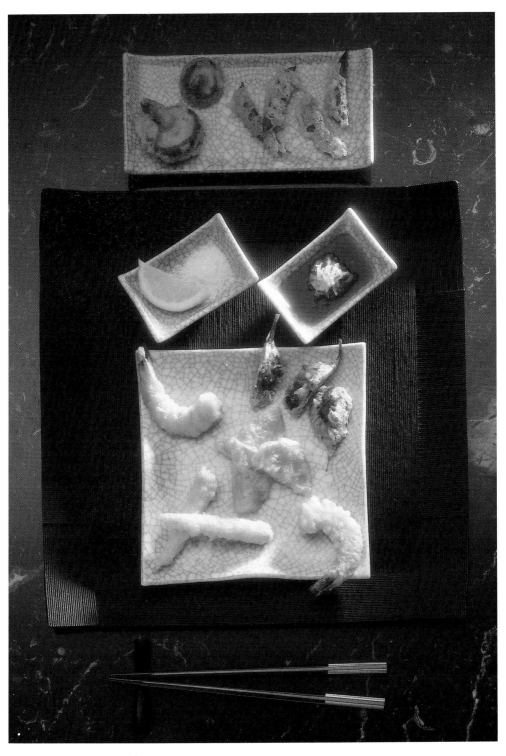

Deep-fried Prawns and Vegetables in Batter – Tempura *(pages 241–2)*

Clockwise from top: *Crab Savouries (page 265); Side-saddle Devils (page 266);*
Mushrooms on Toast (page 267); Anchovy Straws (page 264)

Double-crust Apple Pie (pages 277–8)

Plum and Almond Slice (page 279)

Praline Pancakes (page 282)

Orange Bavarois in Chocolate Genoese Sponge with Orange Sauce (page 296)

Pavlova (page 301)

Clockwise from top: *Flowerpot Bread (page 306); Irish Brown Bread (page 308); Tomato and Onion Bread (page 307)*

Clockwise from top: *Orange and Almond Cake (pages 312–13);*
Sticky Gingerbread (page 310); Coconut Tarts (page 313)

The following vegetable curries can either be served as a starter or with the main dish.

Pea Curry

This is a multi-purpose recipe, which you could also apply to broad beans, chickpeas, potatoes and so on.

SERVES 4

2 oz (50 g) ghee, see page 217, or fat
2 large onions, finely chopped
2 large tomatoes, roughly chopped
2 lb (900 g) fresh peas, shelled
½ teaspoon ground chilli
½ teaspoon ground coriander

½ teaspoon ground cumin
¼ teaspoon ground turmeric
2 teaspoons salt
2 large potatoes, diced
2 green chilli peppers, seeded and chopped

Heat the ghee or fat and fry the onions to a golden brown. Add the tomatoes and continue to fry until brown. Now add the peas, all the spices and the salt. Add 4 fl oz (100 ml) water and cook for 15 minutes. Stir in the potatoes and chillies. Cook over a low heat until the potatoes and peas are soft, 15–20 minutes. Add a little water if the mixture looks too dry.

Cauliflower and Lentil Curry

SERVES 4

2 oz (50 g) ghee, see page 217, or fat
2 onions, finely chopped
1 cauliflower, cut into small pieces
4 fl oz (100 ml) lentils, par-boiled
½ teaspoon chilli powder

¼ teaspoon ground turmeric
½ teaspoon curry powder
2 tablespoons desiccated coconut
1 teaspoon salt
juice of 1 lemon

Heat the ghee or fat in a pan and fry the onions for 4–5 minutes. Add the cauliflower, lentils and all the spices, desiccated coconut and salt. Add 8 fl oz (250 ml) water and cook on a low heat until the cauliflower is soft, about 25 minutes. Stir in the lemon juice and serve.

Potatoes with Fenugreek Leaves

SERVES 4

1 lb (450 g) potatoes
4 oz (100 g) fresh fenugreek leaves or
   1 tablespoon dried fenugreek leaves
3 tablespoons ghee, see page 217, or fat

½ teaspoon ground turmeric
1 teaspoon ground cumin
½ teaspoon chilli powder
1 teaspoon salt

Wash the potatoes, peel and cut them into ¾ inch (2 cm) cubes. If you are using fresh fenugreek, remove the tough lower stalk, wash the leaves thoroughly and chop finely. If you are using dried leaves, soak them in water for about 20–25 minutes, gently squeeze the water out and chop the leaves. Remove any tough stalks.

Melt the ghee or fat in a large frying pan and fry the potatoes, stirring constantly, for about 3–4 minutes. Add the turmeric, cumin, chilli and salt and mix with the potatoes. Cook for a further 1 minute.

Add the fenugreek leaves and mix with the potatoes. Reduce the heat, cover and, stirring occasionally, cook for about 20 minutes, until the potatoes are tender. Add 1–2 tablespoons water if the mixture looks too dry.

Serve with puris or parathas or as a side dish to a main vegetarian curry meal.

Dhall

SERVES 4

8 oz (225 g) lentils (any kind)
¼ teaspoon ground turmeric
½ teaspoon ground chilli
1 teaspoon salt

2 pints (1.2 litres) boiling water
1 oz (25 g) ghee, see page 217, or fat
2 onions, finely chopped
3 tomatoes, quartered

Sort through the lentils and remove any small stones or pieces of grit. Put them in a pan with the turmeric, chilli and salt and pour over the boiling water. Cook until tender, about 1½ hours.

Heat the ghee or fat in another pan and fry the onions and tomatoes together until brown, then add them to the lentils. Cook for 5 minutes more. The dhall should neither be too thick nor like clear soup. It should have the consistency of thick sauce and is best eaten with boiled rice. This simple dish is eaten by the poorest as well as by the wealthiest, because it is cheap, sustaining and tasty.

Spicy Chickpeas

SERVES 4

7 oz (200 g) chickpeas, washed
1½ pints (900 ml) water
4 tablespoons vegetable oil
pinch of ground asafetida
½ teaspoon cumin seeds
½ teaspoon ground turmeric
½ teaspoon chilli powder

1 teaspoon ground coriander
1 teaspoon ground cumin
1½ teaspoons mango powder
½ teaspoon salt
2 tablespoons lemon juice
1 tablespoon chopped coriander leaves
1-2 green chilli peppers, seeded and chopped

Soak the chickpeas overnight in the water. Bring to the boil in the same water, cover and simmer for about 1 hour, until tender. Drain and reserve the liquid.

Heat the oil in a large pan over a medium high heat and add the asafetida and cumin seeds. Let them sizzle for a few seconds. Add the drained chickpeas, turmeric, chilli powder, coriander, cumin, mango powder and salt and stir-fry for 2–3 minutes. Add 8 fl oz (250 ml) of the chickpea stock and cook for 20 minutes, stirring occasionally.

Before serving, pour on the lemon juice and sprinkle with the coriander leaves and chillies.

Chickpea Dhall

I think this is a smashing thing to serve with Tandoori Chicken, see page 219, so you can have a good balance of wet and dry.

SERVES 4

7 oz (200 g) chickpeas
1 large onion, chopped
2 tablespoons desiccated coconut
½ teaspoon ground turmeric
½ teaspoon chilli powder

salt
½ teaspoon garam masala
2 tablespoons groundnut oil
½ teaspoon cumin seeds
½ teaspoon mustard seeds

Thoroughly wash the chickpeas and put in a pan with 1½ pints (900 ml) boiling water. When they have boiled for 4–5 minutes, add the onion, coconut, turmeric, chilli and salt to taste. Cover and cook until the chickpeas are soft, about 50-60 minutes, then mix in the garam masala. Heat the oil in a frying pan and when hot add the cumin and mustard seeds. As soon as the seeds begin to pop, mix into the pan with the chickpeas. Cook and stir for a minute or two, then serve.

Fried Rice

SERVES 4

2-3 tablespoons vegetable oil
1 onion, coarsely chopped or thinly sliced
good pinch of ground turmeric

8 oz (225 g) long-grain rice, boiled, drained
  and dried
2 eggs, beaten

Heat the oil in a frying or sauté pan and fry the onion until pale golden brown. Add the turmeric and rice, forking over well. Add the beaten eggs and continue to cook, forking all the time, until the rice is quite dry. Serve hot.

Wholemeal Flat Bread (Chapati)

MAKES 12-14

10 oz (275 g) wholemeal flour
½ teaspoon salt
about 6 fl oz (175 ml) hot water

2 tablespoons melted ghee, see page 217
  (optional)

Sift the flour and salt together, adding any bran left in the sieve. Slowly add enough hot water to form a soft dough. Knead the dough for about 10 minutes on a floured surface, or until it is no longer sticky. Put back in the bowl, cover with a damp tea towel or cloth and set aside for 1 hour. Divide the dough into 12-14 balls. On a lightly floured surface roll each ball into a 6 inch (15 cm) round.

Heat a frying pan over a medium heat and place a chapati in it. Cook the chapati for about 2 minutes until brown spots appear. Turn and cook the other side for about 15-20 seconds. Take the chapati and place it under a preheated very hot grill for a few seconds so that it puffs up. Turn and cook the other side for a few seconds until it also puffs up.

Place the chapatis in a dish and brush with a little melted ghee, if using. Cover the chapatis as they are made and keep warm while cooking the others in the same way. Serve hot while still soft.

Baked Bread (Naan)

MAKES 7-8

10 oz (275 g) plain flour
1 teaspoon baking powder
½ teaspoon salt
¼ teaspoon bicarbonate of soda
½ teaspoon sugar

1 tablespoon melted ghee, see page 217, plus
a little extra for coating
1 egg, lightly beaten
about 2 fl oz (50 ml) milk

Sift the flour with the baking powder, salt, soda and sugar into a large bowl. Add the melted ghee and egg and stir into the flour mixture. Add enough milk to form a stiff dough. Knead for about 10 minutes on a floured surface.

Place a little ghee in a bowl. Put the dough in the bowl and roll it so that it becomes coated with ghee. Cover with a damp tea towel or cloth and set aside for 3-4 hours.

Preheat the oven to 400°F/200°C (gas mark 6).

Heat two baking sheets. Divide the dough into seven to eight portions. Take one portion and roll it out on a lightly floured surface to a 7 inch (18 cm) round. Pull one end so that the dough takes on a tear shape, and flatten slightly between the palms. Roll out the rest of the dough in the same way. Place the naans on the hot baking sheets and bake for 5-6 minutes. Place under a preheated very hot grill for 15-20 seconds until brown spots appear. Serve hot.

Raita

This is a cooling sort of yoghurt sauce, which helps you to appreciate the spiciness of good curries – but it also goes very well with other dishes, like Chicken Paprika, see page 137.

MAKES ½ PINT (300 ml)

½ pint (300 ml) natural yoghurt
3 tablespoons peeled and finely chopped cucumber
1 tablespoon chopped chives

1 teaspoon finely chopped mint
juice of ½ lemon
salt
freshly ground black pepper

Mix the ingredients together and chill for an hour or so.

SERVING CHINESE FOOD

The secret and joy of most Chinese food is that you can do all the chopping up and preparing at your leisure and then cook it very quickly. It makes ideal dinner party fare because you have plenty of time to have a gin and tonic and natter with your guests, instead of being locked up in the kitchen all night.

However, just like omelettes, Chinese dishes should be served as they are cooked – don't try to keep them warm while you are cooking something else.

Finish up with a banana or fresh pineapple fritters. Anybody can make them. You just dredge the fruit with a little flour, dip it into some very light batter (like that in the *Tempura* recipe, see page 241) and fry in some clean oil. Serve it with some warm syrup and a knob of ice cream. Delicious.

Deep-fried Prawns in Shells

SERVES 4

1 lb (450 g) uncooked prawns, in shells
2 slices of fresh root ginger, finely chopped
1 teaspoon medium or dry sherry
1½ teaspoons cornflour
¾ pint (450 ml) vegetable oil, for deep-frying

1 teaspoon salt
1 teaspoon chilli sauce
chopped coriander leaves, to garnish
grated lemon rind, to garnish

Wash and trim off the legs of the prawns but keep the body shells on. Dry thoroughly. Place the prawns in a bowl (not aluminium) with the ginger, sherry and cornflour. Stir gently to mix, then leave to marinate in the refrigerator for at least 1 hour.

Heat the oil in a wok (pop in a 1 inch [2.5 cm] cube of bread to test the temperature – it should turn golden in 1 minute). Reduce the heat, add the prawns and deep-fry for about 1 minute. Remove the prawns with a slotted spoon and drain on absorbent kitchen paper.

Pour off the oil, then return the prawns to the pan. Add the salt and chilli sauce and mix well. Serve hot, garnished with the coriander and lemon rind.

Stir-fried Crab with Ginger and Spring Onions

In this crazy life I lead I can be eating in the finest restaurants one minute, or going to the dullest receptions, complete with retired British Rail sandwiches, the next. But when I get home and I'm too tired to cook for myself, I always go to my favourite restaurant, The Mandarin, in Bristol. It's not the best restaurant in the world, but if Chinese restaurants were awarded Routier signs, this would certainly get one. It is friendly, reliable and the food is dead good – so a few of the Chinese recipes in this book, like this one, have been unashamedly ripped off from my friends at The Mandarin.

SERVES 4

3 lb (1.4 kg) crab – ask the fishmonger to
  clean it for you
4 eggs, beaten
cornflour
2 tablespoons sesame oil
4 cloves of garlic, crushed
1 small piece of fresh root ginger, finely
  grated

1 small onion, sliced
6 spring onions, trimmed and cut into strips
2 tablespoons rice wine or dry sherry
1 tablespoon soy sauce
1 teaspoon sugar
2 tablespoons Chinese oyster sauce

Detach the claws and cut the body into four pieces. Crack the claws slightly so that the inner flesh will absorb the flavour.

Dip the shell and pieces of crab into the beaten egg and sprinkle with cornflour. Blanch the crab in boiling salted water for 2 minutes and drain.

Heat a wok or a frying pan which has a lid and add the oil. Stir-fry the garlic, ginger and onion until brown, then add the crab and the remaining ingredients. Add a few tablespoons water, cover and cook for 5–10 minutes. Do not overcook the meat or it will lose its tenderness and flavour.

Roast Duck Peking Style

This famous dish is a brilliant combination of flavours and textures – but the most wonderful bit is the crunchy skin, so though the preparation is a little time consuming, the results are well worth it.

SERVES 4-6

3-4¼ lb (1.4-1.75 kg) duckling
1 tablespoon sugar
1 teaspoon salt
½ pint (300 ml) water

For the sauce:
3 tablespoons yellow bean sauce

2 tablespoons sugar
1 tablespoon sesame oil

To serve:
24 Mandarin Pancakes, see opposite page
10-12 spring onion flowers, see below
4 leeks, cut into 3 inch (7.5 cm) strips
½ cucumber, cut into 3 inch (7.5 cm) strips

Wipe the duckling and dunk it in boiling water for a second or two. Insert a meat hook near the neck. Hang it up to dry thoroughly, preferably overnight, in a cool, well ventilated room. Put a pan below the duckling to catch any drips. The next day, dissolve the sugar and salt in the water and rub all over the duckling. Leave for several hours until dry. Place the duckling on a rack over a roasting tin and roast in the centre of a preheated oven, 400°F/ 200°C (gas mark 6), for 1-1¼ hours. Do not prick the skin during cooking.

Place the sauce ingredients in a pan and heat gently for 2-3 minutes, stirring constantly, then pour into a serving bowl.

Carve the duckling into neat slices and arrange on a warmed serving dish. Arrange the Mandarin Pancakes on a separate plate and garnish both dishes with spring onion flowers. To make these, make several cuts from top to bottom along each spring onion, without cutting right through the base. Leave in a bowl of iced water to open. Put the leeks and cucumber on another dish.

To serve, each diner should spread a pancake with a little of the sauce, then place some leek and cucumber in the middle. Top with one or two slices of duckling. Fold over or roll up the pancakes to eat.

NOTE
Cold pancakes can be reheated in a steamer or preheated oven, 400°F/200°C (gas mark 6), for 5-10 minutes.

Mandarin Pancakes

The essential accompaniment to Roast Duck Peking Style. You can make masses in one go and freeze them for later.

MAKES 24

1 lb (450 g) plain flour
½ pint (300 ml) boiling water

vegetable oil

Sift the flour into a bowl. Mix the water with 1 teaspoon oil, then gradually stir into the flour, using chopsticks or a wooden spoon. Knead into a firm dough, then divide into three equal portions. Roll out each portion into a long 'sausage' and cut each sausage into eight equal pieces. Using the palm of your hand, press each piece into a flat pancake. Brush one of the pancakes with a little oil, then place another on top to form a 'sandwich'. Use the remaining dough in the same way to make twelve sandwiches. Flatten each sandwich on a lightly floured surface with a rolling pin into a 6 inch (15 cm) circle.

Place an ungreased frying pan over a moderate heat. When it is very hot fry the sandwiches one at a time. Turn the pancakes as soon as air bubbles appear on the surface. Cook the underside until little brown bubbles appear. Remove the sandwich from the pan and peel the two layers apart very gently. Fold each pancake into four to serve.

Barbecued Chinese Duck

SERVES 4-6

6 lb (2.75 kg) oven-ready duck
1 tablespoon Chinese five spice powder
1 teaspoon aniseed powder
1 teaspoon ground ginger
1 tablespoon salt
1 tablespoon sugar
1 tablespoon MSG

For the marinading sauce:
½ pint (300 ml) malt vinegar
1 tablespoon golden syrup or honey
1 tablespoon Chinese spirit or brandy
1 teaspoon cochineal

Clean the duck well, inside and out. Mix together the five spice powder, aniseed, ginger, salt, sugar and MSG and rub the inside of the duck with this mixture. Tie the neck and tail ends tightly with string, so that no liquid will drip out. Put the ingredients for the marinading sauce into a pan and bring up to the boil. Baste the skin evenly all over with the sauce until it becomes a rosy red colour. Insert a meat hook near the neck and hang up the duck to dry in a cool, well ventilated room for at least 12 hours. Put a pan below the duck to catch any drips.

Place the duck on a rack over a roasting tin and roast in the centre of a preheated oven, 425°F/220°C (gas mark 7), for 1 hour, turning the duck a couple of times. Do not prick the skin during cooking.

Remove from the oven and put the duck on a wire rack to cool for a few minutes before carving.

Stewed Flank of Beef in Hot Pot

This dish gives the lie to the idea that all Chinese dishes are cooked in two minutes flat. In China this is cooked at the table in a special 'hot pot' fuelled by charcoal or spirit. The meat is eaten first and then the stock is drunk as a soup. This version can be eaten all together, with rice.

SERVES 6

3 lb (1.4 kg) lean flank of beef
2 tablespoons sesame oil
1 large onion, chopped
1 small piece of fresh root ginger, crushed
4 cloves of garlic, crushed
1 tablespoon soya bean paste
1 cube of red bean curd
1 teaspoon Chinese five spice powder
1 teaspoon cumin powder

1 teaspoon aniseed powder
1 piece of Chinese dried tangerine peel
1 teaspoon salt
1 teaspoon sugar
2 tablespoons rice wine or dry sherry
½ pint (300 ml) meat stock, see pages 41–2
1 lb (450 g) Chinese dark green cabbage (pak choy), shredded

Cut the beef into bite-sized cubes or strips and trim away any excess fat. Blanch the meat in boiling water for 1 minute and drain.

Heat the oil in a saucepan or wok, add the onion, ginger and garlic and brown over a medium heat. Add the meat and then the remaining ingredients, except the cabbage, adding the stock last. Stir and simmer for 1 hour.

When ready, place the cabbage in a flame-proof casserole or hot pot and lay the cooked meat on top. Cover and cook over a gentle heat for 10 minutes before serving as suggested above.

This 'hot pot' refers to a heavy iron casserole in which the dish is cooked and served and is quite different to the quick cooking Mongolian Hot Pot.

chinese hot pot.

Mongolian Lamb Hot Pot

This is a bit like Japanese *Tempura*, only you are boiling, not frying.

S E R V E S   4 - 6

3-3½ lb (1.4-1.5 kg) boned shoulder, loin or
leg of lamb
1 lb (450 g) spinach leaves, cut into large
pieces
2 lb (900 g) Chinese white cabbage or other
Chinese greens such as pak choy, *cut into*
large pieces
3 cakes of beancurd, each cut into 8-10 slices
4 oz (100 g) transparent (bean thread)
noodles, soaked in warm water for 10
minutes and drained

For the sauces:
3 tablespoons hoisin sauce
3 tablespoons chilli sauce
2 tablespoons soy sauce
1 tablespoon sesame oil
2 tablespoons chopped spring onions
1 tablespoon chopped fresh root ginger
2-3 cloves of garlic, finely chopped

5 pints (2.8 litres) chicken stock, see page
43, or water, for cooking

Cut the lamb into fairly large slices and beat them out with a meat mallet or rolling pin between sheets of greaseproof paper until very thin. Cut the lamb into strips. Arrange the lamb on a serving plate. Place the spinach, cabbage, beancurd and noodles on another serving plate.

Put the hoisin and chilli sauces in separate bowls. Mix together the soy sauce and sesame oil in a third bowl. Mix the spring onions, ginger and garlic in another bowl. Place the meat, vegetables and sauces on the table. Stand the hot pot in the middle and pour in the stock or water. When your guests are seated, bring the stock to the boil. Meanwhile, allow guests to

prepare their own sauces by mixing the different ingredients together, according to taste.

When the stock is boiling vigorously, each guest should pick up a piece of lamb with chopsticks and cook it in the stock or water until just tender. This should take no longer than 20-30 seconds, depending on the thickness of the meat. The meat is then dipped into one of the sauces before eating.

The vegetables can be cooked or eaten in the same way, adding more stock or water to the hot pot as necessary. When all the meat has been eaten, put the remaining vegetables in the pot. Boil vigorously for a few minutes, then serve as a soup in individual bowls.

Barbecued Chinese Pork (Charsiu)

S E R V E S   4 - 6

4 × 12 oz (350 g) pork fillets

For the marinade:
4 cloves of garlic, crushed
2 tablespoons hoisin sauce
2 tablespoons soya bean paste

1 tablespoon soy sauce
3 tablespoons rice wine or Madeira
4 tablespoons sugar
1 teaspoon salt
1 teaspoon cochineal

Mix together all the marinade ingredients in a bowl (not aluminium) and add the pork fillets. Leave to marinate for 4 hours. Lift out the fillets and place them on a rack over a roasting tin. Cook in a preheated oven, 425°F/220°C (gas mark 7), for 1 hour, turning the meat a couple of times.

To serve, cut the meat crossways into slices and pile on top of some stir-fried bean sprouts or Chinese dark green cabbage (*pak choy*).

Chinese Crispy Roast Pork

S E R V E S   4 - 6

3 lb (1.4 kg) belly of pork
1 tablespoon salt
1 tablespoon sugar

1 tablespoon Chinese five spice powder
1 tablespoon MSG
juice of ½ lemon

Make cuts in the pork 1 inch (2.5 cm) apart for marinating and to make cutting the meat easier when cooked. Mix together the salt, sugar, five spice powder and MSG and rub into the meat evenly.

To make the skin crispy, prick little holes in the rind, using a sharp fork, before rubbing a little extra salt and the lemon juice liberally into the skin. Hold the meat together at both ends with skewers. Hang up the pork to dry in a cool, well ventilated room for 12 hours. Put a pan below the meat to catch any drips.

Place the pork, skin upwards, on a rack over a roasting tin and cook in the centre of a preheated oven, 425°F/220°C (gas mark 7), for 1 hour.

To serve, cut between the rib bones to remove slices of meat, then chop into pieces. Serve on a bed of stir-fried bean sprouts and pickled vegetables.

Steamed Spareribs in Black Bean Sauce

In China spareribs are more often steamed than roasted – but you need to cut them up smaller to cook them in this way, so that the meat is tender and juicy.

S E R V E S 4

1 lb (450 g) pork spareribs
1 clove of garlic, crushed
1 slice of fresh root ginger, finely chopped
1 tablespoon vegetable oil

For the sauce:
2 tablespoons black bean sauce
1 tablespoon soy sauce

1 teaspoon sugar
1 teaspoon dry sherry

1 small green or red chilli pepper, seeded and finely shredded, to garnish
1 teaspoon sesame oil, to garnish

Ask your butcher to cut the spareribs into individual ribs and then into small pieces, about ¾ inch (2 cm) long. Alternatively, do this yourself using a heavy cleaver. Put the spareribs in a bowl (not aluminium) with the garlic, ginger and the sauce ingredients. Mix well, then leave to marinate for about 20 minutes.

Brush a heatproof plate or dish with the vegetable oil, then put the sparerib mixture on the plate. Place in a steamer or on a rack in a wok over boiling water, cover and steam for 30 minutes – refill with boiling water, if necessary. Sprinkle with the chilli pepper and sesame oil. Serve hot.

Barbecued Spareribs

These have nothing at all to do with the kind of barbecued ribs that come in boxes from takeaway restaurants. This is the authentic Chinese way of serving them.

SERVES 2-3

1 lb (450 g) pork spareribs
5 tablespoons soy sauce
3 tablespoons water
2 tablespoons dry sherry
2 tablespoons tomato ketchup

1 teaspoon sugar
1 clove of garlic, crushed
1 small piece of fresh root ginger, finely chopped

Cut the spareribs into individual ribs if necessary and remove any excess fat. Mix together the soy sauce, water, sherry, ketchup, sugar and garlic in a wide bowl or casserole dish (not aluminium), and add the ginger. Leave the spareribs to marinate in the sauce for at least 1 hour, turning occasionally.

When you are ready to cook them, remove the ribs from the marinade, reserving the liquid. Cook under a preheated hot grill for 10 minutes on each side, turning once, until the ribs are cooked and a dark brown colour.

Alternatively, the ribs may be baked. Thread the ribs on to a long skewer and place the skewer on an oven rack. Put a large pan or tray below the ribs to catch any drips, and cook in a preheated oven, 375°F/190°C (gas mark 5), for 40–45 minutes, until they are cooked and crisp.

Heat the reserved marinade in a small pan and serve hot as a sauce for the ribs.

Chinese Cabbage in Oyster Sauce

Chinese dark green cabbage or *pak choy*, which looks like spinach or Swiss chard, was originally grown in Shanghai and was considered the king of vegetables in China for its crispness and light fresh taste.

SERVES 4-6

2 lb (900 g) Chinese green cabbage (pak choy)
4 tablespoons oil
4 cloves of garlic, finely crushed
1 small piece of fresh root ginger, sliced

1 tablespoon rice wine or dry sherry
3 tablespoons oyster sauce
salt
freshly ground black pepper

Wash and shred the cabbage. Blanch it in boiling water in a wok for 1 minute and drain.

Heat the oil in the wok over a high heat. Brown the garlic and ginger before throwing in the blanched cabbage and remaining ingredients. Stir-fry for a few minutes, but do not overcook otherwise the cabbage will lose its crispness and much of its vitamin content.

Fried Noodles

The Chinese have endless noodle dishes, but Chow Mein is the best known in the West. This is the basic one that goes with anything from Barbecued Duck to Deep-fried Prawns.

SERVES 4

1 lb (450 g) dried Chinese egg noodles
3 tablespoons groundnut or corn oil
½ small onion, chopped
4 spring onions, trimmed and cut into strips
8 oz (225 g) fresh bean sprouts

1 tablespoon soy sauce
1 tablespoon rice wine or dry sherry
salt
freshly ground black pepper

Cook the noodles in a pan of boiling water for 3–6 minutes – do not overcook them. Drain well and shake to get rid of excess water.

Heat the oil in a wok or frying pan and lightly fry the onion, spring onions and bean sprouts. Add the noodles and the remaining ingredients and stir-fry for a few minutes.

Serve immediately.

SERVING JAPANESE FOOD

The Japanese, even more than the Chinese, eat with their eyes, so freshness and presentation are all. Buy the best ingredients you can find and try your hand at being an artist and a sculptor.

You could serve a little raw fish to start, followed by *Tempura.* Japanese food should always be eaten as soon as it is cooked. At the end of a meal, serve some fresh exotic fruit and plenty of plum liqueur.

The only problem with Japanese food is that you can't make any excuses about being a lousy cook, because most of the ingredients are raw!

Mirin and Soy Dipping Sauce (Soba Tsuyu)

SERVES 6

3 tablespoons mirin *(sweet sake) or substitute 2½ tablespoons Japanese soy sauce*
3 tablespoons usukuchi shoyu *soy sauce or substitute 2½ tablespoons pale dry sherry*
*¾ pint (450 ml) stock (*niban dashi*), see page 242*
*3 tablespoons preflaked dried bonito fillet (*katsuobushi*)*
pinch of salt
MSG

For the garnish:
*2½ tablespoons finely grated Japanese white radish (*daikon*) or substitute 2½ tablespoons peeled, grated icicle radish or white turnip*
1 tablespoon grated fresh root ginger

Heat the *mirin* or Japanese soy sauce in a small pan over a moderate heat until lukewarm. Turn off the heat, ignite the *mirin* with a match and shake the pan gently backwards and forwards until the flame dies out. Add the *usukuchi shoyu* soy sauce or sherry, stock, bonito and salt and sprinkle lightly with MSG. Bring to the boil over a high heat, then strain through a fine sieve into a small bowl. Cool to room temperature and check the seasoning, adding a little salt if necessary.

Garnish with the radish or turnip and the ginger.

Deep-fried Prawns and Vegetables in Batter (Tempura)

This is as much good fun as the old fondue, because you can all gather around this special sort of frying pan and eat little morsels of vegetables and fish cooked freshly, delicately at whim, and the feast can continue for hours. The idea is to present the raw food absolutely beautifully. The Japanese go all out for the look of the thing so you can go mad and serve it on things like black marble. Give everyone a little dish of batter and bowls of sauces and they can cook their own – wonderful group therapy for fazed gastronauts.

SERVES 6

1 small aubergine
18 canned ginnan (ginkgo) nuts, drained (optional)
1 lb (450 g) uncooked king prawns, peeled and deveined, see page 243
2 oz (50 g) flour
12 mangetout peas, topped and tailed
6 white button, oyster or shiitake mushrooms, cut in half
1 medium sweet potato, weighing about 8 oz (225 g), peeled and sliced into ¼ inch (7 mm) thick rounds
12 baby sweetcorn, trimmed
vegetable oil or a mixture of vegetable and sesame oil for deep-frying

For the batter:
1 egg yolk
15 fl oz (425 ml) ice cold water
⅛ teaspoon bicarbonate of soda
6½ oz (180 g) flour

For the dipping sauce:
13 fl oz (375 ml) Mirin and Soy Dipping Sauce, see page 240, or 3 tablespoons Lemon and Salt Dip, see page 243

Peel the aubergine, but leave occasional ½ inch (1 cm) wide strips of purple skin to add colour to the finished dish. Cut the aubergine in half lengthways, then cut into ¼ inch (7 mm) thick slices. Wash in cold water, pat thoroughly dry and set aside. Skewer three ginnan nuts, if using, on each of six toothpicks. Dip the prawns in the flour and shake off the excess.

To make the batter, put the egg yolk, ice cold water and bicarbonate of soda into a large bowl. Sift in the flour and mix well with a wooden spoon. The batter should be thin and watery, but quite lumpy. If it is too thick, thin it with drops of cold water. Ideally, the batter should be used immediately after being made, but it can, if necessary, stand for 10 minutes – no longer.

Since Tempura must be served hot, the most practical way to cook it is to divide the ingredients into individual portions, placing them on separate sheets of greaseproof paper so that a complete serving, consisting of three prawns, two mangetouts, two mushroom halves, three ginnan nuts, if using, a slice of sweet potato and two baby sweetcorn, can be fried at one time and then kept warm in a preheated oven, 250°F/120°C (gas mark ½), while the remaining portions are being fried.

Fill a deep-fat frying pan or a large, heavy-based frying pan, flameproof casserole or *tempura* pan to a depth of 3 inches (7.5 cm) with vegetable oil or mixture of vegetable and sesame oil. Heat the oil to 375°F/190°C on a frying thermometer, or until bubbles form on wooden chopsticks stirred in the oil.

Dip one piece of food at a time into the batter, twirling it around to coat it, then drop it into the pan. Fry only six or eight pieces of food at a time. Turn the pieces with chopsticks after 1 minute and fry for about another minute, until they are light gold. Drain on absorbent kitchen paper, arrange each serving of food on an individual plate or in a basket and keep warm in the oven for no longer than 5 minutes. Skim the oil, check the temperature and fry the remaining portions.

Serve accompanied by a small dish of one of the *Tempura* dipping sauces.

Stock (Niban Dashi)

M A K E S   A B O U T   1   P I N T   (600 ml)

1¾ pints (1 litre) cold water
4 inch (10 cm) square dried kelp seaweed
 (kombu)

½ oz (15 g) dried bonito flakes (hana-katsuo)

Pour the water into a pan and bring to the boil. Wipe the kelp and add it to the pan. Let the water come to the boil again, then immediately remove the kelp from the pan and set aside. Tip the bonito flakes into the liquid and reboil. Turn off the heat. Let this stock rest undisturbed for about 2 minutes, then skim off any surface scum.

Return the cooked kelp to the stock in the pan and bring almost to the boil over a high heat. Reduce the heat to the minimum and simmer, uncovered, for about 5 minutes. Strain the stock through a sieve lined with a double thickness of cheesecloth or clean cloth napkin, set over a bowl, and let it drain through undisturbed. Discard the solids. The stock is now ready to be used.

N O T E

If you really enjoy Oriental food, I'm afraid you are going to have to spend a bit of time ringing up people to find out where you can get the authentic ingredients. It isn't always easy, but if you enjoy your food, it's worth the trouble, and shopping is half the fun.

Lemon and Salt Dip (Ajishio)

SERVES 6-8

2½ tablespoons salt
1½ teaspoons MSG

16 thin lemon wedges

Mix together the salt and MSG in a small bowl, then divide it into equal heaps in the centre of six to eight very small plates.

Garnish each portion with lemon wedges.

Vinegared Rice and Fish 'Sandwiches' (Nigiri-Sushi)

MAKES ABOUT 48

6 medium-sized uncooked prawns, unpeeled
2½ tablespoons Sushi Dressing, see page 245
2 lb (900 g) filleted sea bream, sea bass, red snapper, squid, abalone or tunny fish, in one piece

1¼ pints (750 ml) Sushi Rice, see page 245
2½ teaspoons Japanese green horseradish (wasabi) mixed to a paste with 2½ teaspoons cold water and set aside to rest for 15 minutes

To prevent the prawns curling when cooked, insert a toothpick lengthways along their inner curves. Bring 7 fl oz (200 ml) water to the boil in a small pan and drop in the prawns. Cook only until they turn pink, about 1½ minutes. Drain, remove the toothpicks and peel the prawns. Devein them by making a shallow incision along the top of each prawn and removing the white or black intestinal vein with the point of a knife. Then cut the prawns three-quarters of the way along their inner curves and gently spread them open, butterfly fashion. Flatten them slightly with the side of a cleaver or knife.

Put 4 tablespoons cold water and 1½ tablespoons of the Sushi Dressing in a bowl. Add the prawns, turn them to coat well and leave to marinate for 15-30 minutes.

Cut the filleted fish into ¼ inch (7 mm) thick diagonal slices with a sharp knife. (The thicker tunny fish should be cut into ½ inch [1 cm] thick diagonal slices.)

Put the remaining Sushi Dressing with 2½ tablespoons cold water into a small bowl. This mixture, called tezu, is used to moisten the hands to prevent the rice becoming sticky. Dip your fingers into the tezu and lift out about 1 tablespoon of the rice. Shape it into an oblong. Smear a bit of the horseradish paste down the centre of a piece of fish and put the fish, horseradish side down, on top of the rice, then press the two together. The fish should completely cover the rice. Top the patties of rice with the prawns but do not use any more horseradish.

Arrange on a large dish and serve or cover with a sheet of clingfilm and keep in a cool place (not the refrigerator) for no longer than 30 minutes.

Variations

For the Tekka and Kappa Maki:
2 sheets dried laver seaweed (nori)
1 cucumber, about 4 inches (10 cm) long,
peeled, halved, seeded and cut lengthways
into ¼ inch (7 mm) wide strips

Japanese soy sauce

To make *Tekka Maki*, a variation of *Nigiri-Sushi*, prepare the prawns, raw fish and Sushi Rice as on page 243. Pass the laver seaweed over a gas flame or candle to intensify the flavour and colour. Cut the seaweed in half and lay half a sheet on the edge of a bamboo mat or sturdy cloth napkin.

Spread about 3 tablespoons rice over most of the seaweed sheet, leaving a 1 inch (2.5 cm) border of the seaweed exposed. Spread a streak of the horseradish paste diagonally through the middle of the rice and top with a row of raw fish. Use the mat or napkin to help you roll up the seaweed tightly. Then roll up in the mat or napkin one or two turns, and let it rest for 5 minutes. Remove the mat or napkin and slice crossways into 1–1½ inch (2.5–4 cm) pieces. Use up the remaining ingredients to make rolls in the same way.

To make *Kappa Maki*, another variation, substitute narrow strips of cucumber for the fish on one of the sheets of seaweed, omitting the horseradish.

Serve with Sushi and soy sauce.

Japanese food is not
only good to eat –
its good for your health.
As long as you don't overdo
the Sake.

Rice in Vinegar Dressing (Sushi)

Kelp seaweed, sold dried and packaged, is available from Japanese shops
and is used to give a gelatinous feel to food.

MAKES ABOUT 2½ PINTS (1.4 litres)

For the vinegar dressing:
3 tablespoons rice vinegar or substitute 2½
  tablespoons mild white vinegar
3 tablespoons sugar
2 teaspoons salt
1¼ tablespoons mirin *(sweet sake) or*
  substitute 2½ teaspoons pale dry sherry
½ teaspoon MSG

For the rice:
13 oz (375 g) Japanese rice or 13 oz (375 g)
  short-grain white rice, washed thoroughly
  in cold running water and drained
2 inch (5 cm) square of kelp seaweed
  (kombu), cut with a heavy knife from a
  sheet of packaged kelp and washed under
  cold running water

To make the dressing, put the vinegar, sugar, salt and *mirin* or sherry into a small pan. Bring to the boil, uncovered, and stir in the MSG. Cool to room temperature. You can make this dressing in large quantities and store it, unrefrigerated, in a tightly covered jar for as long as a year.

To make the rice, put 1 pint (600 ml) cold water and the rice into a medium-sized pan and allow the rice to soak for 30 minutes. Then add the square of seaweed and bring to the boil over a high heat. Cover the pan, reduce the heat to moderate and cook for about 10 minutes, until the rice has absorbed all of the water. Reduce the heat to the minimum and simmer for a further 5 minutes. Remove from the heat and allow the rice to rest for an additional 5 minutes before taking off the lid and discarding the seaweed.

Transfer the hot rice to a large dish or tray (not metallic). Immediately pour on the vinegar dressing and mix thoroughly with a fork. The rice is ready to use when it has cooled to room temperature. Or it can be covered and left at room temperature for as long as 5 hours before serving.

NOTE
MSG (monosodium glutamate) powder is used in both Chinese and Japanese cooking to enhance flavour. It is available from supermarkets and specialist shops. Try not to use it very much and omit it, if you like, from any recipe.

Sliced Raw Fish (Sashimi)

The most important factor in the preparation of *Sashimi* is the freshness of the fish. Keep the fish refrigerated, wrapped in cheesecloth, until ready to use. Handle the fish as little as possible. *Sashimi* may be composed of one fish or a variety of fish.

SERVES 4-6

1 lb (450 g) filleted sea bass, halibut, squid, abalone, turbot, bream or tunny fish, in one piece, skinned and all bones removed, squid cleaned

For the dipping sauce:
3-5 tablespoons Japanese soy sauce
*¼ pint (150 ml) spicy dipping sauce (*chirizu*), see page 247*

For the garnish:
*½ teaspoon Japanese green horseradish (*wasabi*) mixed to a thick paste with just enough cold water and set aside to rest for 15 minutes.*
*2 inch (5 cm) section of white radish (*daikon*) or large icicle radish or white turnip, peeled, shredded and soaked in cold water until ready to use*
1 carrot, shredded and soaked in cold water until ready to use
1 stick of celery, cut in half lengthways, shredded and soaked in cold water until ready to use

There are four basic fish cutting methods for *sashimi* and you need a sharp, heavy knife for them all. It's a good idea to use at least two different cutting methods.

■ Flat cut (*hira giri*): this is the most popular shape, suitable for any filleted fish. Holding the fish firmly, cut straight down in slices about ¼–½ inch (7–15 mm) thick and 1 inch (2.5 cm) wide, depending on the size of the fillet.

■ Cubic cut (*kaku giri*): this style of cutting is more often used for tunny fish. Cut the tunny fish as above (flat cut) then cut into ½ inch (1 cm) cubes.

■ Thread shape (*ito zukuri*): although this method may be used with any small fish, it is especially suitable for squid. Cut the squid straight down into ¼ inch (7 mm) slices, then

cut lengthways into ¼ inch (7 mm) strips.

■ Paper-thin slices (*usu zukuri*): place a fillet of bass or bream on a flat surface and, holding the fish firmly with one hand, slice it at an angle into almost transparent sheets.

Arrange the fish attractively on individual serving plates. Garnish each plate with the horseradish paste and decorate with the strips of radish or turnip, carrot and celery. Cover with clingfilm and refrigerate for no more than 1 hour before serving. Pour the dipping sauce into tiny individual dishes and accompany each serving with its own sauce. The horseradish paste may be mixed into the soy sauce to taste.

Spicy Dipping Sauce for Sashimi (Chirizu)

M A K E S   A B O U T   ¼   P I N T   (150 ml)

5 teaspoons sake (rice wine)
3 tablespoons peeled and finely grated white
*   radish (*daikon*) or substitute 3 tablespoons*
*   finely grated icicle radish or white turnip*
2 spring onions, including the green stalks,
*   trimmed and sliced into thin rounds*

3 tablespoons Japanese soy sauce
3 tablespoons lemon juice
MSG
*⅛ teaspoon seven pepper spice (*hichimi
*   togarashi)*

Warm the sake in a small pan. Remove from the heat, ignite it with a match and shake the pan gently until the flame dies out. Pour the sake into a small dish and allow to cool.

Put the sake, radish or turnip, spring onions, soy sauce, lemon juice, a sprinkling of MSG

and the seven pepper spice in a small bowl. Mix well.

To serve, pour the dipping sauce into tiny individual dishes and serve with sea bass, sea bream or plaice *Sashimi*.

N O T E
If you can't get sake, sherry is an acceptable, but second-rate substitute.

Delicate Soy-based Dipping Sauce for Sashimi (Tosa Joyu)

M A K E S   A B O U T   ¼   P I N T   (150 ml)

3 tablespoons Japanese soy sauce
2½ teaspoons sake (rice wine)

5 teaspoons preflaked dried bonito fillet
*   (*katsuobushi)*
MSG

Put the soy sauce, sake, bonito and a sprinkling of MSG into a small pan and bring to the boil, uncovered, stirring constantly. Strain through a fine sieve into a small bowl and allow to cool to

room temperature. Divide the dipping sauce among six individual dishes and serve it with *Sashimi* of any kind.

White Radish and Red Pepper Garnish (Oroshi)

MAKES ¼ PINT (150 ml)

3 inch (7.5 cm) round section of Japanese white radish (daikon)*, peeled*
4 dried whole red peppers (takano tjume)
6 tablespoons equal parts soy sauce and lemon or lime juice (pon-su)

2 spring onions, including 3 inches (7.5 cm) of the green parts, sliced into thin rounds, to garnish

Make four openings in the flat side of the radish with chopsticks or the tip of a sharp, pointed knife. Insert a pepper deep into each opening, so that its tip is level with the surface of the radish. Set aside for at least 4 hours or chill overnight. By then, the radish's moisture will have reconstituted the red peppers and they in turn will have spiced the radish.

Grate the pepper-stuffed radish, divide into six and roll each part into a small ball.

To serve, pour the soy and lemon or lime juice into six tiny dishes and add a grated radish and pepper ball to each dish. Garnish with the spring onions and serve with *Sashimi*.

VEGETABLES AND SALADS

The Campaign for the Preservation of

the Dignity of Vegetables

One of the most misunderstood and maligned dishes in the world is Ratatouille. Where people go wrong is not caring that aubergines, peppers and courgettes each have their own special taste, and they get very hurt if they're chopped up crudely and thrown into the pot with the rest, covered with tinned tomatoes and boiled. You have to let them maintain their individual flavours while sharing them with one another at the same time. The same neglect is evident when people boil delicate vegetables until they resemble wet blotting paper.

Well, in this section, I'm campaigning for the Preservation of the Dignity of Vegetables! Thanks to the wonders of modern science, we can enjoy all sorts of vegetables well out of season, and the supermarkets are overrun with Mediterranean sunshine vegetables and exotica. But that doesn't mean you have to shun the good old carrot or potato. There's still nothing to beat a real country market with stalls piled high with fresh root vegetables.

And freshness is the key. If you're going to join my campaign, you need to start by choosing vegetables that are still proud and vigorous and in the bloom of youth.

BAKING

This is the least troublesome way to cook vegetables – just whack them in the oven with your casserole and joint and they'll look out for themselves.

Artichokes
Wash and trim young globe artichokes and stuff with finely chopped garlic, parsley and seasoned fresh breadcrumbs. Place in an ovenproof dish and drizzle lightly with olive oil. Cook in a preheated oven, 350°F/180°C (gas mark 4), for about 40 minutes, or until tender. Serve immediately.

Aubergines
Make long, thin incisions along the length of each aubergine and place small pieces of bacon, tomato, garlic and sprigs of herbs (marjoram and basil, for example) in these. Place in a shallow ovenproof dish and drizzle with olive oil. Season with salt and pepper and cook in a preheated oven, 325°F/160°C (gas mark 3), for about 1 hour.

Mushrooms
Wipe small mushrooms and mix with a little diced bacon, butter, parsley and chopped spring onions in an earthenware ovenproof dish. Cook, uncovered, in a preheated oven, 350°F/180°C (gas mark 4), for 30–40 minutes, until the bacon is crisp and browned and the mushrooms are tender. Serve sprinkled with chopped parsley.

Onions
Place unpeeled onions in a large baking dish that they will fit into snugly and add a little water to cover the base of the dish. Cook in a preheated oven, 400°F/200°C (gas mark 6), for about 1–1½ hours, or until soft. Remove the skins with a sharp knife. Serve dotted with butter and sprinkled with salt and pepper to taste.

Potatoes and Sweet Potatoes
Scrub the potatoes well and arrange on a baking sheet or on an oven rack. Cook in a preheated oven, 375°F/190°C (gas mark 5), for about 1 hour, or until a skewer inserted into the skin penetrates easily. To serve, cut a cross in the top of each potato and squeeze the potato at both ends to reveal the cooked flesh. Add a generous dollop of butter, soured cream or cheese to serve.

Tomatoes
Remove the stalk end of the tomatoes and seeds. Place in a shallow ovenproof dish and scatter lightly with garlic- and parsley-flavoured fresh breadcrumbs or use to stuff the centres. Drizzle with olive oil and cook in a preheated oven, 400°F/200°C (gas mark 6), for 15–20 minutes, or until the tops are golden.

We all have memories of Brussels sprouts, cooked until they disintegrate into a grey pulp, tasting of nothing and losing all their nutritional value. That shouldn't be what boiling vegetables is all about. Dignity, remember, Dignity at all times!

Since the water you cook your vegetables in is also a precious commodity for adding to stocks and gravies, I suggest you use plenty of it. Boil green vegetables quickly to keep them colourful and still looking the way they did when raw. Root vegetables take longer and should be turned down to simmer after you've brought them to the boil as too much fast boiling will turn them to mush.

This is my guide to approximate cooking times:

And I really do mean approximate

Vegetable	Boiling Time	Steaming Time
Artichoke, Jerusalem	30 minutes	40 minutes
Asparagus	10 minutes	12–15 minutes
Beans, French	8–10 minutes	8–12 minutes
Beans, runner	7–10 minutes	8–12 minutes
Beetroot (young)	1–2 hours	1½–2½ hours
Broad beans	7–10 minutes	10–12 minutes
Broccoli	8–15 minutes	10–20 minutes
Brussels sprouts	6–12 minutes	10–15 minutes
Cabbage, Chinese	4–6 minutes	7–9 minutes
Cabbage, spring	5–7 minutes	7–10 minutes
Carrots	8–10 minutes	12–14 minutes
Cauliflower	12 minutes	15 minutes
Celery	15–20 minutes	18–22 minutes
Chicory	15–20 minutes	20–30 minutes
Courgettes	4–6 minutes	6–10 minutes
Leeks	10–15 minutes	15–20 minutes
Mangetout peas	4–6 minutes	6–8 minutes
Marrow	8–10 minutes	10–20 minutes
Onions	20–30 minutes	25–35 minutes
Parsnips	20–30 minutes	25–35 minutes
Peas	5–20 minutes	8–25 minutes
Potatoes	15–25 minutes	20–30 minutes
Pumpkin	8–10 minutes	15–25 minutes
Salsify	15–20 minutes	20–30 minutes
Spinach	4 minutes	5–8 minutes
Swedes and turnips	20 minutes	25–30 minutes
Sweetcorn	5–6 minutes	12–15 minutes

BRAISING

Braising is a way of cooking vegetables fairly slowly either on top of the stove or in the oven with a relatively small amount of liquid. Unlike boiling, when the vegetables are cooked as quickly as possible to preserve the textures and flavours, braising is designed to allow the ingredients to intermingle and blend to create new flavours.

The choice of the liquid used is therefore very important not just for the cooking process but also as it forms a vital part of the finished dish. Veal or chicken stock or wine can be used depending on the character of the finished dish. Other flavouring elements should be used, such as garlic, herbs, finely chopped onion or bacon. The perfect stock for braising vegetables should have sufficient flavour to enhance the dish but not to drown the flavour of the vegetable. It should also be of good enough quality to reduce to a syrupy texture during the cooking process without an additional thickening agent. However, certain vegetables that have a very pungent taste, such as celeriac and celery, can benefit from par-boiling first.

Braised Chicory

SERVES 4

6 heads of chicory
4 oz (100 g) butter
salt

freshly ground black pepper
2-3 tablespoons lemon juice

Trim the heads off the chicory, core and wash well. Grease a shallow casserole dish with some of the butter, then add the chicory. Dot with the remaining butter and season well with salt and pepper. Cover and cook in a preheated oven, 350°F/180°C (gas mark 4), for about 1 hour, until tender.

Just before serving sprinkle with the lemon juice. Serve hot.

DEEP-FRYING

Deep-fried vegetables can be extremely Undignified unless you follow the golden rule of getting the fat to the right temperature before adding the vegetables. Test by dropping either a piece of vegetable or a cube of bread into the fat. If it sinks to the bottom, the fat isn't hot enough – it should immediately frizzle up and float. Unless the vegetables are coated in batter they must be absolutely dry before you fry them.

The British are renowned as a chip-loving nation, but we frequently make a mess of them. This is how to make chips properly.

SERVES 4

1½ lb (675 g) potatoes

corn oil for deep-frying

Peel the potatoes and cut them into ½ inch (1 cm) thick slices, then cut each slice into ½ inch (1 cm) sticks. Wash them in plenty of cold water to remove the starch. Pat dry in a clean tea towel or with absorbent kitchen paper.

Half-fill a chip pan with oil and heat to the right temperature – test by dipping in a stick of potato to see if it sizzles. When it is ready, dip a chip basket into the oil, then remove and put the chips in it. Lower the basket gently into the fat. Fry over a moderate heat until the chips are almost cooked – they should be waxy, but not browned. Remove from the oil and increase the heat slightly. Cook the chips again rapidly until crisp and golden brown. Drain on absorbent kitchen paper and serve immediately.

Basic Batter Recipe

Onion rings, sliced courgettes and so on are delicious dipped in batter and deep-fried. Slice the vegetables uniformly or the thinner ones will cook faster than the thick ones. And don't overload the basket – it is better to cook the vegetables in batches so that they are evenly done. The simplest way to coat vegetables for deep-frying is to soak them in milk and dust with seasoned flour, or you can use this basic batter recipe.

MAKES ENOUGH TO COAT ABOUT 1½ LB (675 g) PREPARED VEGETABLES

4 oz (100 g) plain flour
½ teaspoon salt
3 tablespoons melted butter or olive oil

2 eggs, separated
7 fl oz (200 ml) milk, water or beer

Mix together the flour, salt, butter or oil and egg yolks in a bowl. Gradually add the liquid and whisk until smooth. Leave to stand for 1 hour, then whisk the egg whites until they hold stiff peaks and fold them into the batter. You can vary the consistency by adding more or less liquid. A runny batter is lighter, though it will tend to spread while cooking. A thick batter clings better to the vegetables, but is more stodgy.

RAPID FRYING OR SAUTÉING

Rapid frying, or sautéing, is a way of crisping moist vegetables, as the heat causes the moisture to evaporate. You must cut the vegetables into thin slices or small, regular shapes so that

they cook through evenly. I use a combination of butter and oil to give a rich flavour – and also because butter alone burns at a lower temperature than oil.

Sautéed Potatoes

SERVES 4-6

1½–2 lb (675–900 g) potatoes
1 tablespoon oil
1½ oz (40 g) butter

salt
freshly ground black pepper

Wash the potatoes and cook them in a pan of boiling salted water for about 15 minutes, until just tender. Drain well and remove the skins. With a sharp knife, cut the potatoes into ¼ inch (7 mm) slices. Heat together the oil and butter

in a frying pan, add the potato slices and cook until golden brown and crisp. Drain on absorbent kitchen paper and season to taste with salt and pepper before serving.

This is a sophisticated – and pretty Dignified – way of serving vegetables, which gives you all sorts of artistic licence to invent different shapes and colour schemes on side plates. Try yellow swede, red beetroot and green Brussels sprouts for an unsubtle combination!

The process doesn't have to be elegant – you just pummel the vegetables with your everyday potato masher, or you can rub soft root vegetables through a sieve. Make sure all vegetables are well drained first.

Beat in a little butter, salt and plenty of freshly ground black pepper, nutmeg or whatever seasoning you fancy. Some drier vegetables might like a little cream too.

ROASTING

Root vegetables are delicious roasted in the oven. This method will work well for potatoes, parsnips, turnips and so on.

Roast Potatoes

S E R V E S 4

1½ lb (675 g) potatoes
2 oz (50 g) lard or dripping

freshly ground black pepper

Peel the potatoes and cut them into large even-sized pieces. Place in a pan of cold salted water and bring to the boil. Cook for at least 10 minutes, then drain well. Roughen the outsides by either shaking the potatoes in the covered pan or by running a fork over them.

Melt the lard or dripping in a roasting tin in a preheated oven, 425°F/220°C (gas mark 7).

Season the potatoes with plenty of pepper and add to the tin, turning them in the fat to ensure they are well coated. Roast, turning and basting them frequently, for about 45 minutes, until they are crispy and golden brown. If roasting a joint at the same time, this should ideally be placed on a wire rack directly above the potatoes so that the meat juices can drip over them.

STEAMING

The joy of steaming vegetables is that their delicate flavours are preserved by their not leaking any juices into the cooking water. Not an iota of Dignity lost here!

You can steam vegetables in anything from bamboo baskets stacked up like a multi-storey car park to a metal colander that fits into your saucepan. The major thing to remember is that the water beneath must be kept at a brisk, rolling boil. Cooking times are longer than those for boiling, see page 251. Remember to get up a good head of steam first.

Green is probably the word that first springs to mind at the mention of salad. In this section I have given you a few dressings and these show the many different ways you can dress a humble lettuce. Wash the lettuce leaves, shake them dry and, unless you have a super efficient salad spinner, dry each piece on a tea towel or with absorbent kitchen paper. This prevents the dressing becoming diluted. Just before serving, stir the dressing, add the lettuce and toss thoroughly to ensure each leaf is well coated.
All the dressings given here are enough to dress one salad for 4-6 people.

French Dressing

If you are serving a dressed green salad after the main course there is nothing to better a classic French dressing. Never, never use malt vinegar or cheap oils.

1 clove of garlic
½ teaspoon sea salt
freshly ground black pepper
pinch of sugar

½ teaspoon made French mustard
1 tablespoon white wine vinegar
3 tablespoons olive oil

Depending on your taste for garlic, either cut it and rub it round the salad bowl or crush the clove with the salt in the bowl. Add pepper and sugar to the salt and stir in the mustard and vinegar. Beat in the oil and mix well with a fork.

Light Summer Dressing

This light dressing is ideal for salads with poultry and fish.

2 tablespoons olive oil
sea salt
freshly ground black pepper

pinch of sugar
1-2 tablespoons lemon juice
finely chopped chives

Place your lettuce, washed and dried as described on page 257, in a large bowl. Pour over the oil and turn the leaves to coat well. Sprinkle on the salt, pepper and sugar and the lemon juice. Toss thoroughly and check the seasoning. Scatter over the chives and serve immediately.

Creamy Dressing

Very simple and delicious with lettuce and cucumber.

2 tablespoons single cream
salt
freshly ground black pepper

squeeze of lemon juice
finely chopped mint

Wash the lettuce, drain well and dry gently with a tea towel or absorbent kitchen paper. Mix together the cream with salt and pepper to taste and a good squeeze of lemon juice. Add the mint and pour over the salad. Toss and allow to stand for 30 minutes before serving.

Flemish Salad Dressing

This is a substantial hot dressing that produces a quick and simple meal.

4 eggs
2 tablespoons white wine vinegar
salt

freshly ground black pepper
1 oz (25 g) butter

Wash and dry the lettuce as described on page 257 and place in a large bowl. Just before serving, break the eggs into another bowl, add the vinegar and season to taste with salt and pepper. Beat with a fork. Melt the butter in a heavy pan, pour in the eggs and stir over a gentle heat until they start to thicken. Pour quickly over the lettuce, toss well and serve immediately.

Warm Butter Dressing

An unusual dressing. Use with the Italian radicchio (red chicory) or a
combination of green and red leaves. This is also delicious as a starter.

2 oz (50 g) butter
juice of ½ lime
juice of ½ lemon

salt
freshly ground black pepper
finely chopped basil

Wash and dry the lettuce as described on page
257 and place in a salad bowl. Melt the butter
very gently in a pan, add the lime and lemon
juices, salt and pepper and basil. Stir well in the
pan, pour over the lettuce, toss thoroughly and
serve immediately.

Bacon Dressing

Use slightly bitter salad leaves for this such as curly endive or very young
dandelion leaves freshly picked from the garden.

4 oz (100 g) streaky bacon, rind removed
2 tablespoons white wine vinegar

salt
freshly ground black pepper

Wash and dry the leaves as described on page
257. Cut the bacon into small pieces and fry,
without additional fat, until crisp. Remove the
bacon from the pan, leaving the fat, and toss on
to the leaves. Add the vinegar to the bacon pan,
season to taste with plenty of salt and pepper
and bring to the boil. Stir well to loosen any bits
in the bottom of the pan. Pour quickly over the
salad. Serve immediately.

Chicken Liver Salad

This also makes a lovely starter.

S E R V E S 2 (O R 4 A S A S T A R T E R)

4 oz (100 g) chicken livers
2 oz (50 g) butter
1 teaspoon made French mustard
1 tablespoon white wine vinegar

3 tablespoons olive oil
1 egg yolk
salt
freshly ground black pepper

Prepare the lettuce as described on page 257. Wash and dry the chicken livers and chop them roughly, removing any strings or bitter green bits. Melt the butter in a frying pan and sauté the livers for 2–3 minutes. Remove from the pan and chop finely. Place the remaining ingredients in a small bowl and stir well with a fork to mix. Add the chicken livers. Pour over the lettuce and serve.

For the Perfect Side Salad

Batavia: This is similar to curly endive in colour and flavour, but with larger leaves.

Cabbage lettuce: The ordinary round lettuce, which is good in summer; the winter variety is not worth its price.

Chicory: A white, bitter and crunchy leaf best added to other sweeter leaves like cos.

Cos lettuce: A firm lettuce with a lot of character and good flavour.

Curly endive: Endive, sometimes called *frisée*, has a slightly bitter flavour – use tender pale leaves only.

Dandelion leaves: Pick young and small – delicious, bitter, iron taste. Make a sweet dressing or add to sweeter leaves.

Escarole: A strong, curly leaf, which is slightly bitter. It is good on its own with a sweetish dressing of olive oil, mustard and sugar.

Iceberg lettuce: A very crisp lettuce with good texture and unremarkable flavour.

Lamb's lettuce: A small leaf, slightly bitter, also called corn salad, or *mâche*. It is expensive; mix with other leaves.

Radicchio: This is expensive, but a small head goes a long way mixed with other leaves.

Watercress: Spicy and crunchy, this should be served dry and never be dressed. It is best with fatty, grilled meats with a little sprinkled salt.

Webb's lettuce: A firm lettuce, quite substantial.

SAVOURIES

One of the highlights of my illustrious but truncated sojourn in the military was the occasional 'dining in' night when, dressed in our ceremonial finery, we feasted in pomp at a long polished table groaning with the regimental silver while the band played Bach and Mozart from the minstrels' gallery.

Although the food was not of the top drawer it was classical in its way. We would begin with mulligatawny soup – a gritty brown liquid with a remarkable, spicy after-taste. Then a thin (and only slightly stale) fillet of white fish masked in a bland cornflour-based white sauce, which had possibly been flecked with grated Cheddar cheese and lightly browned under the grill before being left to weep in the hotcupboard until it was required to be served. This was followed by the ceremonial changing of the wine, from some mildly sweet German white to some cheap Burgundy, to accompany the meat course. As a very junior officer (which I was) you constantly minded your Ps and Qs, and timed your eating to match the colonel's. Finally, after the dessert – usually a pear and sponge flan with evaporated milk or thin custard – came the best bit of all. The savoury. Sometimes prunes wrapped in bacon grilled on toast, sometimes Scotch woodcock. I loved them then as I do now.

There is no better way to end a meal than to munch a savoury or morsel as you sip the last glass of red wine, before you turn to the dessert (and here I beg to differ from those who think dessert is served before either the cheese or savoury) and some excellent Australian dessert wine – fortified Muscat – which, if you can find it, is about the best in the world.

Yes, the savoury is making a comeback and deserves recognition. I have included some of my personal favourites, both classical and modern. I hope you enjoy them.

Sardine Toasties

My version of one of the traditional savouries.

MAKES 12

4 oz (112 g) can sardines, drained, skinned
and boned
dash of anchovy essence
dash of lemon juice
1 oz (25 g) butter, softened
dash of Tabasco sauce

salt
freshly ground black pepper
3 thin slices of white bread, preferably a little
stale
oil and butter for frying

Mash the sardines, add all the remaining ingredients except the bread and oil and butter for frying, and mix well. Cut the bread into 2 inch (5 cm) rounds, using a small pastry cutter or glass, to make 12 rounds. Heat together the oil and butter in a pan, using half oil and half butter to prevent the butter burning, and fry the bread until golden brown. Drain on absorbent kitchen paper. Just before serving spread each round with a generous amount of the sardine mixture and pop under a preheated hot grill for 1 minute. Serve hot.

Devilled Sardines on Toast

SERVES 4

4 oz (112 g) can sardines in oil, drained
½ oz (15 g) butter, softened
1 teaspoon grated onion
1 teaspoon made French mustard

2 teaspoons lemon juice
pinch of cayenne pepper
pinch of ground paprika
4 fingers of hot buttered toast

Place the drained sardines on the rack of a grill pan. Mix the butter with the onion, mustard, lemon juice and peppers until smooth. Spread half of this mixture over the sardines and cook, under a preheated hot grill, until bubbly, about ½–1 minute. Turn over, dot with the remaining mixture and cook for a further 30 seconds.

Serve on the fingers of hot buttered toast while still hot.

Kippered Toasties

2 kipper fillets, each cut in half, or half
1 large kipper, cooked and filleted, to give
4 small fillets

1 oz (25 g) butter
freshly ground black pepper
4 strips of hot buttered toast

Place the kipper fillets under a preheated hot grill for 1 minute on each side until cooked, turning them once. Place half in a bowl with the butter and pepper to taste and beat well. Spread over the hot buttered toast strips. Cut the remaining fillets in half and place a small piece of fillet on top of the toasts. Season again with a little pepper, grill very quickly just to reheat, about 30 seconds, then serve very hot.

Scotch Woodcock

2 oz (50 g) can anchovies in oil, drained
1 oz (25 g) butter
freshly ground black pepper
4 slices of hot toast, crusts removed
4 egg yolks

¼ pint (150 ml) single cream
1 tablespoon chopped parsley
pinch of cayenne pepper
salt

Mash the drained anchovies with the butter and black pepper to taste. Spread on to the hot toast and keep warm.

Place the egg yolks, cream, parsley, cayenne pepper and a pinch of salt in a pan and mix well. Cook over a moderate heat, beating or whisking constantly, until thick and creamy. Pour over the hot, prepared anchovy toasts and serve immediately.

Anchovy Savouries

SERVES 4

1 oz (25 g) butter
½ teaspoon anchovy essence
pinch of cayenne pepper
2 hard-boiled egg yolks

2 oz (50 g) cheese, grated
4 large strips of toast, about 1 × 3 inches
  (2.5 × 7.5 cm)
2 oz (50 g) can anchovy fillets, drained

Mash the butter with the anchovy essence, cayenne pepper, egg yolks and cheese until smooth. Spread the toast strips with this mixture and top each with the anchovy fillets. (Of course, you can do all of this well in advance.)

Just before serving, cook under a preheated hot grill or in a very hot oven until bubbly, about 3 minutes.

Anchovy Straws

Instead of buying Bombay Mix or crisps to nibble while drinking 'At Home', why don't you make these simple *amuse-gueules* – just like cheese straws really – but it will show the poets you can smoke!

SERVES 4

8 oz (225 g) frozen puff pastry, thawed
8 anchovy fillets

4 black olives, stoned and cut in half
1 egg yolk, beaten

Roll the pastry out very thinly on a lightly floured surface into a long rectangle. Cut into sixteen equal rectangles, about 1–1¼ inches (2.5–3 cm) × 2½–4 inches (7–10 cm) each. Put one anchovy fillet and one olive half cut into quarters on eight of the rectangles. Moisten the edges with water. Sandwich the other rectangles on top, pinching the edges firmly together.

Make a criss-cross pattern on each rectangle and paint with egg yolk to glaze. Place on an oiled baking sheet and bake in a preheated oven, 425°F/220°C (gas mark 7), for 20–25 minutes, or until golden brown.

Crab Savouries

SERVES 4

1 oz (25 g) butter
1 tablespoon finely chopped gherkins
1 tablespoon fresh white breadcrumbs
4 oz (100 g) crabmeat

3 teaspoons lemon juice
2 tablespoons double cream
pinch of cayenne pepper
4 squares of hot buttered toast

Melt the butter in a pan. Add the gherkins, breadcrumbs, crabmeat, lemon juice, cream and cayenne pepper. Mix well and cook over a gentle heat for 2–3 minutes, stirring constantly.

When very hot, pile on to the squares of hot buttered toast, dust with a little cayenne pepper and serve immediately.

Angels On Horseback

SERVES 4

2 oz (50 g) butter
4 rounds of bread, about 2 inches (5 cm) in
    diameter
2 rashers of streaky bacon, rind removed

4 oysters
pinch of cayenne pepper
lemon juice
watercress sprigs, to garnish

Melt half of the butter in a pan and fry the bread rounds until golden. Drain on absorbent kitchen paper and keep warm.

Flatten the bacon rashers with the back of a knife and cut in half. Roll around the oysters after sprinkling with a little cayenne and lemon juice. Secure with wooden cocktail sticks.

Melt the remaining butter in the pan and cook the angels until the bacon browns on all sides, about 2 minutes.

To serve, place each cooked angel on the rounds of fried bread and garnish with watercress sprigs. Serve immediately.

Chicken Livers on Toast

SERVES 4

4 oz (100 g) chicken livers
2 tablespoons seasoned flour
1 oz (25 g) butter
½ small wineglass of Madeira

1 oz (25 g) mushrooms, thinly sliced
salt
freshly ground black pepper
4 squares of hot buttered toast

Wash and dry the chicken livers, removing any strings or bitter green bits. Coat the livers lightly in the seasoned flour, shaking off any excess. Melt the butter in a frying pan and cook the chicken livers until lightly browned but still pink, about 3–5 minutes. Add the Madeira with the mushrooms and salt and pepper to taste. Cook gently to mix and to allow the flavours to develop.

To serve, spoon on to the hot buttered toast.

Side-saddle Devils

My own version of these savouries that can also be served as one of your 'nibbles' at a drinks party. The waterchestnuts create a lovely difference in texture from the chicken livers.

SERVES 12-16

4 oz (100 g) chicken livers
2-3 tablespoons soy sauce
8 oz (225 g) streaky bacon

10 oz (283 g) can waterchestnuts, drained
and sliced

Wash and dry the chicken livers and cut into walnut-sized pieces. Marinate in the soy sauce for a few hours. Remove the rinds from the bacon and cut each rasher into two or three pieces of about 2–3 inches (5–7.5 cm). Drain the chicken livers and wrap each with a slice of waterchestnut in a length of bacon. Spear the rolls on to cocktail sticks. Either place under a preheated hot grill for 3–5 minutes, turning frequently, or if heating food for a drinks party, place on a baking sheet in a preheated oven, 425°F/220°C (gas mark 7), for 5–8 minutes until the bacon is cooked. Serve hot.

Devils On Horseback

S E R V E S 4

4 large, plump prunes (cooked in a little red
wine to plump if dry)

2 rashers of streaky bacon, rind removed
4 rounds of hot buttered toast

Remove the stones from the prunes. Flatten the bacon rashers with the back of a knife and cut in half. Roll around the prunes and secure with wooden cocktail sticks. Cook under a preheated hot grill, turning frequently, until the bacon is golden on all sides.

To serve, place each cooked devil on a slice of hot buttered toast.

Mushrooms on Toast

This very simple savoury is best made just before it is to be eaten.

S E R V E S 4

8 oz (225 g) mushrooms
1 oz (25 g) butter
1 tablespoon lemon juice
salt

freshly ground black pepper
1 tablespoon cream
chopped parsley
4 triangles of hot buttered toast

Place the mushrooms in a pan with the butter and lemon juice and cook gently for about 5 minutes, until cooked and tender and the liquid has evaporated. Season with salt and pepper and stir in the cream and a little chopped parsley.

To serve, spoon on to the hot buttered toast triangles and serve immediately.

Welsh Rarebit

S E R V E S 4

8 oz (225 g) mature Cheddar cheese, grated
1 oz (25 g) butter
4 tablespoons beer
salt

freshly ground black pepper
1 tablespoon dry mustard
4 slices of hot buttered toast

Put the cheese, butter and beer in a small pan and melt gently over a low heat, stirring in one direction only. Add the salt and pepper to taste and the mustard and mix well. Spoon over the toast and brown under a preheated hot grill. Serve immediately.

Cheese Aigrettes

M A K E S A B O U T 30
(T O S E R V E 4 - 6)

3½ oz (90 g) plain flour
½ teaspoon dry mustard powder
pinch of cayenne pepper
salt
freshly ground black pepper
7½ fl oz (225 ml) water

3 oz (75 g) butter
3 eggs, beaten
2 oz (50 g) mature Cheddar cheese, grated
oil for deep frying
grated Parmesan cheese, to serve

Sift the flour with the mustard, cayenne and salt and pepper to taste. Place the water and butter in a pan and heat slowly to melt, then bring to the boil. Add the flour, all at once, and beat well to make a smooth paste that leaves the sides of the pan clean. Allow to cool slightly, then gradually beat in the eggs until smooth and shiny (when ready the mixture should have a soft dropping consistency – you may not need all of the third egg). Finally, fold in the cheese.

Heat the oil until a cube of bread sizzles and browns in 1 minute. Drop in balls of the cheese mixture, about the size of a walnut, and fry until cooked and golden, about 6–7 minutes. The aigrettes will rise and puff as they cook, so cook in batches for the best results. Alternatively, the mixture can be placed in a piping bag with a star-shaped nozzle and pieces can be cut with scissors and dropped into the hot oil for frying.

Remove with a slotted spoon and drain on absorbent kitchen paper. Dust with grated Parmesan cheese and serve immediately while still warm.

These are cigar-shaped savouries that can be made in advance and frozen uncooked or part-baked and finished when required.

VARY THE QUANTITIES DEPENDING ON
THE NUMBER YOU ARE SERVING

filo pastry, available from good delis
melted butter

For the cheese filling:
cream cheese and Feta cheese, half and half
clove of garlic, crushed
parsley or mint, finely chopped
generous shake of cayenne pepper
pinch of salt

For the meat filling:
1 tablespoon vegetable oil
lamb, finely minced
onion, finely chopped
clove of garlic, crushed
cayenne pepper, to taste
large pinch of ground cumin

To make the cheese filling, mash the cheese with a fork and mix in the garlic, herbs, cayenne pepper and salt.

To make the meat filling, heat the oil in a pan and fry the minced lamb, onion and garlic until cooked – about 10 minutes. Stir in the remaining ingredients and allow the mixture to cool.

Filo pastry dries out very quickly once it is unwrapped, so keep in a pile, work swiftly and cover any pieces you are not using with a clean, damp tea towel. Cut the sheets of filo into 6 inch (15 cm) squares. Brush each square lightly with melted butter. Lay about 1–2 teaspoons of the filling in a thin line diagonally across the centre, but do not go close to the edges or it will squidge out while cooking. Fold the square in half diagonally, corner to corner, and brush again with a little melted butter, leaving the corner uncovered. Roll up like a cigar and wet the corner with a little water to seal.

Place on a greased baking sheet and bake in a preheated oven, 425°F/220°C (gas mark 7), for 5–10 minutes until crisp and golden brown.

Savoury Fritters

This light fluffy beer batter is used as a base to which you add
the flavouring of your choice. A few of my own suggestions are below.

For the batter:

1 egg, separated
4 fl oz (100 ml) beer
*2 oz (50 g) rice flour – this is a gluten-free
flour, but use ordinary plain flour if you
can't get it*

salt
freshly ground black pepper
½ oz (15 g) butter, melted

Beat the egg yolk with the beer. In a separate bowl sift the flour with the salt and pepper. Make a well in the centre, pour in the egg yolk mixture and beat well until smooth. Allow the batter to stand for about 30 minutes. Stir in the melted butter. Whisk the egg white until it holds stiff peaks and fold this into the batter.

Prawn

Spear peeled prawns on to wooden toothpicks, dip in the batter to cover on all sides and deep fry in hot oil until golden, about 1½–2 minutes. Drain on absorbent kitchen paper.

Chicken

Marinate walnut-sized pieces in soy sauce, and cook as for prawns.

PUDDINGS AND DESSERTS FOR HAPPY GASTRONAUTS

Since this book is personal, opinionated, biased and even, yes though I say it myself, pedantic, I have chosen the puddings, desserts, afters, call them what you will, on the grounds that I like them and to hell with fashion, trends or gastronomic one-upmanship.

While I admire and indeed support the stratospheric efforts of the modern chef to dazzle our eyes and thrill our taste buds with exqui-site flights of culinary fancy served in magically-wrought, spun sugar baskets or expressed as fruit mosaics that would have bewil-dered a Byzantine swimming pool maker, I still believe that a per-fectly made caramel cream or a steamed suet pudding takes a lot of beating. And since cooking as well as eating should be fun and not a nail biting chore, you'll have a better time making simple things taste good rather than submitting yourself to some culinary Ph.D as you frantically try to unravel the mysteries of filo pastry, sugar baskets or go mad trying to buy *fraises des bois* at 5.30 on a Saturday afternoon. After all, if you want to keep up with the culinary fron-tiersmen you only have to reach for the telephone and your wallet, book a table at some brilliant restaurant and pay for it. But life is full of contradictions so I *have* included a few really difficult ones from some of my chums in the trade: for example, Orange Bavarois in Chocolate Genoese Sponge with Orange Sauce, see page 296.

So, to return to the point, here are a few of my favourites that have never failed to give delight and satisfaction.

Hot Chocolate Soufflé

Stephen Ross at Homewood Park, Hinton Charterhouse

Stephen's choc soufflé is excellent – as is most of his food – and I'm jolly
pleased that as a former, dare I say, pupil of the legendary Kenneth Bell,
he has progressed to glory at Homewood Park.

SERVES 6

8 oz (225 g) plain chocolate
1 oz (25 g) butter
½ small cup of rum

4 large egg yolks
7½ fl oz (225 ml) egg whites

Break the chocolate into a pan, add the butter and melt over a low heat. Remove from the heat, add the rum and allow to cool slightly. Beat the egg yolks and, still beating, pour in the chocolate mixture. Whisk the egg whites until they hold soft peaks, then beat one-quarter into the chocolate mixture.

Fold in the remaining egg whites. Pour into six ramekin dishes and arrange on a baking tray. Cook in a preheated oven, 375°F/190°C (gas mark 5), for 10–12 minutes, until they are puffed and lightly set. Serve immediately.

Soufflés are so good because if you've got a sweet tooth like me you can go to the Carved Angel a Albert's place and order 2 – and you won't really feel awfully bloated!

Hot Apple and Honey Soufflé
with Blackberry Cream

Ramon Farthing at Calcot Manor, Tetbury

Another offering from Calcot, again beautifully exploiting good country fruit.

S E R V E S 4

For the soufflés:
8 fl oz (250 ml) thick apple purée (about 2-3
tart cooking apples, peeled, chopped and
cooked in a little water)
honey, to taste
1 teaspoon cornflour (optional)
juice of ½ lemon
4 eggs, separated
caster sugar, for dusting

For the blackberry cream:
3 fl oz (75 ml) double cream
caster sugar (optional)
2 oz (50 g) blackberries, hulled and sliced

Sweeten the apple purée with honey to taste. If the mixture is not thick at this stage, then add the cornflour, dissolved in a little water, and cook until thickened. Allow to cool.

Add the lemon juice and egg yolks and beat well. Whisk the egg whites until they hold stiff peaks. Fold into the apple mixture. Butter and then dust four individual ramekin dishes with caster sugar and fill each with a quarter of the apple soufflé mixture.

Bake in the centre of a preheated oven,

425°F/220°C (gas mark 7), for 7-10 minutes, or until well puffed and golden.

Meanwhile, make the blackberry cream. Whip the cream until it forms soft peaks. Add a little sugar to taste, if liked, then add the sliced blackberries. Continue to whisk the cream mixture slowly until thick.

Finally, shape the cream between two warm spoons to make four mounds and place each on a small side plate with a cooked soufflé. Serve immediately.

Pear Tart

This is the most wonderful pear dessert using ratafias or little Italian Amarettis and pear liqueur to enhance the delicate flavour of the fruit. It should really be served warm with whipped cream to tickle the taste buds.

S E R V E S   6

For the pastry:
4 oz (100 g) butter, softened
2 tablespoons cold water
1 oz (25 g) icing sugar
8 oz (225 g) flour

For the fruit:
3 even-sized Comice pears
3 oz (75 g) sugar
¼ pint (150 ml) water

For the filling:
2 oz (50 g) ratafia biscuits or little Italian Amarettis, available from good delicatessens
2 tablespoons pear liqueur
6 fl oz (175 ml) double cream
2 large eggs
icing sugar

To make the pastry, make sure that the butter is soft enough to work with, but do not melt it – room temperature is ideal. Put the butter, water, sugar and one-third of the flour in a large bowl. Mix well, using a wooden spoon, to make a tacky paste. Gradually work in the remaining flour, then knead until smooth. Roll the pastry out thinly on a lightly floured surface and use a little over half of this to line a deep 8 inch (20 cm) flan ring. Don't roll the pastry too thickly or it will not cook evenly or become crisp. Bake 'blind' in a preheated oven, 375°F/ 190°C (gas mark 5), for about 20 minutes, or until it is lightly browned and firm. Allow to cool. The remainder of the pastry can be used to make some fruit tartlets or a smaller fruit flan.

Thinly peel, halve and core the pears. Put the sugar and water in a pan, add the pears and poach until just tender, about 10 minutes.

Sprinkle the ratafias or Amarettis with the pear liqueur. Whisk together the cream and eggs and stir into the biscuits. Drain the pears and arrange neatly over the base of the flan case, cut-side down. Spoon over the filling and bake in the centre of a preheated oven, 375°F/ 190°C (gas mark 5), for 45 minutes, until firm and set. Sprinkle with icing sugar and return to the oven for a few minutes to lightly brown.

Marmalade and Spice Suet Pudding

Bring back the steamed pudding! I will! So here is one of my family's favourite suet puds.

SERVES 6

4 oz (100 g) self-raising flour
pinch of salt
1 teaspoon ground mixed spice
4 oz (100 g) shredded suet

4 oz (100 g) fresh white breadcrumbs
1 oz (25 g) brown sugar
6 oz (175 g) orange or grapefruit marmalade
milk, water or orange juice to mix

Sift the flour, salt and spice into a bowl. Add the suet, breadcrumbs and sugar and mix well. Stir in the marmalade and a little milk, water or orange juice to make a stiff but manageable dough.

Tip into a well-greased 2 pint (1.2 litre) pudding basin – the mixture should two-thirds fill the basin. Cover the top of the pudding with a sheet of buttered greaseproof paper, then cover the basin with a piece of foil pleated across the centre and secure with string. Steam for 2½ hours (remembering to top up the water level in the pan with boiling water as necessary).

P. S. don't forget the custard

Real Custard Sauce

SERVES 4-6

2 egg yolks
1 tablespoon sugar

1 vanilla pod
½ pint (300 ml) milk

Beat the egg yolks lightly in a bowl. Heat the sugar with the vanilla pod and milk in a pan until hot but not boiling. Remove the vanilla pod and whisk the mixture into the egg yolks. Place the bowl over a pan of hot water or place the mixture in the top of a double boiler and cook, stirring constantly, until the custard thickens slightly and will coat the back of a spoon, about 20–25 minutes.

Serve warm or cold.

Christmas Pudding

Q. Do you know the best way to enjoy Christmas pud?
A. Don't have it on Christmas Day – but eat it the first weekend AFTER Christmas following a lunch of consommé, poultry (a turkey, duck or chicken), and roast pork with crackling and apple sauce. This way you can enjoy Christmas cake and mince pies for tea on Christmas Day! Geddit?

MAKES 1 × 2 PINT (1.2 litre) PUDDING TO SERVE 6-8

5 oz (150 g) fresh white breadcrumbs
4 oz (100 g) plain flour
4 oz (100 g) shredded suet
4 oz (100 g) soft brown sugar
5 oz (150 g) currants
4 oz (100 g) sultanas
4 oz (100 g) seedless raisins
1 small eating apple, peeled, cored and
  chopped
3 oz (75 g) chopped mixed candied peel and
  cherries

pinch of salt
pinch of ground mace
pinch of ground ginger
pinch of freshly grated nutmeg
pinch of ground cinnamon
grated rind and juice of ½ small orange
grated rind and juice of ½ small lemon
2 large eggs, beaten
2 tablespoons brandy
milk to mix

Grease a 2 pint (1.2 litre) pudding basin. Place the breadcrumbs, flour, suet, sugar, dried fruit, apple, peel and cherries, salt, spices and fruit rind and juices in a large bowl and mix well together. Add the beaten egg, brandy and sufficient milk to mix to a soft dropping consistency. Cover with a damp cloth and leave to stand overnight. Stir the mixture well, then place in the prepared basin. Cover the pudding with buttered greaseproof paper, then with a piece of foil pleated across the centre and secure with string. Steam steadily for 6–7 hours (remembering to top up the water level in the pan with boiling water as necessary). When cooked, store in a cool, damp-free place.

To serve, steam as above for a further 3 hours, then turn out on to a serving plate. Serve with clotted cream, brandy butter or rum sauce.

It's a good idea to make Christmas puds in September or October. They mature splendidly.

Baked Stuffed Apple Dumplings

This is my Somerset childhood on a plate – especially with yellow crusted clotted cream AND home-made custard!

S E R V E S   4

1½ quantities of shortcrust pastry, see page 71
4 medium cooking apples
1 oz (25 g) sugar

1 oz (25 g) mixed dried fruit
beaten egg or milk, to glaze
caster sugar, to sprinkle

Cut the pastry into four even-sized pieces and roll each one out on a lightly floured surface to an 8–10 inch (20–25 cm) round.

Peel and core the apples, keeping them whole, and place each on a round of pastry. Mix the sugar with the dried fruit and use to fill the centres of the apples. Brush the pastry edges with water then gather the pastry edges over the top of the apples to completely enclose. Press the edges well together to seal. Turn over so that the seam side is down and place on a greased baking sheet. Glaze with beaten egg or milk and dust with caster sugar.

Bake in a preheated oven, 425°F/220°C (gas mark 7), for 10 minutes. Reduce the oven temperature to 325°F/160°C (gas mark 3) and cook for a further 30 minutes, or until the pastry is golden and the apple is tender.

Double-crust Apple Pie

S E R V E S   6 - 8

For the shortcrust pastry:
10 oz (275 g) plain flour
pinch of salt
2½ oz (65 g) lard
2½ oz (65 g) butter or margarine
3-4 tablespoons cold water

For the filling:
2 lb (900 g) cooking apples, peeled, cored and
  sliced
4 oz (100 g) soft light brown sugar
2 tablespoons cornflour
½ oz (15 g) preserved ginger, chopped
  (optional)
milk or beaten egg, to glaze
caster sugar, to sprinkle

Lightly grease the base and sides of a 10 inch (25 cm) shallow pie dish. Prepare the pastry by sifting the flour with the salt into a large bowl. Rub in the lard and butter or margarine, using your fingertips, a food processor or a pastry blender, until the mixture resembles fine breadcrumbs. Add the water and mix to a firm dough. Roll out two-thirds of the pastry on a lightly floured surface to a round large enough to line the base and sides of the pie dish. Ease the pastry into the dish and trim away any excess. Roll out the trimmings and remaining pastry to make a round large enough to cover the pie and set aside.

To make the filling, place half of the apples in the pastry-lined dish. Mix together the brown sugar and cornflour and sprinkle half over the fruit. Scatter with the ginger, if using, then cover with the remaining apples. Top with the rest of the sugar mixture.

Brush the rim of the dish with milk or beaten egg and carefully lift on the pastry lid. Trim away any excess pastry and seal the edges.

Flute the pastry rim and make a small hole in the top of the pie to allow any steam to escape (a pie funnel may be used in the centre of the pie to hold up the crust during cooking). Glaze with milk or beaten egg and sprinkle with the caster sugar. The pie can be decorated with any pastry trimmings, if liked.

Place on a baking sheet and bake in a preheated oven, 425°F/220°C (gas mark 7), for 30–40 minutes, or until golden brown and cooked through.

Serve hot or cold with thick clotted or whipped cream or with custard.

Old-fashioned Bread Pudding

I know that Anton Mosimann's Bread and Butter Pudding is the best in the WORLD – but my Mum's humble BREAD PUDDING is great too.

S E R V E S   6

8 oz (225 g) stale bread and crusts
6 oz (175 g) mixed dried fruit
2 oz (50 g) sugar
½ teaspoon ground mixed spice

3 oz (75 g) butter, melted
1 egg, beaten
1 tablespoon milk

Soak the bread in a little water for at least 30 minutes. Squeeze out all the water and place the bread in a bowl. Add the dried fruit, sugar and spice, then the butter, egg and milk and mix well. Tip the mixture into a greased 2 pint

(1.2 litre) ovenproof dish and bake in a preheated oven, 325°F/160°C (gas mark 3), for about 40–50 minutes, until just set.

Serve hot, warm or cold.

Real Rice Pudding

S E R V E S 4

3 tablespoons short-grain rice
1 pint (600 ml) creamy milk
1 vanilla pod

1 oz (25 g) caster sugar
¼ pint (150 ml) double cream

Mix the rice with the milk, vanilla pod and sugar in a pan and bring to the boil. Either place in the top of a double boiler and cook gently for 1½ hours until tender or place in an ovenproof dish and cook in a preheated oven, 300°F/150°C (gas mark 2), for about 2 hours. Remove the vanilla pod and allow the pudding to cool slightly.

Whip the cream until it holds soft peaks. Fold the cream into the rice and serve hot or cold.

Plum and Almond Slice

This is a simple and effective way to use up those lovely plums on your trees rather than leaving them for the wasps, so rush out and pick them now and impress your family and friends.

S E R V E S 6

For the base:
4 oz (100 g) butter, diced, at room
    temperature
4 oz (100 g) caster sugar
1 large egg (size 1 or 2)
8 oz (225 g) self-raising flour
pinch of salt
few drops of almond essence

For the filling:
1 lb (450 g) plums – two colours look
    effective
1 oz (25 g) whole almonds, blanched
1 oz (25 g) Demerara sugar
1 tablespoon runny honey, to glaze
icing sugar (optional)

Put all the ingredients for the base into a bowl and beat for a couple of minutes, or whizz for a minute in a food processor. Spread the mixture over the base of a greased shallow baking tin, about 12 × 8 inches (30 × 20 cm).

Halve the plums and remove the stones. Place the halved plums in lines lengthways down the tin, cut-side and skin-side upwards alternately. Put an almond in the centre of each upturned plum and sprinkle the whole pudding with the sugar. Bake in the centre of a preheated oven, 375°F/190°C (gas mark 5), for about 30 minutes, until the plums are cooked and the base is golden brown. Glaze with the honey, thinned with a little water.

Dust with a little icing sugar, if liked, and serve warm or cold with thick clotted or whipped cream.

Apple and Raspberry Nest

This is a wonderful pudding that you can eat in front of a log fire on a
blustery cold day feeling very smug indeed.

SERVES 6

For the pastry:

7 oz (200 g) self-raising flour
1 teaspoon baking powder
4 oz (100 g) butter, diced
1 oz (25 g) sugar
1 egg, beaten
3 tablespoons milk

For the filling:

3-4 tablespoons good raspberry jam
1 lb (450 g) cooking apples, peeled, cored and
  thinly sliced
1 oz (25 g) Demerara sugar

To make the pastry, sift the flour and baking powder into a large bowl. Rub in the butter until the mixture looks like very fine breadcrumbs – this is easiest done in a food processor. Stir in the sugar, egg and milk and mix to a smooth dough. Turn the dough on to a lightly floured surface and knead gently. Roll out two-thirds of the pastry and use to line the base and sides of a greased 2 pint (1.2 litre) pudding basin.

Spread the jam in the bottom and fill with the prepared apples and sugar. Roll out the remaining pastry and use to make a cover. Moisten the edges with a little water and pinch to seal. Cover the top with buttered grease-proof paper, then cover the basin with a piece of foil pleated across the centre and secure with string. Steam for about 2 hours. Don't forget to check the water level occasionally to ensure that your pud does not boil dry. Top up with boiling water as necessary.

When ready, turn out the pudding on to a serving plate and serve with a lovely home-made custard, see page 275.

Spiced Apple and Prune Crumble

SERVES 6

7 oz (200 g) prunes
1½ lb (675 g) cooking apples
4 oz (100 g) butter
4 oz (100 g) sugar

2 teaspoons ground mixed spice
6 oz (175 g) wholewheat flour
2 oz (50 g) chopped toasted hazelnuts

Soak the prunes overnight in water, then transfer to a pan and simmer until tender, about 20 minutes. If you are using tenderised prunes, they do not require prior soaking. Drain the prunes, quarter them and remove the stones.

Peel, core and slice the apples into a large pan and add 1 oz (25 g) of the butter, 2 oz (50 g) of the sugar and half the mixed spice. Cover and cook gently until they are tender. Do not overcook them – we do not want a mush. Carefully stir in the prunes and turn into a shallow 2 pint (1.2 litre) ovenproof dish.

To make the crumble, sift the flour and remaining spice into a bowl. Cut the rest of the butter into pieces and rub it into the flour until the mixture has the texture of fine breadcrumbs. Stir in the hazelnuts and the remaining sugar. Sprinkle the crumble mixture over the fruit. Bake in a preheated oven, 350°F/180°C (gas mark 4), for about 45 minutes. The top should be golden brown and crispy.

Serve warm with home-made custard, see page 275, or whipped cream.

Grilled Bananas with Butterscotch Sauce

Clive Imber at Michael's Brasserie, Newcastle upon Tyne

SERVES 4

8 bananas
sugar, to taste

For the butterscotch sauce:
4 oz (100 g) Demerara sugar
2 tablespoons golden syrup
2 oz (50 g) unsalted butter
½ pint (300 ml) whipping cream

To make the butterscotch sauce, put the sugar, syrup and butter in a heavy-based pan and cook over a moderate heat until the mixture is golden brown. Remove from the heat and whisk in the cream. Allow to cool.

Lightly butter a grill pan. Slice the bananas in half lengthways. Sprinkle with sugar to taste and cook under a preheated hot grill until they are brown but not mushy, about 3–5 minutes.

Serve immediately with the butterscotch sauce and perhaps with some vanilla ice cream.

Praline Pancakes

I adore praline and pancakes and this recipe combines the two.
Serve them with a raspberry sauce.

S E R V E S   4 - 6

For the batter:
4 oz (100 g) flour
pinch of salt
1 egg
1 egg yolk
½ pint (300 ml) milk
1 tablespoon melted butter
1 teaspoon sugar

For the praline:
2 oz (50 g) unblanched almonds
2 oz (50 g) caster sugar

For the praline butter:
3 oz (75 g) butter
2½ oz (65 g) caster sugar
Kirsch, to taste

oil or clarified butter, see page 35,
    for frying

½ pint (300 ml) Raspberry Sauce,
    see the recipe for Iced Hazelnut Mousse
    on page 291

To make the batter, sift the flour with a good pinch of salt into a large bowl. Make a well in the centre and drop in the whole egg and egg yolk. Start adding the milk to the egg and mix from the centre, very gradually drawing in the flour to make a thick, smooth batter. When half of the milk has been added, beat well and stir in the melted butter and sugar. Whisk in the remaining milk. Cover and leave to stand in a cool place while you make the praline butter.

To prepare the praline, place the almonds and sugar in a small, heavy-based pan over a gentle heat. When the sugar is a liquid caramel, stir carefully with a metal spoon to toast the nuts on all sides. Turn on to an oiled slab or oiled foil and leave to set. When it is completely cold, crush it with a rolling pin as finely as possible.

To make the praline butter, cream the butter in a bowl and beat in the sugar until the mixture is light and fluffy. Mix in the praline and flavour with Kirsch.

To cook the pancakes, heat a heavy 6 inch (15 cm) frying pan. Grease very lightly with oil or clarified butter and put a generous tablespoon of batter into the centre. Swirl it to cover the base by tipping the pan. Cook the pancake over a brisk heat until the underside is golden. Loosen round the edge with a palette knife, toss or turn over and cook the other side. Cook the remaining batter in the same way, making the pancakes as thin as possible. Quickly spread the inside of each with praline butter and roll up like a cigar. Heat for a moment in a preheated oven and serve immediately with the Raspberry Sauce.

Iced Rhubarb Parfait

Clive Imber at Michael's Brasserie, Newcastle upon Tyne

Delicious! I've eaten this many times, cooked by my chum Clive Imber.
It's an elaborate way of serving the humble rhubarb – the sort of
invention that must be encouraged.

S E R V E S 8

6 egg yolks
7 oz (200 g) sugar
8 fl oz (250 ml) milk
12 fl oz (350 ml) double cream
¾ pint (450 ml) cooked rhubarb purée,
  sweetened to taste (you'll need about 1½ lb
  [675 g] raw rhubarb for this)

For the apricot and ginger purée:
1 lb (450 g) apricots, halved and stoned
2 pieces of preserved ginger in syrup, finely
  chopped
sugar
squeeze of lemon juice

Whisk together the egg yolks and sugar in a bowl until pale and creamy. Put the milk in a pan and bring to the boil. Remove from the heat and pour on to the egg yolk mixture, whisking constantly. Transfer the mixture to a clean pan and return to the heat. Cook the custard over a low heat, stirring continuously, until it thickens a little, just enough to coat the back of a spoon – do not allow it to boil. Pour the mixture into a bowl and allow it to cool, beating with an electric whisk, then chill it well.

Whip the cream until it holds stiff peaks. Fold the rhubarb purée and cream into the custard mixture. Line a 2½ pint (1.4 litre) loaf tin or terrine with clingfilm and pour in the custard. Cover and freeze for 4–6 hours, until firm.

To make the apricot and ginger purée, poach the apricots in a little boiling water for 5–10 minutes with the ginger, sugar to taste and the lemon juice. Purée in a food processor or blender or pass the mixture through a fine sieve. Chill.

To serve, turn out the ice cream, remove the lining and slice on to cold plates. Serve with the apricot and ginger purée.

Raspberry Parfait

This is a terribly simple dessert to make and is very refreshing after a substantial meal.

SERVES 4

1 lb (450 g) raspberries – frozen ones can be used as long as they are unsweetened
2 egg whites

4 oz (100 g) caster sugar
½ pint (300 ml) double cream

Rub the raspberries through a sieve, or process the fruit lightly, and pour the purée into a freezer tray. Cover and leave in the freezer overnight.

About 1 hour before serving, whisk the egg whites until they hold stiff peaks. Gradually add the sugar, about 1 tablespoon at a time, and continue beating until the mixture stands in firm peaks. Whip the cream lightly until

very soft peaks are beginning to form.

Tip the frozen purée into a bowl and mash it with a wooden spoon to break down the ice crystals. Fold together the cream and egg whites and then quickly, but carefully, fold in the semi-frozen raspberry purée. Pile into tall glasses and keep in the coolest part of the refrigerator until wanted, but for no longer than 15–30 minutes.

Syllabub with Strawberries

This must be one of the simplest desserts to make. Make it in tall glasses so that you can see the lovely contrasts in colours. Please use decent sherry as the flavour is most important.

SERVES 6

4 oz (100 g) caster sugar
½ pint (300 ml) double cream
4 tablespoons medium dry sherry

juice and finely grated zest of 1 lemon
1 lb (450 g) strawberries
caster sugar

Place the sugar, cream and sherry together with the lemon juice and zest in a large bowl. Whisk well, until quite thick. This is easiest done with an electric beater and will take several minutes if done by hand.

Do not wash the strawberries, but wipe them carefully. Keep six of the best ones with

stalks for decoration. Hull and core the remainder, slicing them into the base of six glasses. Carefully spoon over the syllabub mixture. Chill for several hours.

Just before serving, dip your reserved strawberries in a little caster sugar and pop on top.

Ice Cream

This is the ultimate ice cream, unrecognisable from that nasty yellow stuff
that forms an oily puddle if you happen to drop it on the floor! This
recipe is ideally suited for those of you who do not own an ice cream
maker as it is based on an egg mousse, which enables you to produce a
creamy result more easily. Try it with one of the delicious naughty sauces
that follow, which are not for the calorie counters.

SERVES 4-6

3 oz (75 g) sugar
4 fl oz (100 ml) water
4 egg yolks, well beaten
½ pint (300 ml) single cream

¾ pint (450 ml) double cream, partially
whipped
vanilla essence

Put the sugar and water into a small, heavy-based pan (not non-stick as it will not take the heat) and stir over a gentle heat until the sugar has dissolved. Then boil steadily without shaking or stirring until the sugar reaches 'thread' stage. When it is ready, a dribble of syrup dropped into a glass of water will form a crunchy string.

Have the well beaten egg yolks ready, preferably with an electric beater. Remove the pan of syrup from the heat and, as soon as the bubbles have subsided, pour on to the yolks, beating well. Continue whisking until the mixture is thick and mousse-like. Add the creams and vanilla essence to taste – freezing diminishes the flavour of cream ices so take this into consideration – and mix well. Pour into a freezer container, cover and chill well before freezing until set, about 2–4 hours.

Variations

Chocolate Ice Cream
When you have reached the mousse-like stage, stir in 3 oz (75 g) melted plain chocolate, then continue as above. Omit the vanilla essence.

Coffee Ice Cream
When you have reached the mousse-like stage, stir in 4 teaspoons instant coffee that have been dissolved in a few drops of boiling water, then continue as above. Omit the vanilla essence.

Praline Ice Cream
Put 3 oz (75 g) unblanched almonds and 3 oz (75 g) sugar in a heavy-based pan. Heat until the sugar caramelises, then turn on to an oiled slab or on to oiled foil. When cold, crush it, using a rolling pin or a pestle and mortar, to the texture required. Stir this praline into the vanilla ice cream just as it starts to set and return to the freezer.

Ice Cream Sauces

These are all wickedly rich sauces to serve with home-made ice cream.

S E R V E S   4 - 6

For chocolate sauce:

Break 7 oz (200 g) plain chocolate into a bowl or the top of a double boiler and melt it over hot but not boiling water. Meanwhile, bring ¼ pint (150 ml) milk and 2 tablespoons double cream to the boil, then pour on to the melted chocolate. Return to the pan and bring back to a simmer. Remove from the heat and stir in ½ oz (15 g) butter to make the sauce glossy. This sauce should be served hot, but it can be made in advance and kept in the refrigerator. Reheat carefully.

For tipsy coffee sauce:

Make as for the caramel sauce but substitute black coffee for half of the cream. When cool, add whisky or brandy to taste.

For caramel sauce:

Put 5 oz (150 g) caster sugar and ¼ pint (150 ml) double cream in the top of a double boiler or a bowl and heat it over hot but not boiling water. Meanwhile, melt 4 oz (100 g) caster sugar in a heavy-based pan and heat until it turns a golden caramel brown. As soon as it caramelises, pour it into the hot cream. Stir well over the heat, until the caramel has dissolved and the sauce thickened. Beat in a knob of butter.

Rich Lemon Ice Cream

Kate Smith at Royal Oak Hotel, Sevenoaks

SERVES 8

8 eggs, separated
3 oz (75 g) caster sugar
juice and grated rind of 6 lemons
Cointreau or Grand Marnier, to taste
  (optional)

1½ pints (900 ml) double cream (preferably
  Guernsey or Jersey)
mixture of fruit, sliced starfruit, blackberries,
  fraises des bois, raspberries, to serve

Whisk the egg yolks and sugar in a bowl set over a pan of gently simmering water until they are thick and frothy and form a continuous thread or ribbon when you hold the whisk well above the bowl. Take care not to scramble the eggs and keep whisking all the time. Remove from the heat and add the lemon juice and rind and a little Cointreau or Grand Marnier, if liked.

Whip the cream until it holds soft peaks. Whisk 4 egg whites to a similar consistency and mix with the cream. Fold into the lemon mixture and stir well. Pour into a freezer container, cover and freeze for 4 hours or more – the ice cream should have a soft consistency.

Serve scooped in tall, elegant glasses with biscuits and small fruits or arrange the ice cream on a large plate surrounded by sliced starfruit, blackberries, *fraises des bois*, raspberries, peaches, mangoes or loganberries.

If all this hand work is too daunting save up your pennies and buy an ice cream maker!

Caramel Apple Tart with Honey and Almond Ice Cream

Shaun Hill at Gidleigh Park, Chagford

You have to drive a long way to eat Shaun's cooking on Dartmoor – but the results are divine.

SERVES 4-6

1 quantity of shortcrust pastry, see page 71
4 firm eating apples
6 oz (175 g) unsalted butter
9 oz (250 g) sugar
2 tablespoons Calvados

For the ice cream:
4 oz (100 g) ground almonds
½ pint (300 ml) milk
½ pint (300 ml) double cream
8 egg yolks
4 oz (100 g) caster sugar
clear honey

To make the ice cream, put the almonds, milk and cream in a pan and bring to the boil. Whisk the egg yolks and sugar in a bowl until pale and thick. Strain the almonds, milk and cream and pour on to the egg yolk mixture. Set the bowl over hot water and whisk over a gentle heat until the mixture thickens enough to coat the back of a spoon. Remove from the heat, add honey to taste and allow to cool. Pour into a freezer container, cover and freeze until firm, about 2–4 hours.

Roll out the pastry on a lightly floured surface to about ⅛–¼ inch (4–7 mm) in thickness and use to line four small tartlet tins. Prick the pastry and bake 'blind' in a preheated oven, 400°F/

200°C (gas mark 6), for 10–15 minutes, until cooked. Allow to cool.

Meanwhile, peel, core and chop two of the apples. Cook in a small pan with a teaspoon of water until soft, then purée in a food processor or blender. Spoon the purée into the pastry cases.

Put the butter and sugar in a pan and cook until they turn a golden caramel brown. Add the Calvados. Slice the remaining apples and arrange in a thin fan shape across the purée. Coat with the Calvados caramel. Allow to cool, then serve with scoops of the honey and almond ice cream.

Sliced Poached Pear and Sorbet with Butterscotch Sauce

Christopher Oakes at Oakes Restaurant, Stroud

Chris used to feed me well at the Castle in Taunton before he opened on his own account. A great cook.

S E R V E S 6

1½ pints (900 ml) water
juice of ½ lemon
10 oz (275 g) sugar
9 medium pears, peeled, halved and cored

For the shortbread biscuit:
4 oz (100 g) butter
2 oz (50 g) caster sugar
4 oz (100 g) flour

For the butterscotch sauce:
¼ pint (150 ml) double cream
2½ oz (65 g) butter
2½ oz (65 g) Demerara sugar

For the chocolate sauce:
2 oz (50 g) plain chocolate
2 tablespoons double cream

Mix together the water, lemon juice and sugar in a pan. Add the pears and bring to a simmer. Cook gently for about 10–15 minutes, depending on the pears' ripeness, until they are tender. Cool in the syrup.

To make the sorbet, purée three of the poached pears in a food processor or blender, then rub the purée with about one-third of the syrup through a fine sieve. Freeze the mixture in an ice cream maker according to the manufacturer's instructions. Alternatively, pour the sorbet into ice cream trays and freeze. After 30 minutes, when partly frozen, remove and beat until smooth. Do this two or three times during the freezing process, which will take 2–3 hours.

Meanwhile, prepare the shortbread. Cream together the butter and 1½ oz (40 g) of the sugar in a bowl. Stir in the flour and leave to rest in the refrigerator for 10–15 minutes. Place in a piping bag with a star-shaped nozzle and pipe into flat, thin rosette shapes, about 2½ inches (6 cm) in diameter. Put on a buttered baking sheet and bake in a preheated oven, 400°F/ 200°C (gas mark 6), for 10–15 minutes. Do not allow the biscuits to colour too much. Sprinkle with the remaining sugar.

To make the butterscotch sauce, put the cream and butter in a pan over a gentle heat and bring to a simmer. Add the sugar and cook until the sauce thickens enough to coat the back of a spoon. Pass the sauce through a fine sieve set over a bowl and allow to cool.

Break the chocolate into a bowl or the top of a double boiler and melt over hot but not boiling water. Add the cream and stir well. Do not overheat the chocolate.

To serve, cut each of the remaining six poached pears into very thin slices. Arrange in a spiral pattern around the serving plates – leaving a 1 inch (2.5 cm) border around the outside. Pour the butterscotch sauce around the outside. Pour a ribbon of chocolate sauce on top of the butterscotch sauce. Using a small knife, run the blade back and forth through the chocolate line to give a 'feather' effect. Spoon a neat ball of sorbet into the middle of the sliced pears. Place a shortbread biscuit on top of the sorbet and serve immediately.

Lemon Soufflé

I once had to put a dessert together for an unexpected dinner party. Trouble was that my son ate the lot before dinner so they had bread and cheese for pud instead! Anyway, this is an impressive one to make with ingredients that most keen cooks would have to hand.

S E R V E S 4

3 tablespoons cold water
½ oz (15 g) powdered gelatine
4 large eggs (size 1 or 2)
3 oz (75 g) caster sugar

juice and finely grated zest of 3 lemons
½ pint (300 ml) double cream, lightly
whipped
finely chopped walnuts, to decorate

Prepare a 2 pint (1.2 litre) soufflé dish by making a paper collar of double thickness greaseproof paper and tying this so that it stands at least 2 inches (5 cm) above the rim of the dish.

Place the water in a small pan, sprinkle in the gelatine and allow to stand for 5 minutes. Separate the eggs, putting the whites in a large bowl. Add the sugar and the lemon zest to the yolks. Add the lemon juice to the gelatine mixture. Heat the gelatine mixture gently until it has dissolved completely, but do not allow to boil. Set aside.

Set the bowl with the egg yolk mixture over a pan half-filled with gently simmering water and whisk until thick and light. Remove from the heat and, beating constantly, pour in the gelatine mixture. Continue whisking until the mixture shows signs of setting. Whisk the egg whites until they hold stiff peaks. Fold the cream and egg whites into the egg yolk mixture.

Pour into the prepared soufflé dish and chill for 2–4 hours, until firmly set. Just before serving, run a knife around the inside of the collar, remove, and coat the sides with the walnuts. I don't feel this dessert needs any more decoration.

Iced Damson Soufflé

Colin White at Whites, Cricklade

S E R V E S 8

2 lb (900 g) damsons
1 lb (450 g) sugar
8 fl oz (250 ml) water

8 egg whites
1 pint (600 ml) double cream, whipped until
semi-stiff

Prepare eight ramekins by making paper collars of double thickness greaseproof

paper, which stand at least 2 inches (5 cm) above the rims.

Wash the damsons and remove the stalks. Place in a pan and cover with water. Bring to the boil and simmer gently until the fruit is very soft. Rub the damsons through a fine sieve to get a smooth purée. Discard all skins and stones and allow to cool.

Place the sugar and water in a pan and stir until dissolved. Boil to the soft-ball stage or 225°F/110°C. To test without a thermometer, drop a little of the syrup from a spoon into a bowl of water to see if it forms a soft ball. Add a few drops of water to hold it at that temperature.

Whisk the egg whites until they hold stiff peaks and slowly add the syrup mixture, beating constantly, and continue to whisk until cool. Fold the damson purée into the meringue mixture and gently but thoroughly fold in the cream. Pour the mixture into the prepared ramekins and freeze, uncovered, for about 3–6 hours.

Remove from the freezer and put in the refrigerator about 10–15 minutes before serving. Peel the paper bands from the ramekins and serve.

Iced Hazelnut Mousse

Juan Martin at Sharrow Bay Hotel, Ullswater

I love this mousse so much that I've planted two hazelnut trees in my garden in Devon so I can (one day) pick my own nuts to make this excellent recipe.

SERVES 4

2 oz (50 g) hazelnut
2 oz (50 g) caster sugar
3 egg whites
4½ oz (125 g) icing sugar
½ pint (300 ml) double cream, lightly whipped
raspberries or strawberries, to decorate

For the sauce:
8 oz (225 g) strawberries or raspberries
juice of 1 lemon
about 1–2 oz (25–50 g) sugar

Roast the hazelnuts in the oven or under the grill. Place the caster sugar in a small pan and heat until it turns a golden caramel colour. Stir in the hazelnuts. Turn on to an oiled tray. Allow to cool and harden. When cold, crush it, using a rolling pin or a pestle and mortar, until it is coarsely ground.

Put the egg whites and icing sugar in a bowl and set over a pan of boiling water. Whisk until they are fairly hot. Remove from the heat and continue to beat with an electric beater until

cool and thick. Fold in the cream and the ground nut mixture. Spoon into four small wetted moulds. Cover and freeze for 2–4 hours, until firm.

To make the sauce, purée all the ingredients in a food processor or blender. Pass through a fine sieve. Dip the moulds briefly into hot water before turning out on to plates.

To serve, surround with the sauce and decorate with a little fruit.

Berry Mousse

Ramon Farthing at Calcot Manor, Tetbury

A brilliantly refreshing dessert from one of my favourite
restaurants – Calcot Manor in Glo'shire.

SERVES 4-6

*½ pint (300 ml) fruit purée (blackcurrants,
redcurrants, raspberries or strawberries, for
example)
icing sugar
1 sachet of powdered gelatine soaked in a
little cold water*

*¼ pint (150 ml) whipping cream
red and black fruits, picked over and sliced, to
decorate*

Top and tail blackcurrants and redcurrants or pick over raspberries and strawberries and place in a pan. Cook over a gentle heat until soft. Cool slightly, then purée in a food processor or blender. Rub through a fine sieve set over a bowl and sweeten to taste with icing sugar.

Put the soaked gelatine with a small ladleful of purée in a pan and heat gently until it has dissolved completely. Mix into the remaining purée and whisk to combine. Lightly whip the cream and fold into the purée. Spoon the mousse into four to six small cups and chill for 4–5 hours.

To serve, put the cup bases under running warm water, loosen the edges with a knife and turn out on to a cold plate. Decorate around the mousses with the sliced fruits.

Chocolate Mousse

The wickedest, richest chocolate mousse I know. Not for the faint-hearted.

SERVES 6

*6 fl oz (175 ml) double cream
6 oz (175 g) plain chocolate
1 egg
6 egg yolks*

*6 oz (175 g) caster sugar
5 tablespoons water
grated chocolate, to decorate (optional)*

Whip the cream until it is very thick but not stiff. Break the chocolate into small pieces and place in a bowl or the top of a double boiler. Melt the chocolate over hot but not boiling water. (This can also be done very easily in a bowl in a microwave on a low power setting.) Beat the egg and egg yolks in a separate large bowl until they are frothy and pale.

Place the sugar and water in a heavy-based pan (not non-stick) and stir over a gentle heat until the sugar has dissolved. Increase the heat and bring to the boil. Boil steadily until a dribble of syrup dropped into a glass of water forms a crunchy string. Do not overcook or it will turn to caramel. As soon as this stage is reached, plunge the base of the pan into cold water for a few seconds to halt the cooking process. Beating constantly, pour the hot syrup on to the egg mixture in a steady stream. Continue beating for a few minutes until the mixture is nearly cold. Stir in the melted chocolate and, when well mixed, carefully fold in the whipped cream. Divide the mixture between six individual ramekin dishes and chill for a few hours until set.

Decorate with a little grated chocolate, if liked. Serve at room temperature with a plain biscuit such as my Almond Crisps, see below.

Almond Crisps

These delicious thin crispy biscuits are perfect to serve with your home-made ice cream or chocolate mousse. They are very fragile and, once made, should be stored carefully in an airtight tin (or you can munch them for your midnight feasts!)

MAKES ABOUT 20

3 oz (75 g) unsalted butter, at room temperature
4 oz (100 g) caster sugar
1½ rounded tablespoons flour

juice and grated zest of 1 orange
6 oz (175 g) almonds, blanched and roughly chopped

Working with a wooden spoon, cream the butter in a bowl. Stir in the sugar and beat well until the sugar has dissolved. Sift in the flour and mix thoroughly. Add the orange juice and zest and continue beating until smooth. Stir in the almonds.

Drop teaspoonfuls of the mixture on to buttered baking sheets, allowing plenty of room for the biscuits to spread out. Bake in a preheated oven, 400°F/200°C (gas mark 6), for about 5 minutes, or until the edges turn a biscuit colour. Remove from the sheets with a spatula and immediately curl them round a rolling pin for a few seconds, pressing gently to make them curve. Remove when firm and allow to cool on a wire rack.

Chocolate Galette

The most outstanding chocolate cake-cum-biscuit in the world and
invented by me. He said modestly.

SERVES ABOUT 8

For the pastry:
1 oz (25 g) cocoa powder
7 oz (200 g) flour
3 oz (75 g) icing sugar
2 egg yolks, beaten
5 oz (150 g) butter, softened

For the filling:
8 oz (225 g) butter
3 oz (75 g) cocoa powder

2 oz (50 g) icing sugar
1 measure of brandy

For the covering:
8 oz (225 g) expensive dark chocolate
1 oz (25 g) butter
4 tablespoons milk
grated chocolate, to decorate (optional)

To make the pastry, mix together the cocoa, flour and icing sugar in a large bowl. Add the egg yolks and knead in the butter. Allow the dough to rest for 1 hour before rolling out. Divide the pastry into three and roll out each piece as thinly as possible on a lightly floured surface to a round about 11 inches (28 cm) in diameter. Place on greased baking sheets and bake in a preheated oven, 400°F/200°C (gas mark 6), for 5–6 minutes.

Mix together all the filling ingredients to make a rich chocolate butter cream. Spread the cream over the rounds to make a three-tiered sandwich. By now the whole thing should be about ¾ inch (2 cm) in height.

Finally, break the chocolate into a pan with the butter and milk and melt over a low heat, stirring constantly until smooth. Pour the sauce over the galette. If you like you could grate over a little hard chocolate when the top has set.

Serve cut into wedges.

Compotes

This method of cooking fresh fruit produces the best flavour and appearance. Great for desserts or breakfast – with a little iced dessert wine!

FOR EACH 1 LB (450 g) FRESH FRUIT – ABOUT
2 LB (900 g) FRUIT WILL SERVE 4 - 6

12 fl oz (350 ml) water   *6 oz (175 g) sugar*

Put the water and sugar into a pan that is large enough to hold the fruit in one layer. Add the flavouring for the fruit being used, as described below, and bring to simmering point over a gentle heat. Stir occasionally until the sugar has dissolved and the syrup boils. Tip the fruit into the pan and, as soon as the syrup simmers again, slowly cook, uncovered, until the fruit is not quite tender. Remove the pan from the heat, cover and leave until absolutely cold.

Raspberries, strawberries and other soft fruit
After being added to the syrup, these should be removed from the heat as soon as it has been brought up to boiling point again. Coat the fruit thoroughly with the syrup and allow to cool without covering.

Pears
Peel and core the pears, then thinly slice them. They are delicious if red wine is substituted for half the water and a vanilla pod is added. Remove the pod before serving.

Prunes
Add a cinnamon stick or the grated zest of 1 lemon to the syrup. Cook the prunes according to the packet instructions.

Rhubarb
Trim and wash the rhubarb, then cut into short sticks. Add the juice and grated zest of 1 lemon to the syrup. As soon as the syrup has reboiled, remove from the heat, cover and allow to cool. This will ensure that the fruit remains whole.

Apples
Peel and core the apples and either leave them whole or cut into halves or thick rings. The syrup can be flavoured with the juice of 1 lemon or a vanilla pod. Remove the pod before serving.

Orange Bavarois in Chocolate Genoese Sponge with Orange Sauce

Juan Martin at Sharrow Bay Hotel, Ullswater

A little burst of skilful wizardry to dazzle your friends, when you have the time!

SERVES 6-8

For the sponge:
3 eggs
4 oz (100 g) caster sugar
1½ oz (40 g) butter, melted
2½ oz (65 g) flour
1 oz (25 g) cocoa powder

For the bavarois:
½ pint (300 ml) milk
4 egg yolks
4 oz (100 g) caster sugar
*2 teaspoons powdered gelatine soaked in a
little cold water*

grated rind of 3 oranges
*½ pint (300 ml) double cream, lightly
whipped*

For the sauce:
2 oranges
7 fl oz (200 ml) water
2 oz (50 g) sugar
Cointreau, to taste

*chopped oranges, sprig of mint or lemon
balm, to decorate*

To make the sponge, whisk the eggs and sugar until thick and creamy. Fold in the butter, flour and cocoa powder. Butter a 9½ × 11 inch (24 × 28 cm) Swiss roll tin, line it with greaseproof paper and pour on the mixture. Bake in a preheated oven, 375°F/190°C (gas mark 5), for about 15 minutes. Turn out on to sugared greaseproof paper. Trim to fit and line a greased 2 pint (1.2 litre) mould. Allow to cool.

Next, prepare the bavarois. Heat the milk but do not allow it to boil. Whisk the egg yolks and sugar until thick. Pour the milk into the egg mixture, stirring constantly. Return the mixture to the pan and cook, stirring with a wooden spoon, until the custard has thickened and coats the back of the spoon. Remove from the heat, then stir in the soaked gelatine and mix until it has dissolved. Strain and add the orange rind. Allow to cool. When the custard is cold and almost at setting point, gently fold in the cream. Pour into the sponge-lined mould and leave to set, about 2–4 hours.

To make the sauce, peel the oranges, cut away the white pith and finely shred the peel. Place in a pan with the strained juice of the oranges, water and sugar. Reduce the sauce over a high heat for about 5 minutes. Allow to cool and add a little Cointreau to taste.

To serve, turn out the sponge bavarois, slice thinly and arrange in overlapping slices on top of chopped oranges on individual plates. Surround with the orange sauce and decorate with a sprig of mint or lemon balm.

Lovers' Hearts

A wonderfully romantic dessert to impress your loved one with at the end of an intimate meal. I cannot be held responsible for the consequences.

You will need six heart-shaped *coeur à fromage* moulds, which have little drainage holes and are available from kitchen shops. Line them with muslin before making this dish.

SERVES 6

For the hearts:
12 oz (350 g) cream cheese, unsalted
¾ pint (450 ml) soured cream
4 tablespoons caster sugar
juice and grated zest of 1 lemon
4 egg whites
icing sugar, to decorate

For the sauce:
about 4 oz (100 g) sugar
4 fl oz (100 ml) water
1 ½ lb (675 g) blackcurrants, topped and tailed
blackcurrant liqueur or crème de cassis
  (optional)

Beat together the cheese, cream, sugar, lemon juice and zest in a large bowl. Whisk the egg whites until they hold stiff peaks and fold them into the cream mixture. Divide into the dishes, stand them on a plate or a baking sheet and leave in a cool place to drain overnight.

To make the sauce, put the sugar and water in a pan and heat gently until the sugar has dissolved, then bring to the boil. Tip in the prepared blackcurrants. Allow these to simmer for a few minutes in the syrup, until just tender. Rub through a sieve. The sauce should be of a light syrupy consistency; if it is not, return to the pan and bubble until it is. When cold, stir in the alcohol, if using, to taste.

Next day, tip out the hearts from their pots on to a large white plate, remove the muslin and dust with a little icing sugar. Float around some of the sauce and serve the remainder separately.

P. S. you can eat
the other 4 tommorow

Caramel Cream

A smooth indulgent pudding , best served at room temperature to appreciate the delicate flavour fully.

SERVES 6

7 fl oz (200 ml) milk
½ pint (300 ml) single cream
1½ tablespoons caster sugar
2 eggs
2 egg yolks
few drops of vanilla essence

For the caramel:
4 oz (100 g) sugar
2 tablespoons water

To make the caramel, put the sugar and water in a heavy-based pan and heat gently until the sugar dissolves. Bring to the boil, but do not stir while the syrup is boiling. Boil rapidly until the sugar turns a rich caramel colour. Plunge the base of the pan into cold water to halt the cooking process. Pour into six individual ramekin dishes, turning the dishes so that the caramel coats the bases and part of the sides.

Mix the milk and cream with the sugar in a pan and heat until steaming. Meanwhile, beat together the eggs, egg yolks and vanilla essence, but do not allow them to become frothy. Add the milk mixture and stir well. Strain into the ramekins over the caramel.

Place the ramekins in a roasting tin half-filled with cold water and bake in a preheated oven, 350°F/180°C (gas mark 4), for about 20 minutes, until set. Allow to cool completely before turning out.

A classic little number
that I never tire of.
Yum yum.

Macaroon Cream

This has a delicate flavour and colour. It must be made at least six hours or preferably a day ahead to allow the macaroons time to soften. Do not use macaroons from the cake shop but go to a good deli and buy a box of miniature macaroons or ratafias. I like to serve this with a raspberry sauce – see the recipe for Iced Hazelnut Mousse on page 291.

SERVES 4-6

4 oz (100 g) packet of macaroons or ratafias
3 eggs
1 oz (25 g) caster sugar
½ pint (300 ml) milk

½ oz (15 g) powdered gelatine soaked in 3 tablespoons cold water
½ pint (300 ml) double cream, lightly whipped
1 tablespoon Kirsch

Crush the macaroons or ratafias lightly with a rolling pin and place on a baking sheet. Bake in a preheated oven, 350°F/180°C (gas mark 4), until lightly browned. Allow to cool.

Separate the eggs, putting the three yolks in a large bowl and two of the egg whites in a smaller one. We shall not be using the third egg white. Whisk the egg yolks with the sugar until creamy. Heat the milk in a pan but do not allow it to boil. Slowly stir the milk into the yolk mixture, then return to the pan and heat gently, stirring constantly, until it has thickened slightly – do not let it boil. Remove from the heat.

Pour the soaked gelatine into the hot custard and stir until it has dissolved completely. Set aside to cool, stirring occasionally. You can speed up this process by setting it over a bowl of iced water. When the custard is cold and beginning to thicken, fold in the cream, macaroons or ratafias and Kirsch. Whisk the two egg whites until they hold stiff peaks and fold in. Turn at once into a wetted 2 pint (1.2 litre) mould – I like to use a pretty fluted dish – and leave until firm.

Just before serving, dip the mould briefly in hot water and turn out on to a serving dish.

Profiteroles

Old-fashioned maybe – but an excellent dish when properly made. Don't
be put off by the factory-made versions you find in supermarket chests.

SERVES 4 - 6

For the choux pastry:
3¾ oz (100 g) plain flour
7½ fl oz (225 ml) water
3 oz (75 g) butter
3 eggs

For the chocolate sauce:
3½ oz (90 g) plain chocolate
2½ fl oz (65 ml) milk
1 tablespoon double cream
½ oz (15 g) butter

½ pint (300 ml) Pastry Cream, see below

The first rule is to sift the flour on to a sheet of
paper. Put the water and butter in a fairly large
pan and bring to the boil. When bubbling,
remove from the heat and, as soon as the bubbles have subsided, 'shoot' in the flour at once
and beat like crazy until it is smooth. Allow to
cool for a few minutes, then beat in the eggs
one at a time. The second rule is to beat the
mixture thoroughly between the addition of
each egg until it is firm again. When all the eggs
have been added, beat the pastry for a few minutes until it looks glossy, thick and smooth.

Place the mixture in a piping bag fitted with
a large plain nozzle and pipe walnut-sized balls
on to a dampened baking sheet. Bake in a
preheated oven, 400°F/200°C (gas mark 6),
for about 25 minutes, until they are crisp and
golden brown. Lift the choux balls off the sheet
and prick the sides to allow the steam to
escape. Leave to cool.

To make the chocolate sauce, break the
chocolate into a bowl or the top of a double
boiler and melt it over hot but not boiling
water. Meanwhile, bring the milk and cream to
the boil, then pour on to the melted chocolate
and return to the pan. Allow to bubble for 20
seconds, remove from the heat and whisk in
the butter until glossy.

To assemble the profiteroles, make a slit in
the sides and spoon or pipe in the Pastry
Cream, see below. Pile them on a dish and, just
before serving, pour over the chocolate sauce
or hand it round separately.

Pastry Cream

This recipe makes a firm cream that holds its shape and is suitable for filling
all types of patisseries. If it is too firm it can be softened with a little cream.

MAKES ½ PINT (300 ml)

1 egg yolk
1 egg, separated
2 oz (50 g) caster sugar

1 oz (25 g) cornflour
½ pint (300 ml) milk
1 vanilla pod or 1 teaspoon vanilla essence

Beat together the two egg yolks with the sugar until pale and creamy, then add the cornflour and a little of the milk to form a smooth paste. Scald the remaining milk with the vanilla pod or essence. Remove the vanilla pod, if using. Pour the milk on to the egg mixture, mix well and return to the pan. Stir over a gentle heat until it boils. The pastry cream must be smooth before it boils; if lumps form remove from the heat and beat thoroughly before returning. Whisk the egg white until it holds stiff peaks and fold carefully into the pastry cream. Cover with dampened greaseproof paper and allow to cool and set before using.

Pavlova

This is a delicious and impressive yet simple dessert, which uses up those egg whites after making your chocolate mousse.

SERVES 6

3 egg whites
6 oz (175 g) caster sugar
½ teaspoon vanilla essence
½ teaspoon vinegar
1 teaspoon cornflour

For the topping:
½ pint (300 ml) clotted or whipped cream
1 lb (450 g) fruit – ripe apricots, stoned
*   and quartered, strawbs, raspberries, sliced*
*   mangoes etc*

Draw a circle 7 inches (18 cm) in diameter on bakewell, greaseproof or rice paper and place on a baking sheet.

Whisk the egg whites until they hold stiff peaks, then gradually beat in half of the sugar. Add the vanilla essence, vinegar and cornflour and continue to beat until the mixture is glossy. Fold in the remaining sugar.

Spread one-third of the mixture on the marked circle, then use the remaining mixture to form a 'nest', either spooning it or piping it to form sides. Bake in a preheated oven, 275°F/140°C (gas mark 1), for about 45 minutes, or until the meringue is firm. If the meringue starts to go brown, reduce the temperature and allow it to cook for a little longer. Ideally, the pavlova should be left in the oven after it has been switched off, until completely cold.

When the meringue is cold and just before serving, fill it with the cream and arrange the fruit on top.

For a special occasion, it is delicious to make a pouring sauce to accompany this. Use the same or a complementary fruit, such as raspberries, and boil these with a cup of water and sugar to taste until they form a light syrupy consistency. Strain and hand round separately.

My Trifle

A trifle is among the simplest puddings to make yet one of the loveliest if done well. A good trifle does not need jelly to set it or nasty angelica or hundreds and thousands sprinkled on the top, as I am sure you will agree if you make this.

SERVES 4-6

6 trifle sponge cakes
good raspberry jam
3-4 fl oz (75-100 ml) decent sherry
1 lb (450 g) good-quality mixed fruit (I like
   raspberries, bananas, grapes etc)
whipped cream
toasted flaked almonds - if you must!

For the custard:
3 egg yolks
1 oz (25 g) caster sugar
1 teaspoon cornflour
½ pint (300 ml) double cream

Trifles are best made in beautiful crystal bowls so that you can see the different layers and textures, but you don't need to rush out and buy one if you don't have one.

Split the sponge cakes and spread with a generous amount of raspberry jam. Sandwich them together again and use to line the base of the bowl attractively. Drench with the sherry and set aside.

To make the custard, mix together in a bowl the egg yolks, sugar, cornflour and a little of the cream to form a smooth paste. Heat the remaining cream until very hot, then pour on to the egg mixture, stirring briskly. Return the mixture to the pan and cook very gently, stirring constantly, until the custard has thickened. Allow to cool.

Meanwhile, prepare your fruit. If you are using apples or bananas, remember to dip them in lemon juice to prevent them going brown. Arrange the fruit on top of the sponge base and pour over the cooled custard. Pop the trifle in the refrigerator until cold.

Spoon whipped cream over the trifle and toss on some toasted flaked almonds to decorate if you wish, but that is all. Easy and delicious.

BAKING -
THE ESSENTIALS

The way to approach baking is with peace in your heart and a jug of cider by your side. It's a generous, warm-hearted, sexy business and my favourite bakers are generous, warm-hearted, sexy people. Baking folk have a terrific sense of the goodness of the earth, the warmth of the sun and the coolness of the rain on the wheat in the fields; the ploughing and the sowing, and the harvest at the end of the day.

Making a loaf of bread is a celebration. It's therapeutic and fun. You can rope in the children to help and they'll have a whale of a time covered in dough and flour. The important thing is to devote time, space and patience to it. If you don't get it right on the first go, give the dough a rest and start again tomorrow.

As for the cakes I've chosen for this chapter – they're all unashamedly English. Well, they'd have to be wouldn't they? After all, the Viennese make very fine pastries, the French are brilliant with fruit tarts, but no one understands The Cake like the English.

These are my favourites, evoking all those comforting childhood memories of 'tea'. Be it posh tablecloths and the best china, or muffins toasted by the hearth while the winter howls outside, the English do it like nobody else in the world.

White Bread

I like my breads to serve specific purposes – for me the honest white loaf
is the one for accompanying soups and mopping up simple stews.

M A K E S 1 (2 lb/900 g) L O A F

1 lb (450 g) strong plain flour
½ teaspoon salt
1 oz (25 g) butter
½ oz (15 g) fresh yeast

½ pint (300 ml) lukewarm water
1 teaspoon caster sugar
beaten egg, to glaze (optional)

Sift the flour and salt into a bowl. Rub in the butter until the mixture resembles fine bread-crumbs. Meanwhile, blend the yeast with the water and sugar. Add to the flour mixture and mix well to a smooth dough.

Turn the dough out on to a lightly floured surface and knead until smooth and elastic, about 10 minutes. Place in an oiled bowl and cover with clingfilm or lightly greased poly-thene. Leave to rise in a warm place until doubled in size. This can take anything from 1–1½ hours – don't let it rise too quickly or it will have a yeasty, unpleasant taste.

On a floured surface, knock the dough back to release all the air bubbles and knead again for about 5 minutes. Shape the dough into a rectangle and place in a greased 2 lb (900 g) loaf tin. Cover as before and leave to rise in a warm place until doubled in size, or until the dough reaches the top of the tin, about 1 hour.

Score along the top of the bread with a sharp knife and brush with beaten egg to glaze, if liked. Alternatively, brush with lightly salted water. Bake in a preheated oven, 425°F/220°C (gas mark 7), for 30–40 minutes, or until golden and firm. When cooked the loaf should sound hollow when rapped on the base with the knuckles. Cool on a wire rack.

N O T E
If using dried rather than fresh yeast, use half the amount of fresh yeast specified in these recipes. Sprinkle over a quarter of the warm liquid to which a teaspoon of sugar has been added, mix well and leave in a warm place until frothy, about 10–15 minutes to actuate.

Wholemeal Bread

This is the one to eat all by itself, except for the butter – or alfresco with cold meats and sauces.

M A K E S 2 (2 lb/900 g) O R 4 (1 lb/450 g) L O A V E S

3 lb (1.4 kg) plain wholemeal flour
2 tablespoons salt
1 oz (25 g) lard

2 oz (50 g) fresh yeast
1½ pints (900 ml) lukewarm water
2 tablespoons caster sugar

Sift the flour into a bowl, adding any bran left in the sieve, and mix with the salt. Rub in the lard until the mixture resembles fine breadcrumbs. Meanwhile, blend the yeast with the water and sugar. Add to the flour mixture and mix well to a smooth dough.

Turn the dough out on to a lightly floured surface and knead until smooth and elastic, about 10 minutes. Place in an oiled bowl and cover with clingfilm or lightly greased polythene. Leave to rise in a warm place until doubled in size, about 1–1½ hours.

On a floured surface, knock the dough back to release all the air bubbles and knead again for about 5 minutes. Divide into two or four pieces and shape to fit two 2 lb (900 g) or four 1 lb (450 g) greased tins. Cover as before and leave to rise until doubled in size, or until the dough reaches the tops of the tins, about 1 hour.

Brush the loaves with lightly salted water and bake in a preheated oven, 450°F/230°C (gas mark 8) for 30–40 minutes, or until cooked and firm. When cooked the loaves should sound hollow when tapped on the base with the knuckles. Cool on a wire rack.

Flowerpot Bread

I find the crust on these loaves has a delicious flavour and texture – but the terracotta pots need to be greased with oil and baked several times before you use them to prevent sticking (and do remove last year's azaleas first!).

MAKES 3 LOAVES

1 lb 14 oz (850 g) strong plain flour
2 teaspoons salt
½ oz (15 g) butter or lard

1 oz (25 g) fresh yeast
¾ pint (450 ml) lukewarm water
1 teaspoon caster sugar

Wash and dry three 8 inch (20 cm) terracotta flowerpots and oil them inside and out. (Remember to bake them four to five times with anything else before using so that they become 'non-stick'.)

Sift the flour and salt into a bowl. Rub in the fat until the mixture resembles fine breadcrumbs. Meanwhile, blend the yeast with the water and sugar. Add to the flour mixture and mix well to a smooth dough.

Turn the dough out on to a lightly floured surface and knead until smooth and elastic, about 10 minutes. Place in an oiled bowl and cover with clingfilm or lightly greased polythene. Leave to rise in a warm place until doubled in size, about 1 hour.

On a floured surface knock back the dough to release all the air bubbles and knead again for 4 minutes. Divide the dough into three pieces and roll each into a ball. Place in the prepared flowerpots (they should be about two-thirds full with dough). Cover as before and leave to rise until the dough reaches the tops of the pots, about 25–30 minutes.

Bake in a preheated oven, 425°F/220°C (gas mark 7), for about 30 minutes, or until golden and firm. When cooked the loaves should sound hollow when tapped on the base with the knuckles. Cool on a wire rack.

Tomato and Onion Bread

This is brilliant topped with Cheddar cheese and toasted.

MAKES 4 (10 oz/275 g) LOAVES

1½ lb (675 g) strong plain flour
½ teaspoon salt
½ oz (15 g) dried milk powder
½ oz (15 g) lard
1 oz (25 g) fresh yeast
2 tablespoons lukewarm water

½ oz (15 g) caster sugar
14 oz (400 g) can tomatoes, drained and
   chopped
1 oz (25 g) butter
1 large onion, thinly sliced into rings
beaten egg, to glaze

Sift the flour with the salt into a bowl and mix in the milk powder. Rub in the lard. Meanwhile, blend the yeast with the water and sugar. Add to the flour mixture with the tomatoes and mix well to a smooth elastic dough.

Turn the dough out on to a lightly floured surface and knead for 10 minutes. Place in an oiled bowl and cover with clingfilm or lightly greased polythene. Leave to rise in a warm place until doubled in size, about 1–1½ hours.

On a floured surface, knock the dough back to release all the air bubbles and knead again for 5 minutes. Divide into four pieces and shape to fit four well-greased loaf tins. Cover as before and leave to rise until doubled in size,

or until the dough reaches the tops of the tins, about 30–40 minutes.

Meanwhile, melt the butter in a pan and soften the onions. Drain on absorbent kitchen paper. Brush the loaves with a little beaten egg and cover the tops with the onion rings, overlapping them slightly.

Bake in a preheated oven, 425°F/220°C (gas mark 7), for 30–35 minutes. When cooked, the loaves should sound hollow when tapped on the base with the knuckles. If, towards the end of the cooking time, the onion slices are getting too brown, cover them with greaseproof paper or foil. Cool on a wire rack.

Irish Brown Bread

I first tasted this while filming in Ireland. It is a lovely nutritious bread, with a slightly nutty, sweet flavour produced by the treacle. You could even use this for those soirees when you are serving things like rollmop herrings, caviar and smoked eel.

MAKES 3 LOAVES

2 lb (900 g) stoneground wholemeal flour
4 teaspoons salt
1½ teaspoons black treacle

about 1 pint (600 ml) lukewarm water
2 oz (50 g) fresh yeast

Sift together the flour and salt in a large bowl and put in a warm place. An airing cupboard, the bottom of an Aga or the oven as it is heating are ideal. Dissolve the treacle with a little of the water in a small bowl – the water needs to be warm enough to activate the yeast but not too hot or it will kill it. Crumble or sprinkle on the yeast, then set aside in a warm place until the yeast has dissolved and frothed up, about 5 minutes.

Pour the yeast mixture into the flour and add the remaining warm water. The amount of water needed depends a lot on the flour. Mix to a wettish dough that is too soft to knead.

Turn out on to a lightly floured surface, divide into three equal pieces and shape each into a rectangle the same length as that of a greased 1 lb (450 g) loaf tin. Place in the tins, cover with clingfilm or lightly greased polythene and leave in a warm place until the dough has doubled in size. Depending on the heat, it will take about 30 minutes. Bake in a preheated oven, 450°F/230°C (gas mark 8), for 50 minutes, or until they sound hollow when tapped on the base. Cool on a wire rack.

Quick Soda Bread

In Scotland, Wales and Ireland they make this at the drop of a hat – it's rich and moist and delicious with farmhouse butter. And it's so quick to make that if your friends phone up at two in the afternoon saying that they're arriving for tea, you can have made it by three.

MAKES 1 LOAF

1½ lb (675 g) plain flour
1½ teaspoons salt
1½ teaspoons bicarbonate of soda

1½ oz (40 g) butter
¾ pint (450 ml) buttermilk or milk with
1 dessertspoon cream of tartar

Sift the flour with the salt and bicarbonate of soda into a bowl and mix well together. Rub in the butter, then add the buttermilk or milk and cream of tartar to make a soft dough.

Turn out the dough on to a lightly floured surface and shape into a 2 inch (5 cm) thick round. Place on a floured baking sheet and cut nearly through into quarters. Bake in a pre-heated oven, 425°F/220°C (gas mark 7), for 30 minutes. The bread should sound hollow when tapped on the base with the knuckles. Cool on a wire rack.

Cheese Muffins

These little delights, toasted and spread with farmhouse butter, are scrumptious with cold ham and pickles on a wintry Sunday afternoon.

MAKES 40

4 lb (1.75 kg) strong plain flour
pinch of salt
4 oz (100 g) lard

2 lb (900 g) Cheddar or strong cheese, grated
4 oz (100 g) fresh yeast
2 pints (1.2 litres) lukewarm water

Sift the flour and salt into a bowl. Cut the lard into pieces and rub into the flour. Stir in the cheese. Blend the yeast with the water and pour it into the flour mixture. Mix to a dough.

Leave to rest for 10 minutes, then turn the dough out on to a lightly floured surface. Roll it out to approximately ½ inch (1 cm) in thickness and cut into 4 inch (10 cm) rounds using a scone or biscuit cutter. Place on greased baking trays and bake in a preheated oven, 400°F/200°C (gas mark 6), for about 20 minutes. Cool on a wire rack.

Sticky Gingerbread

This recipe was discovered on a worn page that had fallen out of an old cookery book. It is wonderfully moist.

MAKES 1 LOAF

4 oz (100 g) butter
4 oz (100 g) dark moist brown sugar
6 oz (175 g) black treacle
6 oz (175 g) golden syrup
4 fl oz (100 ml) warm milk
2 tablespoons ground ginger
1½ teaspoons ground cinnamon
1½ teaspoons ground mace
1½ teaspoons freshly grated nutmeg

2 fl oz (50 ml) sweet sherry
1 teaspoon cream of tartar
12 oz (350 g) plain flour
3 eggs, well beaten
juice and grated rind of 1 orange
1 teaspoon bicarbonate of soda, dissolved in
*   2 tablespoons warm water*
4 oz (100 g) sultanas or seedless or stoned
*   raisins*

Cream together the butter and sugar until the mixture is pale and fluffy. Add the treacle, syrup, milk, spices and sherry. Beat well. Mix the cream of tartar with the flour and then add alternately with the beaten eggs to the butter and sugar mixture. Add the juice and grated rind of the orange, the dissolved soda and the sultanas or raisins. Pour the mixure into a well greased shallow 12 × 9 inch (30 × 23 cm) baking tin and bake in a preheated oven, 350°F/180°C (gas mark 4), for 45–60 minutes. Cool on a wire rack and serve cut into squares.

Farmhouse Treacle Loaf

This loaf contains no fat, so it does not keep well, but it's delicious sliced and buttered while still warm.

MAKES 2 LOAVES

8 oz (225 g) wholemeal flour
8 oz (225 g) plain white flour
4 oz (100 g) sugar
5 oz (150 g) stoned or seedless raisins
1 oz (25 g) chopped nuts

½ pint (300 ml) milk
6 oz (175 g) black treacle
1 teaspoon bicarbonate of soda
1 egg, beaten

Sift together the flours into a large bowl and mix in the sugar, raisins and nuts. Make a well in the centre.

Heat the milk and treacle to lukewarm. Add the bicarbonate of soda, then pour into the flour. Add the beaten egg. Stir well and turn into two generously greased 1 lb (450 g) loaf tins.

Bake in a preheated oven, 350°F/180°C (gas mark 4), for 1½ hours, or until a skewer plunged into the centre of the loaf comes out clean. Cool on a wire rack.

Nutty Teabread

Slice and butter this delicious sweet bread and serve with tea, around a wonderful log fire, while the snow piles up outside your windows.

MAKES 2 LOAVES

2 eggs
8 oz (225 g) dark brown sugar
1 lb (450 g) plain flour
4 teaspoons baking powder

½ teaspoon salt
16 fl oz (475 ml) milk
6 oz (175 g) finely chopped nuts

Beat the eggs well in a bowl and add the brown sugar. Sift together the flour, baking powder and salt. Add the flour mixture alternately with the milk to the egg mixture. Stir in the chopped nuts. Divide between two greased 1 lb (450 g) loaf tins and allow to stand for 30 minutes before baking. Bake in a preheated oven, 350°F/180°C (gas mark 4), for about 45 minutes, until a skewer plunged into the centre of the loaves comes out clean. Allow to stand for 10 minutes before turning out. Cool on a wire rack.

Rich Christmas Cake

The definitive recipe my Mother used to make.

MAKES 1 (9 inch/23 cm) CAKE

1-2 oz (25-50 g) currants
8 oz (225 g) sultanas
8 oz (225 g) stoned raisins
4 oz (100 g) chopped mixed candied peel
6 oz (175 g) glacé cherries, halved
10 oz (275 g) butter
10 oz (275 g) soft brown sugar
grated rind of 1 lemon

grated rind of 1 orange
6 eggs, beaten
10 oz (275 g) plain flour
pinch of salt
¼ teaspoon ground mixed spice
¼ teaspoon ground cinnamon
3 tablespoons brandy

Line a 9 inch (23 cm) deep cake tin using double thickness greaseproof paper and tie a double piece of brown paper around the outside of the tin. Also have ready a double piece of greaseproof paper with a hole about the size of a 50p cut in the middle to cover the cake before putting in the oven.

Wash the fruits if necessary, then mix together. Cream the butter and sugar in a large bowl until pale and fluffy. Add the grated rind of the lemon and orange. Add the beaten egg a little at a time, beating well between each addition. Sift and fold in half the flour and the salt and spices, then carefully fold in the remaining

flour. Stir in the fruit and brandy, mixing together evenly. Turn the mixture into the prepared tin, making sure there are no air pockets and make a slight dip in the centre.

Cover with the greaseproof paper and place on top of a layer of newspaper in the lower part of a preheated oven, 275°F/140°C (gas mark 1). Cook for about 4-4½ hours. The cake is cooked when a skewer plunged into the centre comes out clean. Cool in the tin, then turn out. When the cake is completely cold wrap it in several layers of greaseproof paper and store in an airtight tin or wrap well in foil.

Orange and Almond Cake

This is a foolproof cake with a strong orange flavour. The ground almonds make it very rich and moist. Yum Yum!

MAKES 1 CAKE

3 eggs
4 oz (100 g) caster sugar
2 oz (50 g) fine, fresh white breadcrumbs
4 oz (100 g) ground almonds
finely grated rind of 1 orange
juice of 3 oranges

To decorate:
6 fl oz (175 ml) double cream, whipped
toasted flaked almonds

Separate the eggs, putting the yolks into a large bowl and the whites into a medium-sized one. Add the sugar to the yolks and beat with a wooden spoon until light and creamy. Add the breadcrumbs, ground almonds, grated rind and strained orange juice and beat well. Whisk the egg whites until they hold stiff peaks and, using a metal spoon, fold carefully into the mixture.

Pour into a greased and lined 8 inch (20 cm) cake tin. Bake in the centre of a preheated oven, 350°F/180°C (gas mark 4), for 30 minutes. When ready it will be golden brown and the centre spongy to the touch. Loosen the sides and leave to cool in the tin for 15 minutes before turning out. Cool on a wire rack.

Before serving, cover the top and sides with the whipped cream and toasted almonds.

Coconut Tarts

MAKES 16 TARTS

For the pastry:
4 oz (100 g) self-raising flour
pinch of salt
2 oz (50 g) butter
cold water to mix

For the filling:
jam
2 oz (50 g) butter
2 oz (50 g) caster sugar
1 large egg (size 1 or 2), beaten
few drops of almond essence
6 oz (175 g) desiccated coconut

Grease 16 patty tins. Sift the flour and salt into a bowl. Rub in the butter, using your fingertips, a food processor, or a pastry blender, until the mixture resembles fine breadcrumbs. Add a little cold water to mix to a firm dough.

Turn on to a lightly floured surface and knead lightly. Allow it to rest for 30 minutes, then roll out the pastry and cut into rounds the size of the patty tins. Use to line the tins and

put about half a teaspoonful of jam into each.

To make the filling, cream the butter and sugar until pale and fluffy. Add the beaten egg a little at a time, beating well between each addition. Stir in the almond essence and coconut and place in spoonfuls in the lined patty tins. Bake towards the top of a preheated oven, 375°F/190°C (gas mark 5), for 15–20 minutes, or until golden brown. Cool on a wire rack.

INDEX

ACKNOWLEDGEMENTS

No cookery writer, if he is honest, can produce a whole book in which all the recipes are entirely his own. And I certainly couldn't have done this one without a little help from my friends or for that matter all those other folk, whose names none of us knows, but who taught us how to make Coq au Vin, or a simple Cornish pasty; all those traditional, classic dishes handed down through countless generations, which we have all cooked and enjoyed.

So thanks to them and to this little bunch below – some of the good guys who like to share their skills with others. I've unashamedly picked their brains, enjoyed their food and, I hope, passed on a bit of their expertise to you.

Ramon Farthing, Calcot Manor, Tetbury, Gloucestershire
Paul Gayler, Inigo Jones, London
Robert Harrison, Congham Hall, Grimston, Norfolk
Shaun Hill, Gidleigh Park, Chagford, Devon
Allan Holland, Mallory Court, Bishops Tachbrook, Warwickshire
Clive Imber, Michael's Brasserie, Newcastle upon Tyne, Tyne and Wear
Mandarin Restaurant, Bristol, Avon
Juan Martin, Sharrow Bay Hotel, Ullswater, Cumbria
Tony Marshall, Dukes Hotel, London
Joyce Molyneux, Carved Angel, Dartmouth, Devon
Christopher Oakes, Oakes Restaurant, Stroud, Gloucestershire
Stephen Ross, Homewood Park, Hinton Charterhouse, Avon
Kate Smith, Royal Oak Hotel, Sevenoaks, Kent
Colin White, Whites, Cricklade, Wiltshire